IN THE FACE OF INEQUALITY

IN THE FACE OF INEQUALITY

How Black Colleges Adapt

Melissa E. Wooten

Published by State University of New York Press, Albany

For information, contact State University of New York Press, Albany, NY
www.sunypress.edu

Production, Jenn Bennett
Marketing, Kate Seburyamo

Library of Congress Cataloging-in-Publication Data

Wooten, Melissa E.
  In the face of inequality : how Black colleges adapt / Melissa E. Wooten.
      pages cm.
  Includes bibliographical references and index.
  ISBN 978-1-4384-5691-1 (hardcover : alk. paper)
  ISBN 978-1-4384-5690-4 (paperback : alk. paper) — ISBN 978-1-4384-5692-8
(e-book) 1. African American universities and colleges. 2. African Americans—
Education (Higher) I. Title.
  LC2781.W67 2015
  378.7308996073—dc23
                                        2014030655

10 9 8 7 6 5 4 3 2 1

For all the good that came from in and around 249 Eason,
especially Charles J. Wooten Sr.

Contents

Figures and Tables

Figures

Tables

Preface

The twentieth century represented a pivotal moment in American racial politics. Large-scale, multiracial movement organizations assaulted the systems that denied black Americans equal protection under the law. This revolution brought millions of previously disenfranchised individuals into the citizenry. There was nothing inevitable about this revolution. Nor was there anything in American history to suggest that this revolution's effects would be long lasting. After all, conservative forces were able to dismantle the revolutionary gains achieved following the Civil War. Not surprisingly then, the rights-based revolution of the mid-twentieth century has served as a rich source of scholarly inquiry.

Many scholars have found themselves fascinated with explaining the origins of this political movement and the interrelated question as to why this movement succeeded. Unraveling such dynamics ultimately sheds light on how the civil rights era reshaped inequality within America. While not denying the importance or necessity of these investigations, this book takes a different approach to the study of inequality. Organizations, not individuals, are the primary characters in this story. The very laws and social customs that created conditions of inequality that stifled individual choice were consequential to organizations, especially those serving racial and ethnic minority group members. By concentrating on the fate of organizations that continued to maintain a missionary focus on black Americans, this book seeks to understand how such organizations fared as rights for black Americans expanded. Was increasing equality for black Americans a good thing for black organizations? How did the needs of black Americans diverge from those of black organizations in the midst of the civil rights era? These are questions that few social scientific studies have pondered.

I first became intrigued by the possibility of studying organizations that maintained a missionary focus on serving black Americans after watching a documentary about Jackie Robinson, the first black American to play in the previously racially segregated major leagues. Toward the end of this documentary, several participants reflected on the ramifications of blacks entering the major leagues on the Negro leagues. Teams and players were not the only casualties. Reporters on the Negro league beat suffered, as did the black newspapers for which they worked. Concession stands, radio broadcasters, and many other ancillary organizations that supported the Negro leagues were hard hit as black players migrated toward the major leagues.

I was struck by the duality of this historical moment. Indeed, equality of opportunity in the major leagues represented "progress for the race." But what did it mean that this progress came at the expense of organizations, many of which were operated by blacks, and many of which had seen it as their mission to serve this community. As a graduate student studying organization theory at the time, I turned to the literature only to discover that my discipline had not set its collective mind to studying this particular quandary. As a result, I set out to study the effect of state-sanctioned racial segregation and its decline for organizational development. Choosing what type of organizations to study came next.

The very nature of state-sanctioned racial segregation meant that there were a number of organizations from which to choose. Black hotels, black newspapers, black advertising agencies, and black sport leagues are but a few of the examples. Yet, in the end, I chose to focus on black colleges because they represented an anomaly of sorts. Few organizations that catered specifically to black clientele survived the demise of state-sanctioned racial segregation. Once hotels that declined to serve black Americans began to do so, black hotels could not compete. While black newspapers still exist, especially in large urban centers, the numbers are far fewer now that black Americans are more dispersed. Contrary to the pattern present among these other industries, black colleges never witnessed such losses. Yes, a few schools closed, but all in all the number has remained fairly stable following state-sanctioned racial segregation. Among black political leaders, the closing of black hotels and other organizations was taken as a sign of growing equality. The closing of black colleges has never had quite the same allure. Even as inequality lessened for black individuals, the defense of black colleges and the need for black educational organizations never waned. This seemed like an ideal context to ponder the intersection of inequality and organization theory.

Studying black colleges afforded the opportunity to think through the ways in which race as a social structural system influences organizations

and the process of organizing. To me, this was an important and necessary step. Race and its ability to shape organizations is a topic often over-
looked or perhaps avoided within the organization theory tradition. At its
core, organization theory concerns itself with explaining why organizations take the particular form and character that they do. When trying to
understand the rise of bureaucracy or the division of labor, scholars such
as Max Weber and Émile Durkheim looked outward. They sought to understand what social need these particular forms of organization served.
Rarely is such introspection brought to bear on the role of organizations
whose mission was and continues to be in the service of black Americans. Understanding the social needs these organizations fulfilled during
state-sanctioned racial segregation is easy to surmise. Black colleges were
necessary; their existence enabled Americans to proclaim that blacks had
access to higher education. Black colleges were key to America's system
of inequality. Understanding how societal needs around racial inequality
shifted and how these organizations subsequently adapted is less evident
and consequently deserving of scholarly attention.

Acknowledgments

A number of people provided intellectual and emotional support as this manuscript came to fruition. As members of my dissertation committee, Jerry Davis, Kathleen Sutcliffe, Mary Ann Glynn, Mark Mizruchi, and Michael Jensen nurtured my interest in applying an organizational lens to black colleges. When I ventured to Atlanta, Georgia, to craft this project Karyn Lacy provided me with affordable housing and good conversation. This allowed me to immerse myself in the archives and map out my dissertation project. Mary Ann Glynn, then a faculty member at Emory University, helped me secure office space within the Organizational Behavior department and facilitated my integration within the department's intellectual community. Mike Kaatz, Krysia (Wrobel) Waldron, and Joseph Walton were especially gracious and welcoming during my time at Emory. During the graduate program at Michigan, I forged a community that has sustained me personally and academically. Modupe Akinola, Peter Anderson, Sekou Bermiss, Anne Bowers, Ebony Bridwell-Mitchell, Arran Caza, Josh Cohen, Karen Hebert, Jason Kanov, Jacoba Lillius, Chris Marquis, Eric Neuman, Francisco Polidoro, Aradhana Roy, PK Toh, Mike Trolio, Timothy Vogus, and Erica (Ryu) Wong are but a few of the graduate school colleagues who have enriched my life immeasurably. Emily Heaphy and Cedric de Leon, both of whom I met at graduate school, have become a surrogate family of sorts. Their friendship and investment in my scholarly growth has meant more than words can express.

Since leaving Michigan I have seen my network of supporters expand evermore. I thank Marvin Washington and Marc Schneiberg for their willingness to read multiple drafts of anything I've sent them over the years. During my post-doc year at Dartmouth College, I had the good fortune to meet Deborah King and Denise Anthony. Both helped me transition fully into my role as a professional academic. I cannot imagine a better place to have landed than UMass Amherst. The sociology department provided the space and time necessary for me to craft this manuscript. My colleagues, faculty and staff, have extended themselves on numerous occasions Joya Misra, Don Tomaskovic-Devey, and Robert Zussman were particularly generous with their time, providing extensive comments on this manuscript and other projects through the years. The friendship and constant cheerleading of Amel Ahmed, Steve Boutcher, Enobong (Anna) Branch, Noriko Milman, and Amy Schalet made the tenure track grind manageable. Anna Branch was especially helpful in the early stages of this manuscript's development. I'll always be thankful for the time we spent outlining the manuscript's aims and goals. Online writing communities have played a large role in my academic career and I'd like to thank the Academic Ladder's Social Science Professors Group 6 for their virtual support, encouragement, and motivation. I thank Grace Bricker for her research assistance. I thank the University of Massachusetts, Amherst for honoring this project with a publication subvention award.

As a comparative historical sociologist, archives and archivists have played a key role in this project's development. In particular, the staff of the Rockefeller Archive Center provided me with monetary support on several occasions. While at the archive, Nancy Adgent, Jim Allen Smith, Teresa Iacobelli, and Ken Rose were particularly helpful and welcoming. The editorial team at SUNY Press made the publication process easy to navigate. I thank Beth Bouloukos for her shepherding of this project and the anonymous reviewers for providing critical and developmental feedback. Responding to it strengthened the manuscript infinitely.

Finally, I'd like to thank my family. My family has always encouraged me to pursue my passion and share my gifts with the world. My immediate, extended, and fictive family is vast, but Maggie Nelson, Dorothy Moore, and the Eaddy family are just a few that I'd like to thank in particular. My interest in black colleges is undoubtedly connected to my parents' involvement with radical black labor politics. Labor and community leaders such as General Gordon Baker were a constant presence within Gracie and Charles Wooten's household. I can't think of a better training ground for an intellectual life. This book was written shortly after my father's passing. Writing it has offered me a chance to reflect on the work that he and others like him did in the name of black progress and liberation. I can think of no better way to extend my family's legacy.

Introduction

"Are black colleges still necessary?" This is a dilemma facing not just black colleges, but all organizations whose mission is to serve racial, ethnic, and other minority group members. Black colleges, like other such organizations, operate within stigmatized spaces. For black colleges, the stigma is a result of historic processes that ensure that "blackness" continues to be understood as inferior to "whiteness." Asking whether black colleges are still necessary forces us to contemplate why we as a society continue to invest in these organizations given that historically better, superior colleges—that is to say, traditionally white colleges—now admit black students.

Questioning the necessity of black colleges is understandable. The category "black" stigmatizes individuals and collectivities alike. Black applicants with clean criminal records have similar employment opportunities as white felons. With few exceptions, black neighborhoods are cognitively associated with violence, disorder, and poverty.[1] American society rests upon the perpetuation of these stigmatized ways of understanding black bodies and the spaces they inhabit. Yet and still, there is another question. What if, instead of defending the relevance and necessity of black colleges, we turned to this question: "What has prevented black colleges from acquiring the resources, honor, and prestige typically reserved for traditionally white colleges?" Answering this question takes us down an entirely different path. We would not emphasize the necessity of black colleges given other alternatives. Rather, we would suggest that black colleges have the same potential as traditionally white colleges. What then, impeded, diverted, or stymied black colleges as organizational actors?

The adaptive challenges facing black colleges have made it difficult for them to compare well to their better-resourced traditionally white

1

counterparts. Critics argue that average SAT scores and slower graduation rates at black colleges are evidence of these schools' lower quality
relative to traditionally white colleges.[2] That black colleges enroll a high
proportion of students who qualify for Pell Grant and other forms of financial aid counts for little to these detractors. Neither does it seem to
matter that as a mere 3 percent of all colleges, black colleges grant 25
percent of all bachelor's degrees to black students.[3] The areas in which
black colleges fare better than traditionally white colleges are discounted.
All this is built into the racial structure of the United States. The racial
dynamics of the United States that relegated black Americans to a subordinate class did the same to the organizations that sought to serve this
community, making it difficult for black colleges to succeed in the areas
that critics now use to judge their relevance.

Like all colleges, black colleges have needed to adapt to a changing educational landscape. Black colleges, however, have faced quanda-
ries particular to the category of "blackness" that other schools did not.
Traditionally white colleges are held out as the "norm" to which black
colleges are expected to adapt. They are judged and valued according to
how they measure up against benchmarks and standards associated with
traditionally white colleges. Educators, legislators, and aspiring students
alike have demanded that black colleges adapt to this norm. However, in
a society privileging whiteness, black colleges cannot be as good as traditionally white colleges. As a result, when black colleges attempt to garner
resources, express rights, and develop distinctive capabilities,[4] in short,
to adapt, they inevitably embark upon a racial project[5] that runs contrary
to the interests of all those invested in keeping traditionally white colleges superior. Adaptation, even if intended to make black colleges "better," represents an ever-present threat to white privilege.

Lacking the political, financial, and moral resources to *fully* adapt
to the white model, black colleges historically made *partial* adaptations,
emulating but never equaling (at least on their own terms) the white colleges against which they are constantly judged. Moreover, these partial
adaptations created hierarchies between and among black colleges. Perhaps even worse, these partial adaptations meant that black colleges abandoned structural configurations and practices that made them unique
and special relative to traditionally white colleges. Thus, black colleges
were neither perceived as equals of traditionally white colleges nor were
they organizationally distinct from those colleges. The consequences of
these dynamics for black colleges are not well understood. With this volume, I hope to change that.

Few scholars investigate how organizations are raced and what this means for their ability to adapt.[6] When race is the subject of an organizational investigation, the primary concern is whether and how racial categories create conditions of inequality. Sociological accounts dissect the ways in which organizations create and reify social inequality and the untoward effect of this for racial minority group members. Inequality regimes or the "loosely interrelated practices, processes, actions and meanings" that produce "systematic disparities between participants in power" and those lacking power, are politically, historically, and culturally specific.[7] Accordingly, in the American context, these regimes have privileged whiteness within organizations such that for much of the country's history blacks faced near exclusion.[8] These regimes then provide whites with scripts that enable them to make claims for more organizational rewards (e.g., jobs, wages, promotions).[9]

How such regimes affect organizations, not the individuals located within them, is less appreciated. We tend to overlook organizations as social actors, failing to completely comprehend what this means. It is important to remember that though populated by people, these people are expected to subjugate their own needs in favor of those of the organization. Their job is to help the organization acquire the resources it needs to flourish and pursue its goals. The organization is an entity in and of itself. Race, as an attribute of social systems, is capable of shaping the organizing process or the organization's ability to claim rewards relative to its competitors. Thus, inequality regimes not only make it possible for whites within organizations to make claims that disadvantage blacks, they also make it possible for actors supporting white racial projects to construct claims that disadvantage organizations serving blacks. Hence, inequality regimes empower claims that organizations serving black Americans should have fewer financial, moral, and political resources than organizations serving white Americans.

Analyzing these regimes can help explain why we have the type of organizations that we do. Inequalities of race created black colleges as subordinate institutions. That is well known. Less obvious is that interrogating inequality regimes can help explain why black colleges took the shape, form, and structure that they did historically and the contemporary implications of this. Racial inequalities continue to limit the ability of black colleges to adapt to new circumstances. By studying black colleges, I am able to demonstrate how adaptation among black colleges threatened inequality regimes among all those interested in black higher education. No one individual or organization took sole responsibility for providing, or limiting for that matter, black Americans with access to higher education. Religious societies, community members, the state (Southern at first, then later Federal), and individual and foundation donors collectively endeavored to provide and at times curtail access. Consequently, black higher education is best understood as an activity undertaken by a community of actors, that is, an activity that takes place within the context of an organizational field.[10] With this premise in mind, I am able to systematically introduce inequality into the study of organizational fields.

Understanding how inequality influenced the growth and development of black colleges necessitates a multifaceted approach. Accomplishing this task requires more than an accounting of black history, culture, or particular black colleges. It requires a focus on the organizational field that black colleges operated within so as to illuminate the effect of particular historical configurations and constellations on their growth and development. The stories and actions of the leaders of colleges, foundations, and government bureaus will not be taken at face value. From the standpoint of organization theory, such individuals represent mere symbols or focal points for an organization's success or failure. The environment and social milieu will take center stage and black college adaptation will be analyzed in relation to them.

Organization theory provides a lens through which to interpret both the types of adaptive maneuvers undertaken by black colleges and how inequality shaped those maneuvers. This requires extending the scope of analysis beyond the colleges to include students, sponsors, donors, labor markets, the state, and the judiciary. Studying the colleges in isolation from this field of actors would hide the impediments to, and the sources and consequences of, adaptation. It is virtually impossible to investigate any episode of adaptation among black colleges without situating it within the context of the field of actors interested in promoting black higher education. Despite being on the front line in this effort, black colleges did not hold the most power, prestige, or influence among the field of actors promoting black higher education. Instead, black colleges often had to react and concede to the demands of other actors providing political, financial, and moral support.

It is misleading to think of black colleges in isolation. Colleges and universities rely on elementary and high schools to adequately prepare students for higher education, on other colleges to prepare faculty, and on employers to hire their graduates. Thus, black colleges and universities are enmeshed in a series of relationships that make it possible to provide higher education. Any investigation of black higher education as organizational phenomena must take these relationships seriously and account for whether and how they influenced adaptation among black colleges and universities.

Inequality made it impossible for black colleges to adapt in ways most beneficial to their students and to all those truly invested in these organizations' survival. Allowing black colleges to grow and develop to their best potential ran counter to the goals of a society premised upon the inferiority of blacks and the organizations serving them. The modern day development of black colleges, or in critics' eyes the lack thereof, cannot be understood or properly contextualized absent this historical reality.

This is not to suggest that traditionally white colleges did not face dilemmas. No organization operates without environmental constraints. All organizations must compete to obtain human, financial, and social capital as they attempt to grow and develop. However, in addition to overcoming the obstacles faced by traditionally white organizations, those serving black Americans were straddled with additional burdens. The state could outlaw, divert funding away from, and ignore the needs of organizations serving blacks without fear of repercussion. Any efforts to expand the capabilities of organizations serving black Americans could not contradict, undermine, or question state-sanctioned racial inequality, lest they face extra scrutiny. Even after the system of state-sanctioned racial inequality met its demise, organizations serving black Americans continued to deal with the legacies of this system. Officials who had once used their legislative and administrative powers to ensure that black colleges remained underfunded, understaffed, and underresourced now judged these schools according to whether they met standards they had once been actively prevented from reaching.

Using archival organizational data, both quantitative and qualitative, this book articulates how inequality shaped adaptation and the effect this had on the growth and development of black colleges between the mid- to late twentieth century. These years represent an interesting period within American and black college history. Though black colleges always suffered from the dynamics of inequality, the undoing of state-sanctioned racially segregated education heightened the stigma associated with the organizational field the schools occupied. It is, therefore, important to study the adaptive dilemmas particular to this moment in which society grappled intensely with the rationale of race-specific organizations. The civil rights movement assaulted the system, or as organizational scholars would say, the institutions that many including black college leaders and supporters claimed justified the colleges' existence. When used this way the term *institution* refers to the enduring features of social life that provide meaning and stability to social behaviors,[11] such as the laws and customs that made state-sanctioned racial inequality a reality. These institutions shaped the possibilities for black college adaptation.

The duality of the mid- to late twentieth century then, is striking. On the one hand, individual blacks gained unprecedented access to the American polity and society. On the other, the organizations that had served them, indeed prepared many black Americans to take advantage of these emerging opportunities, were characterized as out of step with the times. Investigating black colleges ten years before and roughly fifty years following the 1954 Supreme Court ruling in *Brown vs. Board of Education Topeka, Kansas* (*Brown*) offers the chance to understand how the unraveling of state-sanctioned racial inequality shaped the adaptation of organizations created under, and in support of, racial segregation.

Two primary research questions are explored throughout this book. How does inequality shape organizational adaptation? How does organizational adaptation shape inequality? The chapters highlight a circular pattern whereby inequality constrains the adaptive capacity of black colleges, and adaptions undertaken by black colleges challenge, yet, in the end, reify existing inequalities. Situating this study at the level of the organizational field makes it clear that inequality emanates from multiple sources, including the differential levels of power, prestige, and influence available to the various types of organizations, or populations,[12] promoting black higher education. Both the state and educational philanthropies had their own ideas about how a black college should structure its curricular offerings. Additionally, controlling financial resources enabled the state and educational philanthropies to dictate adaptive strategies. Yet, it would be too simple to suggest that all black colleges were affected similarly by this source of inequality. Inequities existed among the colleges themselves. Though formal rankings like those distributed by *U.S. News and World Report* had yet to appear, a status order among the colleges had arisen by the mid-twentieth century. As chapter 2 will demonstrate, an adaptive strategy constrained by the inequalities between black colleges and philanthropies formalized the inequalities among more and less developed colleges.

Likewise, situating this investigation at the organizational field level illustrates the organization- and field-level consequences of adaptation. While an adaptive strategy's most direct effect is on an organization's ability to survive, grow, and develop, it also alters the way an organization relates to the broader field of actors. As chapter 5 will demonstrate, black colleges adapted their curriculums to better reflect the employment opportunities facing black college graduates following the civil rights movement. These changes not only had implications for the organizational capacity of black colleges, but also influenced the relationship between black and traditionally white colleges. For much of their history, black and traditionally white colleges had distinct earned degree patterns. The changes black colleges underwent to grow and develop increased their similarity to their traditionally white counterparts.

How Inequality Influences Black College Adaptation

Schools are heavily institutionalized organizations, not judged according to measures such as financial performance or debt-to-equity ratios, but judged according to how well collectively defined interests are accounted for within their activities.[13] Operated for the benefit of society, schools necessarily exist within an open system. Decisions to adapt are influenced by and subject to the input of multiple stakeholders including the government, students, parents, and community members.

Within institutional paradigms, adaptation affords organizations the opportunity to gain social approval and legitimation from important stakeholders. Adopting widely used structural configurations indicates an organization's willingness to conform to prevailing standards. Whether these structures improve organizational performance is beside the point. If stakeholders value linking teacher pay to student performance, then engaging in programmatic and structural change to meet these expectations increases a school's desirability and legitimacy.[14] Consequently, any explanation of adaptation among black colleges should start from the contention that schools use adaptation to gain legitimacy, and then seek to understand how the category of "blackness" created conditions of inequality that complicated matters.

The American state, first through slavery and later through de jure and de facto segregation, endorsed the practice of separating people according to their racial ancestry. The policies associated with these practices led to the proliferation of organizations that served individuals of one race or another. These organizations sustained the system of racial segregation by ensuring that people of different races had access to separate service providers. Black colleges are a reflection of this policy. Because the system of racial segregation favored whites, the organizations catering to them were meant to have better resources and ultimately be of a higher quality than those to which blacks had access. Black colleges' legitimacy and social approval was intricately connected to their ability to fit within this inequality regime. It was expected that black colleges would educate black students while remaining inferior to traditionally white colleges. As a result, when black colleges needed to adapt, their ability to do so *fully* was limited, because Southern society did not welcome an educated black citizenry. In fact, restricted opportunities for blacks were key to its functioning.

Still agrarian following Emancipation, the planter elite needed blacks to labor on farms. The Southern political economy worked only to the extent that blacks were denied the very opportunities higher education promised—the ability to educate one's way out of farm labor. Yes, the Southern polity could sustain a handful of well-educated individuals—a W. E. B. Du Bois, Charles S. Johnson, or Charles Drew—but the education of blacks en masse presented a problem. For what highly educated person would actively pursue employment in an exploitative occupation such as farm labor? The close relationship between the planter elite, foundations, and the educational authorities within Southern states[15] had a severe impact on the adaptive possibilities of black colleges.

Southern state educational authorities routinely diverted funding away from state-sponsored black colleges to traditionally white ones, making it difficult for black colleges to adapt.[16] And educational authorities' reach extended beyond publicly controlled colleges. In their approach to rating black colleges, regional accrediting agencies further reinforced the inequality regimes operating within the South by refusing to accredit black colleges, instead opting to maintain a separate listing of approved Negro colleges or to ignore black colleges altogether.[17] Because of the growing emphasis placed on achieving accreditation by the late 1920s, black colleges had to then adapt to criteria that were not developed with their particular challenges in mind. This made it difficult for many of the schools to attain accreditation or to even be put on the list of approved Negro colleges.[18] This meant that among other things, black colleges would find it difficult to attain financial resources that were only available to accredited or approved schools, making it more challenging to become accredited in the future.

The planter elites' influence was not confined to elected and appointed officials. Even Northern-led foundations sided with the planter elites' desire to limit educational opportunities for blacks. Though Northern industrialists wanted to promote black education, these industrialists did not want the white South to feel antagonized by these efforts. Thus,

Northern industrialists refused to challenge the inequality regimes operating within the South. Therefore, more often than not, industrial philanthropies supported forms of education that ultimately limited the ability of black colleges to adapt beyond industrially or vocationally focused education.[19] For instance, circa 1920s, the Rosenwald Fund's emphasis on vocational education reflected the assumption that because their employment opportunities were limited, blacks did not need training in more academically rigorous subjects. Most blacks were employed in jobs that required no schooling, leading many foundation leaders to feel that "it was idle to educate them [Negroes] beyond their opportunities as the South would never permit them to enter upon professional and business careers in competition with the Whites."[20]

Following the 1954 *Brown* ruling, the Southern state's ability to assert its inequality regime initially weakened. For a brief moment, federal oversight of Southern schools led to real increases in the number of blacks receiving primary and secondary education. In turn, black colleges saw their enrollments increase twofold in some instances. The opportunities for black colleges to adapt to meet this new student demand seemed endless. However, federal oversight waned and the federal court system took up the mantle of reconstituting the white racial project[21] under the umbrella of color-blind public policy. Through various rulings, district courts and the Supreme Court created legal precedents stipulating that schools should not be identified by their race. Schools should be neither black nor white. These policies undercut the rationale for race-specific schools, while simultaneously affirming the perspective that though they were traditionally white, because they no longer intentionally denied blacks admission, traditionally white colleges were no longer racially specific.

The inequality regimes operating within the South produced specific regulative, normative, and cultural-cognitive barriers that affected the ability of black colleges to grow and develop.[22] At the regulative level, for instance, prior to *Brown,* state policies prevented black students from acquiring the skills necessary to be college ready. The law also prevented white students from attending black colleges. Yet, in a federally funded survey, Thomas Jesse Jones criticized black colleges for having small enrollments. [23] While supporters and detractors both recommended black colleges merge with nearby schools, recruiting more students represented an equally viable solution to small enrollments. However, state policies all but foreclosed recruitment as an adaptive strategy for black colleges.[24]

Black colleges also faced difficulty when trying to adapt to prevailing norms within higher education. Much has been written about the curriculum debates between W. E. B. Du Bois and Booker T. Washington.[25] The standard story depicts Du Bois as the champion of liberal arts and Washington as the champion of vocational arts. Yet, an institutional interpretation focuses less on either individual and more on the professional standards that emerged around college curriculum and whether black colleges were free to participate in this wave. When this debate raged among black college leaders, normative standards shifted such that it was no longer acceptable for traditionally white colleges to have a strictly vocationally focused curriculum. When it came time for black colleges to adopt this norm, which was increasingly followed by other colleges within the country, doing so was cast as problematic. Suddenly, the ability of a higher education organization to prepare its students for academically focused pursuits was implausible.

In the post-*Brown* world, culturally, the monikers "black college" or "historically black college" also complicate matters. Over time, traditionally white colleges abandoned their missionary preference for white students in principle if not always in practice. This coupled with the reality that most black students now attend a traditionally white college makes these schools appear as though they have kept up with the cultural shift toward valuing racially integrated education. Other than researchers who refer to these schools as "traditionally white colleges," few think of them as organizations who once made it their goal to maintain an all white student body. They are "just colleges."

Alternatively, black colleges to this day place a premium on the education of black students. Consequently, terms such as "historically black college" mask the adaptations that black colleges have made toward integrating their student bodies. The schools are multiracial, some more so than neighboring traditionally white colleges. Yet, the colleges did not go as far as abandoning their missionary focus on the education of black students. This cultural preference for facilitating black Americans' access to education makes it difficult to appreciate the schools' contribution to society beyond the black community.

The continued perception of inferiority relative to traditionally white colleges represents perhaps, the biggest cultural barrier to black college adaptation. This taken-for-granted assumption allows many to discount the educational achievements, and political and economic importance, of black colleges to the nation. Approximately 40 percent of black doctorates earn their bachelor's degrees at a black college. Eighty-five percent of black doctors attend a black college at some point in their academic career. More than 40 percent of blacks earning degrees in physics, chemistry, astronomy, environmental sciences, mathematics, and biology do so at black colleges. [26] Much empirical research shows that black students fare better emotionally and academically at black colleges than at traditionally white ones.[27] If black colleges were ranked in the same way that private corporations were, their total economic impact would land them on the Forbes Fortune 500 list.[28] Inequality regimes and the resulting stigma prevent black colleges from gaining the social approval and legitimacy that should befall institutionalized organizations responsible for such outcomes.

The presence of powerful inequalities forces a rethinking of black college efforts to adapt and of organization theory more generally. Absent inequality, organization theory would have predicted that the colleges' efforts to adapt would have drastically altered the public's willingness to support the schools while greatly reducing the organizational disparities between black and traditionally white colleges. To a limited extent, when black colleges adapted, progress was made toward these desirable outcomes. But given the inequalities of resources and much else within the field in which black colleges operated, their efforts to adapt also tended to increase the organizational disparities among black colleges, alienate quarters of the black community, and paint the schools into ideological corners that were difficult to emerge from, particularly following the end of state-sanctioned racially segregated education.

The following chapters will show that when inequality is present adaptation is partial at best. Partial because even when it appears as though organizations are doing something radically different, such as fundraising collectively (chapter 2), upon further reflection it becomes apparent that field-level dynamics related to inequality restricted the possibilities. Moreover, these adaptations are partial because the desired results are rarely achieved. Bringing an organizational perspective to bear on black college growth and development allows for analysis of what should have happened versus what actually happened when black colleges tried to adapt. Organization theory offers specific predictions regarding the outcomes that should result from adapting. Be it greater control over material or cultural resources, institutionalized organizations engage in adaptation to gain more legitimacy and social approval, that is, to improve their situation. Thus, it is important to contemplate whether and how inequality moderates potentially positive and lucrative organizational outcomes.

A voluminous scholarship on black colleges exists, however, a focus on partial adaptation is missing. Historically based works tend to chronicle the development of black colleges in particular eras. For instance, Dwight O. W. Holmes's *The Evolution of the Negro College* charted the rise of both private and public black colleges. Holmes drew particular attention to the role of religious societies in the sponsorship and development of black colleges. Though neither James D. Anderson's *The Education of Blacks in the South, 1860–1935* nor Eric Anderson and Alfred Moss Jr.'s *Dangerous Donations: Northern Philanthropy and Southern Black Education, 1902–1930* are strictly focused on black colleges, both volumes provide invaluable insight into the role of Northern industrial philanthropists in black higher education. Desegregation struggles have afforded legal scholars and political scientists the opportunity to investigate black colleges as well. Mark Tushnet highlights the precarious position in which black colleges were placed as a result of the National Association for the Advancement of Colored People's (NAACP) legal strategy to end racially segregated education.[29] In arguing *Brown*, the NAACP criticized single-race institutions and many of the organization's leaders adopted an antagonistic stance toward black colleges. Focusing on black colleges after the *Brown* decision in *Is Separate Unequal? Black Colleges and the Challenge to Desegregation*, Albert Samuels offers a political scientific analysis of legal decisions pertaining to the desegregation of higher education and their effect on black colleges.[30]

The picture that emerges from these works indicates that since the 1800s, blacks and whites, religious groups, the state, philanthropists, and their foundations have endeavored to provide black Americans with access to higher education. Some of these efforts were incredibly earnest and well planned. After establishing Talladega College in 1867, the American Missionary Association provided Northern-trained teachers for the school's eighteen students. At this time, education in Alabama was so dismal that Talladega took it upon itself to offer elementary and high school training. Despite its hopes to prepare black students for college-level work, it was not until 1890 that the first college course appeared in Talladega's catalog.[31]

Other efforts to provide black students with access to higher education occurred with far more haste. To stave off racially integrating their flagship universities, Southern state authorities established graduate schools for black students and instituted programmatic upgrades at previously neglected publicly controlled black colleges. With little forethought, politicians in Texas and Oklahoma created law schools for blacks in response to lawsuits accusing each state of failing to provide black students with access to legal education in 1947 and 1948 respectively.[32]

We also know that the individual liberty of black Americans threatened black colleges in the mid-twentieth century. Though the *Brown* ruling applied mainly to primary and secondary schools, black institutions of higher learning were immediately put on the defense and required to justify their right to exist.[33] Suddenly, affirming the right of individual black Americans to attend any school of their choosing meant that black colleges were no longer a legitimate educational alternative.

Instead of documenting particular historical moments for black colleges, a focus on partial adaptation uses seemingly disparate moments to highlight a more general pattern by which the field structures the adaptive possibilities for black colleges. Black colleges operated within a field rife with inequality that restricted their creativity, ensuring limited adaptive responses. Those that controlled resources (e.g., Southern states, philanthropists, judiciary) essential to black colleges' ability to prosper were committed to maintaining the dominance of traditionally white colleges and the white racial project more widely. Sustaining this inequality regime necessarily foreclosed the most beneficial organizational opportunities, thus significantly limiting black colleges' capacity.

Plan of the Book

Multiple adaptive episodes are used throughout this volume to investigate how inequality influenced the growth and development of black colleges in the mid- to late twentieth century. To set the stage for these episodes, chapter 1, "The Black Higher Education Field," introduces the various organizations involved in promoting the college education of black Americans. A sociological periodization draws attention to the specific adaptive challenges related to particular eras. Through the 1960s, the social context that actively promoted the inferiority of black Americans more generally constrained black colleges' ability to provide black students with a path toward better opportunities. Even when they needed to adapt, black colleges faced obstructions from the social milieu or field in which they resided. If an adaptive strategy appeared to challenge the ideologies associated with racial segregation, then black colleges risked losing their place within Southern society. Though they no longer had to adapt in light of ideologies presuming the inferiority of black students, new adaptive challenges emerged following the end of state-sanctioned racial segregation. Black organizations continued to be seen as inferior. Adding to this, black colleges now had to compete with traditionally white colleges—the historic beneficiaries of racial segregation—for black students. This overview provides the necessary context to understand the inequality regimes operating within the South, and America more extensively, which dogged black colleges from their genesis. From here, four empirical chapters investigate how specific forms or instantiations of inequality structured black college development.

The adaptive episodes covered in the empirical chapters mirror the dominance of particular types of colleges or organizational forms throughout the time period of interest. Chapters 2 and 3 highlight challenges associated with private college adaptation. Private colleges, especially future United Negro College Fund (UNCF) member colleges, dominated the black higher education field in enrollment and public discussion first. The fundraising campaigns that these schools undertook in the mid-1940s placed private black colleges on a national stage. However, in the mid-1950s, following the *Brown* decision, state-controlled or public black colleges eclipsed the private ones. Not only did enrollments at public black colleges outpace their private counterparts, the conversation also shifted toward understanding the role of public black colleges within a society now placing a premium upon racially integrated education. Chapter 4 highlights challenges associated with public college adaptation. As traditionally white colleges entered the black higher education field, attention turns toward understanding how black colleges compared to the schools that became their foremost competitor for black students. Thus, the final empirical chapter highlights challenges associated with black college adaptation vis-à-vis traditionally white colleges.

Focusing on subsets of black colleges provides a means of analyzing how these schools were valued as organizational actors and the relevance of this for adaptation. Again, as institutionalized organizations, black colleges must maintain an awareness of the interests held by the entire field of actors. Adaptation then becomes a way to show that black colleges recognize these interests and are working to gain social approval and legitimacy from this field of actors. Additionally, focusing on subsets of black colleges highlights the difference between sociological and historical treatments of black colleges. My intention is not to document a general history of black colleges but to isolate theoretically significant issues that were critical to shaping the black higher education field. Not all black colleges participated equally in these events. Nevertheless, these events influenced the organizational possibilities for all parties involved in the provision of black higher education.

Chapter 2, "Collective Action and Status Inequality," examines the UNCF's formation. Studying which colleges were invited to and ultimately joined the UNCF illuminates the organizational characteristics valued by major foundations—a key player in the black higher education field. Problematizing who joined the UNCF departs from historical perspectives on this organization's importance. In *Envisioning Black Colleges*, Marybeth Gasman focuses on the UNCF so as to understand the shifting terrain of black higher education philanthropy in the mid-twentieth century. Indeed, this was a novel form of organization. However, the effect of the UNCF's emergence on the relationships between more and less developed black colleges goes unnoticed in her study.

In its selectivity, the UNCF solidified previously implicit status distinctions among private black colleges. Hence, this organization's formation demonstrates the circularity of inequality and adaptation. UNCF affiliates were more developed with regard to their curriculum, enrollment, and income. Historically, a potential affiliate's ability to achieve development in such areas depended upon foundation support. Though initially not invited to join, those schools lacking development in key areas were allowed to join should their position improve. Given that all private four-year black colleges joined the UNCF at some point, this organization's formation is significant beyond the history of philanthropy. The less-developed schools now had to strive toward those status markers valued by the UNCF and foundations if they were to join the fundraising effort. Yet, the less developed schools were initially locked out of a financially lucrative opportunity that could have helped them improve more rapidly. By investigating the UNCF, the causes and consequences of the status inequities within the black higher education field come to light. Moreover, the analysis offers an opportunity to understand how field-level inequality regimes shape definitions of institutional legitimacy and the implications of this for accessing the resources and support necessary to adapt.

Likewise, the UNCF's campaigns provide a record for how private black colleges—and given the organization's reach and influence, I argue, all black colleges—were valued in the years leading up to the *Brown* decision. Chapter 3, "Advocacy and Racial Inequality," investigates the UNCF's first ten (1944–1954) annual campaigns. Much like the formation process, the organization's advocacy highlights how an adaptive strategy strengthened existing inequality. The taken-for-granted assumption of black inferiority and racial segregation's righteousness shaped the words chosen by the UNCF as it advocated for the financial support of private black colleges. The value of black colleges was understood in relation to how these schools helped society fulfill segregationists' goals.

The UNCF raised money by highlighting the need for a talented tenth and claiming private black colleges as protectors of segregated education capable of producing leaders who would not challenge racial segregation or demand political equality. Increases in funding for facilities, faculty, or curriculum were intended to make black colleges better racially segregated institutions. This again points to the significance of the UNCF beyond studies of the history of philanthropy. Investigating the words used to raise money for black colleges provides evidence of the ways in which inequality regimes structure an attempt to adapt.

Chapter 3 highlights how the cultural-cognitive frames supporting the inequality regimes limited the claims black colleges could make about their role within society. This framing proved consequential, not just for its ability to raise money, but also because black colleges, both private and public, were then "stuck" with this interpretation in the years following the *Brown* decision as chapter 4, "Adapting in a World Without State-Sanctioned Racial Inequality," highlights. Thematic emphasis shifts to the public black colleges at this point for two reasons. First, public black colleges are educating the majority of black students. Second, because of their relationship to the state, public black colleges are more intensely scrutinized in this period. Focusing on the public colleges best captures the dilemmas of adaptation in the postsegregationist historical moment. Adaptation in this period was designed to demonstrate the value and relevance of black colleges in a higher education system that supposedly valued racially integrated education. The historical and legal record provides ample evidence with which to trace how black colleges and their advocates responded, that is, adapted to the shifting socio-legal landscape.

Chapter 5, the final empirical chapter, "Building Legitimacy amid Inequality," uses data on earned degrees to demonstrate the organizational consequences of the shifting value placed on black colleges through the end of the twentieth century. Once valued for their role in a segregated society, now valued in comparison to traditionally white colleges—adaptation in this period was toward the "norm" of white colleges more than ever. Adapting in this manner meant that black colleges were no longer teacher training–focused organizations, as they had been historically. Yet and still, critics continued to cast the schools as narrowly focused and as anachronistic. Despite real progress in adapting, the schools found it difficult to escape the perception that they were drastically different from traditionally white colleges. The air of stigma continued to plague black colleges.

Investigating coalition formation (chapter 2), advocacy (chapter 3), institutional work (chapter 4), and isomorphism (chapter 5) highlights the diverse array of adaptive strategies utilized by black colleges. Though it is easiest to detect via structural transformation (e.g., coalition formation, isomorphism), to adapt, organizations do more than this. In several instances, growing and developing black colleges required strategies intended to bring about cultural transformation. Black colleges attempted to manipulate the cultural associations tied to these organizations. Advocacy and institutional work may not lead to structural transformation, but they are efforts to adapt nonetheless. Adapting in this manner focuses on influencing field members' attitudes toward single-race schools and their value in society. Adaptation can be used to reify (chapter 3) or challenge (chapter 4) the characteristics that should be of value to field members. Most importantly, studying a range of adaptive strategies demonstrates the extensive effects of inequality. Inequality has the power to mar both structurally and culturally focused adaptations.

After focusing so intently on specific episodes of adaptation, "The Story of Organizational Adaptation" (chapter 6) highlights what can be learned by comparing across the cases studied within this volume and comparing black colleges to other stigmatized organizational actors such as women's and tribal colleges. Particular attention is given to understanding the consequences of the field's relatively stable structure and hence the field's ability to impose nonoptimal adaptive strategies on black colleges. I argue that if stigmatized actors hope to do something other than partially adapt, they must circumvent interactions with field members committed to projects that perpetuate their stigmatized position.

Conclusion

Created to sustain racial segregation policies, black colleges were and still are a dominant part of the American political, cultural, and economic system. In the current political climate, traditionally white colleges have all but retreated from an emphasis on affirmative action and other programs that led to real increases in the number of black students on campus. Conservative racial projects, with the aid of the court system, act to limit traditionally white colleges' efforts to promote integration and access. If black colleges disappeared from the higher education landscape there is little evidence to suggest that traditionally white colleges would fill the void. Accordingly, questions regarding the necessity of black colleges must acknowledge that black and traditionally white colleges are not substitutes for one another in an economic sense. It's not the difference between margarine and butter.

Though it may seem innocuous, the question, "Are black colleges still necessary?" is actually fundamental to the question of black economic and cultural progress in a color-blind but racist society. In fact, this question offers insight into the taken-for-granted nature of traditionally white organizations. This question is itself a reflection of the inequality that continues to plague black colleges. When racial desegregation occurred, few if any questioned why the universities of Texas, Mississippi, Georgia, or any of the other traditionally white state-run schools were still necessary. This despite the role that each organization had played in perpetuating racial discrimination in the former slaveholding states.

Why was it necessary to perpetuate schools whose organizational practices were ingrained with racist procedures? Traditionally white colleges may have been the "best" the South had to offer but they were complicit actors in the tale of segregated education. Surely if there had been will, imagination, and political pressure the region might have developed a solution that did away with traditionally white colleges in favor of opening schools that had never erected exclusionary admission policies. Not surprisingly, this did not occur. Instead, traditionally white colleges were understood as mainstream organizations while black colleges were seen as deviations from the norm. This despite the proven record of black colleges in creating skilled, educated, African Americans who could take advantage of desegregation policies. Traditionally white colleges of the South lacked any credentials to suggest they could, would, or wanted to educate black students.

Questioning the necessity of black colleges affords people an opportunity to talk about race and education without actually having to engage the thorny subjects of racial disparities in access and outcomes. Inevitably, when debating the necessity of black colleges thoughts about individuals get subsumed in a conversation that is presumably about organizations. In essence, debating the necessity of black organizations provides cover for things that one would not say about black individuals. On the one hand, critiquing the graduation rates and selectivity of black colleges appears innocent enough. Any organization that wants the continued support of the public and policymakers should be held accountable. On the other hand, these critiques of organizational outcomes mask critiques of the type of student that attends black colleges, that is, the type of student who takes longer than average to complete college, has lower SATs, and comes from an impoverished background. Black colleges have different

organizational outcomes than traditionally white colleges because, on average, they educate a fundamentally different type of student. A type of
student that would more often than not be denied admission to a highly
selective, well-resourced, traditionally white college. What schools would
absorb these students if black colleges were no longer an option? Do we as
a society feel these students do not deserve a chance at higher education?
Because they do take these students in and successfully credential them,
black colleges challenge mainstream notions of the "merit" and "qualifications" necessary for higher education.

   If today someone suggested that as a remedy to continued discrimination blacks return to Africa, we would without a doubt question the
integrity of this proponent. Yet, despite continued disparities in educational outcomes between blacks and whites, people genuinely and openly
question the need for and relevance of black colleges without fear of being
identified as bigots. How is questioning the necessity of a set of organizations that has proven its worth with regard to black education a legitimate
intellectual endeavor? If black colleges are still necessary then it means
that American society has not progressed as much as those who proclaim
the value of color-blind educational policies suggest we have. Black colleges represent a constant affront to this ideology. Their presence forces
us to confront the issue of race, a subject with which America has never
easily dealt. Because these organizations are so crucial to black higher education, it is imperative that scholars and practitioners alike comprehend
the challenges facing these schools as they adapt. So in lieu of asking, "Are
black colleges still necessary?" I instead encourage all to ask, "What barriers have historically prevented these schools from effectively growing
their resources, expressing their rights, and developing their distinctive
and much needed capabilities?"

1

The Black Higher Education Field

Ashmun Institute, founded in 1854 and now known as Lincoln University of the Commonwealth of Pennsylvania, holds claim as the first school established with the intent of offering "higher education in the arts and sciences" for youth of African descent.[1] In the course of conducting this research, I identified 154 schools that began with the primary mission to provide higher education to black Americans.[2]

As Figure 1.1[3] indicates, while three black colleges—Lincoln University of Pennsylvania, Wilberforce University of Ohio, and Atlanta University of Georgia—began before the U.S. Civil War (1861–1865), the remaining black colleges opened their doors in its aftermath.

These schools intended to provide the formerly enslaved and the generations following them with the means to participate within a democratic society. Southern Reconstruction provided the groups operating these schools with a window in which to act. Whereas it had been illegal to educate blacks during slavery, and was still a dangerous endeavor in some Southern locales, educating freedmen and women was now an option.[4] Without a doubt, the emergence of black colleges can be understood as an adaptive response to the post-Emancipation environment. Moreover, the story fits neatly within the standard paradigm of adaptation within the organization studies tradition. Groups in favor of educating blacks—missionary societies, ex-slaves, the Freedmen Bureau—seized the opportunities made available by the political cleavages of Reconstruction. The uncertainty of this moment allowed for innovation with regard to the education of blacks.[5] Then again, this depiction provides an incomplete picture of the field's expansion. For though black colleges emerged, they did so against the backdrop of the developing system of state-sanctioned racial segregation.

Figure 1.1 School Foundings per Year

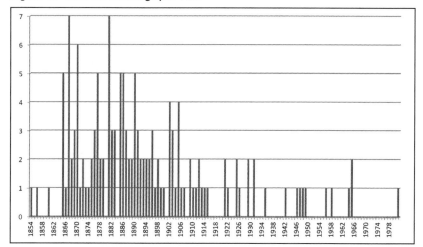

Described as a race-making institution by social theorist Loïc Wac-quant, the system of legally sanctioned racial segregation permeated all realms of life within the American South because it "consisted of an ensemble of social and legal codes that prescribed the complete separa-tion of the 'races' and sharply circumscribed the life chances of African-Americans."[6] Colloquially known as Jim Crow, the system sustained and further developed status distinctions between whites and blacks devel-oped during slavery. The character of black higher education cannot be understood outside of this context.

The proliferation of publicly controlled black colleges illustrates the inescapable effect of Southern racial politics on the growth and develop-ment of the black higher education field. As Table 1.1 illustrates, the aver-age state-controlled black college was established in 1887.

Comparatively, the average state-controlled school for white students was established in 1840. Each state that established a black college al-ready had a college in place. In theory, black students could have attended the state-run schools already in existence. In practice, doing so was unac-ceptable in the Southern states.

As a result, two separate fields—one black, the other white—worked to provide higher education within the South. The organizational conse-quences of this decision for black colleges were severe. Funding for educa-tion in the South traditionally lagged behind all other regions in the nation. Particularly in the Civil War's aftermath, as a region the South's financial

Table 1.1. Southern University Founding Dates

State	First Traditionally White College Founded	First Black College Founded
Alabama	1831	1874
Arkansas	1871	1875
Delaware	1833	1891
Florida	1853	1887
Georgia	1785	1890
Kentucky	1865	1896
Louisiana	1860	1914
Maryland	1856	1886
Missouri	1839	1866
Mississippi	1844	1871
Oklahoma	1890	1897
North Carolina	1798	1877
South Carolina	1801	1895
Tennessee	1794	1912
Texas	1881	1885
Virginia	1819	1883
West Virginia	1867	1891
Earliest Founding Date	1785	1866
Most Recent Founding Date	1890	1914
Average Founding Date	1840	1887

resources were crippled. Operating a dual system of education is necessarily more expensive than a single system, as it required two sets of schools, two sets of certification procedures, two sets of administrative offices, two sets of school boards, etc. Despite the region's financially precarious position, the Southern states' cultural preferences dictated an unsustainable organizational solution. In a system privileging whiteness, starving black colleges of critical resources represented the only way forward.

The establishment of public colleges is but one example of how Jim Crow structured the adaptive possibilities of black higher education. However, the system encouraged more than the expansion of one particular organizational form. It touched every aspect of black college growth and development. To remain viable, institutionalized organizations must gain the public's trust.[7] This was particularly consequential for black colleges, public and private, operating within the Jim Crow South. Those involved in the provision of black higher education had to construct a system of colleges and universities that acknowledged and incorporated the legal rules and cultural norms associated with Jim Crow. Though they would have welcomed white students on their campus, black colleges could not do so. Though college leaders preferred racially integrated campus activities, when prominent whites visited black college campuses, segregation was often enforced. Though leaders preferred to develop their curricula fully, black colleges were encouraged to restrict their offerings to majors that would not put their graduates in direct competition with whites.[8]

The Jim Crow period was not the only historical configuration that influenced the growth and development of black colleges. Other configurations also affected the adaptive capacity of the schools. Though they did not begin as organizations that focused on graduate-level training, by the 1970s a number of state-controlled black colleges had the capacity to offer postbaccalaureate courses. Understanding how the curricular emphasis among black public colleges came to include graduate-level programs requires an understanding of broader events occurring within the black higher education field.

Four time periods are of particular interest for this study. The first time period, 1854–1895, marks the field of black higher education's creation and expansion. The expansion of the field occurred as Southern society struggled to reconfigure itself following the Civil War. By the second period, 1896–1944, the field had taken shape with regard to the number and type of schools that would operate within it. Clear enrollment, degree, and financial patterns had crystalized. Unfortunately, it had become clear that blacks located in the Southern states would not be treated as full citizens. In this era, black colleges felt the full weight of the *Plessy v. Ferguson* ruling that codified state-sanctioned racial inequality.

Several factors collided to make the third time period, 1945–1975, a momentous one for black colleges. Improvements in primary and secondary education for black students led to an increase in the number of students seeking higher education. Taking advantage of the GI Bill, black servicemen returning from World War II swarmed black college campuses. Though mass protests had yet to occur, black colleges began to feel the effects of what we would later call the civil rights movement in the 1940s. As legal challenges against racially segregated education mounted, Southern state educational authorities expanded the capacity of public black colleges. The 1954 *Brown* ruling further hastened state and private efforts to improve black colleges. Between 1945 and 1975, black colleges underwent unparalleled growth and development.

The renaissance would not last forever. During the final time period, 1976–1999, the place of black colleges within the American landscape faced increasing scrutiny. Black students began to enroll in traditionally white colleges. Several black colleges closed. Several black colleges had a majority white student body. While the usefulness of black colleges had always come under attack, the rationale for attacking the colleges shifted. Whereas critics had once wondered aloud whether "savages" could acquire higher learning, they now questioned the necessity of black colleges given the plethora of choices available to black students.

Field Creation and Expansion, 1854–1895

The majority of black colleges (60 percent) began during the field's first forty years.[9] Between 1854 and 1895, ninety-two black colleges emerged amid a general air of optimism. The South was being reconstructed. The political system that oppressed blacks was coming undone. In coalition with white Republicans, black leaders used the Southern state constitutional conventions to lay the foundation for universal education.[10] Promoting higher education represented a natural extension of the idea that every citizen had a right to education within the reconstructed South. With the role of blacks in the postwar South shifting, black colleges emerged to train blacks to participate as full political, social, and economic citizens.[11]

Private colleges dominated the landscape, accounting for 74 percent of the ninety-two schools established in this first period. A small minority (N = 14) operated as independent schools while the rest had ties to black and white religious societies.[12] The denominational boards of these religious groups provided teachers, financial support, and administrative resources for their affiliated colleges.[13] Using northeastern colleges as their models, the private schools, particularly those controlled by religious societies, viewed the classical curriculum as the best way to prepare black students for participation within a democratic society.[14] Many private black colleges even utilized the same admission requirements as the classical New England colleges of the time by limiting admittance to the freshmen class to those students that had taken higher arithmetic, algebra, and Greco-Roman history.[15]

Of the ninety-two schools that began during this period, 24 percent (N = 22) operated as state-controlled or affiliated institutions. Eight of the state-controlled colleges had the additional designation of land grant schools.[16] Passed by the U.S. Congress in 1862, the Morrill Act provided each state with a tract of federal land for the purpose of establishing a college focused on the agricultural and mechanical arts. The founding of public colleges during this period provides a window into the coexistence of contrasting sentiments and foreshadowed what was to come. Like the denominational boards, Southern state legislatures took up the cause of black higher education. Yet, the state legislatures, even when controlled by coalitions in favor of black access to education, faced opposition.

When chartered in 1871 by a Republican state legislature, Alcorn Agricultural and Mechanical College of Mississippi received three-fifths of the state's land grant funds, an annual appropriation of $50,000 from the state legislature, and a four-year scholarship for one student from each legislative district.[17] Indeed, a promising start for any college. However, just one year earlier, the faculty and chancellor at the University of Mississippi threatened to resign should the school admit black students. Alcorn had the backing of the legislature. Yet, Alcorn might not have existed if forces within Mississippi had shown a willingness to integrate the existing state university.

Categorizing black colleges as state or privately controlled masks the fluidity that existed in the early development of the field. The Colored Industrial and Agricultural School of Louisiana, now known as Grambling State University, began as a private college in 1905. Not until 1928 did the school become affiliated with the state. Likewise, St. Philips Normal and Industrial College of Texas opened its doors as an affiliate of the Episcopal Church in 1898. When the church could no longer financially support the school, it affiliated with the state in 1942.

Because they are responsive to their environments, institutionalized organizations are heavily influenced by the societal characteristics present at the time of their founding.[18] Moreover, once established these characteristics tend to carry through for generations. For instance, schools at all levels continue to close for the summer months. Primary, secondary, and postsecondary schools still reflect America's agricultural past even though few children spend their summers farming. The educational backgrounds of the formerly enslaved had profound implications for black college growth and development. The majority of blacks emerged from slavery illiterate. As the black higher education field expanded post Emancipation, those operating the black colleges could not ignore this reality. As a result, black colleges opted for an organizational structure that included collegiate, elementary, and high school divisions.

Chartered in 1868, Hampton Normal and Agricultural Institute focused on the "instruction of youth in the various common-school, academic and collegiate branches."[19] Of the nine hundred students attending Hampton in 1917, all were enrolled in elementary and secondary courses.[20] Not until the 1920s did collegiate-level enrollment at Hampton become significant. Like the privately controlled schools, the public schools also began with small enrollments and gradually evolved into colleges. By 1917 only one public school, Florida Agriculture and Mechanical College, founded in 1887, enrolled students at the collegiate level.[21]

While the majority of black colleges concentrated on both pre- and postsecondary work, a small number of schools concentrated on still higher levels of education. From the outset, those invested in black higher education wanted to ensure access to graduate and professional training. The black community needed trained doctors, lawyers, ministers, and social workers to serve them. Howard University, Atlanta University, Meharry Medical College, and Gammon Theological Seminary were four such institutions founded with a particular focus on graduate and professional training.

As the black higher education field developed it came to include a diverse set of schools. Private, public, undergraduate, graduate, and professional schools each occupied a position within the field. Within each of these broad categories further distinctions applied—religious, independent, land grant.

In the moments following the Civil War, those opening black colleges assumed that blacks would have access to the full range of social, political, and economic opportunities emerging within the South. For a time this was true—blacks accounted for 15 percent of political officeholders in the 1870s South, a higher proportion than in 1990.[22] As the 1890s approached, it became clear that these opportunities would not last. The dynamics that would plague black college development had taken root.

Reconstruction had come to an end. The federal government would not intervene on behalf of black education for decades to come. Opponents of black education, now controlling Southern state legislatures, took an interest in black education for nefarious reasons. As a result of the second Morrill Act of 1890, all states that maintained racially segregated systems of education had to establish land grant colleges for blacks if they chose to utilize the land and monies from the Morrill Act to operate land grant colleges for white students.[23] Southern states fulfilled this requirement by annexing existing schools, some of which had operated as private black colleges until this point, and creating new schools.

The field of black higher education would persist. However, state-sanctioned racial inequality shaped the adaptive capacity of the colleges.

By 1896, blacks located in the Southern states were still not treated as full citizens. In that year, the U.S. Supreme Court held that statutes that imply distinctions between "white and colored races" do not destroy the legal equality of the races. They argued that the Fourteenth Amendment, which guaranteed citizenship, due process, and equal protection under the law to formerly enslaved blacks, had not guaranteed social equality to this group. A ruling against Homer Plessy's right to sit in the "White" car of the East Louisiana Railroad had far-reaching consequences. For years to come, black colleges, public and private, forged ahead amid concerns that black higher education threatened the stability of Southern and America society.

Separate but Equal, 1896–1944

With the Supreme Court's approval, Southern states legalized racial inequality. The role of black education in general, and black colleges specifically, within a racially segregated society became a topic of deliberation. Education should enrich political, social, and economic opportunities—things Southern society denied blacks altogether. Whether and how schools for blacks could exist within such a system became the subject of heated exchanges. The ideological debates over the most advantageous form of black higher education that occurred during the late nineteenth and early twentieth centuries have received much historical attention. Often referenced in relation to Booker T. Washington and W. E. B. Du Bois, these debates reflected the attitudes of a diverse set of parties interested in black higher education—black leaders, Northern industrial philanthropies, Southern education reformers, Southern planters.

In his 1895 speech at the Cotton States and International Exposition in Atlanta, Booker T. Washington claimed, "No race can prosper till it learns that there is as much dignity in tilling a field as in writing a poem."[24] Washington pushed for the development of a black laboring class and emphasized the role of black colleges in this process. Because they educated black teachers, black colleges had the ability to "train a corps of teachers with a particular social philosophy relevant to the political and economic reconstruction of the South."[25] Washington's attitudes reflected a widely held sentiment among those in favor of the "Hampton-Tuskegee Idea" which held that black colleges' pedagogical focus should maintain the inequities of wealth, power, and race.[26] Here, educating blacks was a necessary part of the South's industrial transformation. The "right" type of education would produce more efficient workers and

represented a "sound investment in social stability and economic pros-
perity."[27] In contrast to the Hampton-Tuskegee Idea stood those who
argued that "ex-slaves struggled to develop a social and educational ideology singularly appropriate to their defense of emancipation and one that
challenged the social power of the planter regime."[28] The emerging class
of black intelligentsia and leaders viewed black colleges as tools to liberate
blacks from the inequities inherent to a system such as Jim Crow.

This debate offers evidence of the field coalescing. When actors, individual and organizational, begin to interact and engage one another as
though they are part of the same enterprise this is an important step in a
field's development. Doing so indicates recognition of common purpose
that is essential to field membership.[29] While pedagogical preferences
among the factions differed, the mere fact that one side chose to engage
the other shows that each party knew the other was equally vested in
the provision of black higher education. Moreover, it is through these interactions and others that standardized data about the colleges becomes
available.

When it took an interest in black higher education, the Rockefeller
family's General Education Board, founded in 1902, began to collect enrollment, course, financial, facility, and faculty data from the black colleges. To determine whether to support a college, the foundation sent
field agents to conduct site visits. In his role as a general field agent for the
General Education Board between 1915 and 1933, Jackson Davis visited
black college campuses to assess their progress. Not only would Davis
interview campus officials, he would also attend classes and inspect facilities, all in an effort to determine if a school merited foundation support. Even when the foundation did not visit schools, it would request
that schools submit data on the finances, enrollment, classes, and faculty
using a standardized template internally referenced as the blank form.[30]

The federal government's surveys of black colleges in 1916, 1929, and
1942 further attest to the interconnections that developed within the
black higher education field. Thomas Jesse Jones first affiliated with black
colleges in his role as an associate chaplain and economics instructor at
Hampton Institute in 1902.[31] In 1913 he became the educational director
of the Phelps Stokes Fund, a philanthropy whose interest included black
education.[32] During his time there, Jones directed the 1916 survey, *Negro
Education: A Study of the Private and Higher Schools for Colored People
in the United States.*[33] Notably, the Phelps Stokes Fund sponsored this
survey in cooperation with the U.S. Department of Interior.[34] The movement of key people in and out of organizations related to black higher

education offers further evidence of the field's coalescence. Each organization had a stake in black higher education and the movement of individuals across these organizations reinforced the interconnections of
the field.

College leaders spearheaded efforts to document black colleges as
well. Du Bois, working at Atlanta University, catalogued the "intricate
social problems" affecting black communities.[35] As a result, volumes
such as *The College Bred Negro*, published in 1900, tracked the status and
development of black colleges and their graduates. The *Journal of Negro
Education* published its first issue in 1932. Housed at Howard University, founder and editor-in-chief Charles H. Thompson used the journal to
document the status of black education, particularly the state of black colleges.[36] Around the same time, Dwight O. W. Holmes, dean of Howard's
graduate school, published his study of black colleges, *The Evolution of the
Negro College*. Several coalitions among the colleges began during this
time period as the connections between them deepened—the Association
of Colleges for Negro Youth (1913), the Conference of Presidents of Negro
Land Grant Colleges (1924), the Association of Colleges and Secondary
Schools for Negroes (1934), and the United Negro College Fund (1944).

The government, foundation, and publication data that emerged
during this period make it possible to understand the relationship between the social milieu (e.g., ideological debates, racial segregation) and
black college growth and development. Historical works have established that foundations took sides in the aforementioned pedagogical de-
bates. Northern industrial philanthropies such as the General Education
Board preferred to support black colleges that adhered to the Hampton-
Tuskegee Idea.[37] In the early 1900s, philanthropic groups, including the
General Education Board, pressured schools such as Fisk University, Fort
Valley High and Industrial School, and St. Paul's Normal and Industrial
School to implement elements of vocational training associated with the
Hampton-Tuskegee model in lieu of school leader preferences for the lib-
eral arts by intimating that foundation funding would increase.

Data from several sources contextualize the financial ramifications of such events for black colleges. *The Evolution of the Negro College* illustrates that even among poorly resourced schools differences
existed.[38] Using data from the 1929 *Survey of Negro Colleges and Universities*, Holmes tabulated that as a group, black colleges had a total endowment of $20,713,796.00. While the average black college in 1926–27
had $85,426.00 in its endowment fund, a wide gulf existed between the
most well-endowed schools, Hampton and Tuskegee ($14,135,768.00

combined), and all the others.[39] Foundation preferences for this pedagogical model had more than ideological consequences. A financial pecking order among the colleges took root.

Though public and private colleges existed, as Figure 1.2 documents, at their peak, private black colleges enrolled 90 percent of the students within the field. Given their dominance, private college endowment figures offer a general proxy for the well-being of the entire field. Endowment, and the income from it, are important determinants of a college's ability to grow and develop. It is no surprise then, that the federal government recognized only three black colleges as "true" colleges in 1916. The 1916 survey, *Negro Education: A Study of the Private and Higher Schools for Colored People in the United States*, revealed that thirty-three schools offered work at the collegiate level. However, because the majority of the work undertaken at these schools occurred in primary and secondary education, the survey classified only three as true colleges—Howard University, Meharry Medical College, and Fisk University. The report referred to Howard's endowment as "negligible" and Fisk's endowment as "insufficient."[40] Notwithstanding the poor state of their endowments, in each case the schools had secured external support, which no doubt contributed to their ability to devote the necessary resources to developing their collegiate curriculum. Howard University received an annual appropriation from the federal government; Meharry Medical College received financial support from the Carnegie and Rockefeller family foundations; Fisk University had found success raising funds through the performances of the Fisk Jubilee Singers. The poor financial situation of most schools made it impossible to adequately develop both pre- and postsecondary work. Holmes estimated that "6 per cent of the total income of [schools doing some college work] $3,999,071, or $239,404, for the support of 2,641 college students for a year, or a per capita expenditure of less than one hundred dollars, was a sum entirely inadequate even in 1916."[41]

Ironically, despite their large endowments, given their propensity to focus on vocational training, the government recognized neither Hampton nor Tuskegee as colleges. Foundation preferences aside, this model did not meet the standards by which colleges were judged. Even at this point it is possible to see the problems that result from partial adaptation. The private colleges that aspired to be colleges could not actually achieve this goal because they lacked the financial resources to do so. The Hampton-Tuskegee schools had more financial resources than others, but the money was conditioned upon eschewing the curricular choices

Figure 1.2 Percent of Enrollment by College Type, 1916–1944

that would enable the schools to be recognized as colleges. Thus, neither type of school—the liberal or vocationally focused—was able to achieve its full potential. Foundation policies rooted in theories of black inferiority and inequality curtailed adaptation all around.

High enrollments in the primary and secondary or academy divisions of the black colleges further highlight the implications of the social milieu for growth and development. The colleges were affected far beyond the ideological debates of their merits within a segregated society. The schools continued to bear the burden of educating all black children, not just those interested in pursuing a college degree. The growth and development of their collegiate divisions depended upon the states' willingness to provide black students with an educational alternative. Yet, in 1916, of the roughly twenty thousand blacks enrolled in high schools, approximately 5,300 were enrolled in public high schools. The remaining students attended private high schools or the secondary departments of the land grant and state normal colleges for blacks.[42]

Here again, this results in partial adaptations for black colleges. Black colleges continued to enroll students at the primary and secondary levels while also trying to establish themselves as "true colleges." Black colleges could not easily do away with their lower divisions. For many blacks, the colleges were the only options for elementary and high school training. State policies prevented the black colleges from abandoning lower-level courses, although, as blacks migrated to urban centers in the 1920s, Southern states began to revise their policies toward publicly supported black primary and secondary education. Unschooled children in the rural

South were easily absorbed into the farm labor system. Unschooled children in urban areas walked the streets. Schools became the solution. By 1926, all major Southern cities had at least one publicly supported black high school.[43] By the mid-1930s, black high school enrollment topped 150,000. By 1940, almost one-quarter of the black youth age fifteen to nineteen had enrolled in a publicly supported black high school within the South.[44]

Even though the financial situation of the colleges had changed very little between 1916 and 1928, the *Survey of Negro Colleges and Universities* revealed a tremendous amount of development at the collegiate level. While the majority of the schools included in this survey still offered primary and secondary education, the number of schools offering collegiate-level work increased to seventy-seven. As black students began to rely on state-sponsored primary and secondary education, black colleges could concentrate more of their resources at the collegiate level. According to data from the *Journal of Negro Education*, on average 13 percent of the students enrolled at black colleges were at the primary and secondary levels in the 1938–39 academic year.[45] The implications of the differential speed at which the schools became "colleges" is further explored in chapter 2. By the 1940s, when the United Negro College Fund emerged, these partial adaptations toward the collegiate model became ever so important.

Despite the movement of black students toward state-controlled primary and secondary education, black colleges continued to play a critical role in the overall scheme of racially segregated education. The black colleges provided the bulk of the teaching force for the elementary and high schools that black children attended in Southern communities. Despite the organizational diversity among black colleges—public, private, religious, land grant—the schools operated primarily as teacher training institutions. Admission to some colleges, such as Hampton Normal and Agricultural Institute, was partly based on the student's intention to become a teacher.[46] In *The College Bred Negro*, W. E. B. Du Bois reported that by 1900, 53.4 percent of the graduates from black colleges reported their occupation as teachers.

The *Survey of Negro Colleges and Universities* further confirms the emphasis on teacher training at black colleges. Between 1922 and 1927, education ranked highest among the academic specialties.[47] Other popular majors included agriculture, home economics, and theology. A report issued by the U.S. Department of Interior indicates that the focus on education continued into the 1940s. The Department of Interior's 1942 report, *National Survey of the Higher Education of Negroes*, found that 84 percent of the students surveyed from a subset of black colleges stated they felt most prepared to enter the teaching profession and of these students, 75 percent planned to enter the teaching profession in the following year.

This too offers a chance to reflect on the social milieu's ability to divert the adaptive potential of black colleges. The heavy emphasis on teacher training was not a random outcome. During this time period, black colleges were encouraged to train their students in fields that would not put their graduates in direct competition with whites. This, coupled with the meager resources available to most black colleges, resulted in a limited curricular focus. Teachers were needed throughout the black community, and black teachers would never be assigned to white schools. Though understandable, the heavy focus on teacher training meant that other disciplines did not flourish at black colleges.

The prevailing attitude toward black colleges during this historical moment was that if black colleges had to exist, then these schools should help blacks adjust to their position within a racially segregated society. Consequently, black colleges were used as vessels to provide the black community with its own leadership class.[48] Concerns that black colleges would educate black students out of their "rightful place" within Southern society remained throughout this period. These attitudes not only structured the curricular choices of black colleges, but also shaped the resource mobilization process. Endowment figures from this period indicate that foundations selectively supported black colleges, favoring those schools that did not appear to challenge the status quo of Southern race relations. The contours of the debate changed—by the 1930s, educational reform had made the ideological debate over vocational versus applied curriculum all but moot. Yet, the South's commitment to racial segregation remained; thus, the reality of black colleges did not change.

Civil Rights, 1945–1975

The years following World War II brought significant changes to the American landscape. After sacrificing to secure democracy abroad, efforts on the part of black Americans to secure rights within their own country intensified. As had been the case post Emancipation, education remained high on the list of priorities among black citizens and activists. Though large-scale protests had yet to occur, the National Association for the Advancement of Colored People (NAACP) had initiated a series of lawsuits that would have wide-ranging repercussions for the growth and development of black colleges.

Beginning in the mid-1930s, the NAACP sought to ensure that blacks had access to professional and graduate schools. According to data from the 1942 *National Survey of Higher Education of Negroes*, Alabama, Arkansas, Delaware, Florida, Georgia, Kentucky, Louisiana, Maryland, Mississippi, Missouri, Oklahoma, South Carolina, Tennessee, Texas, West Virginia, and the District of Columbia maintained no graduate programs for blacks in the arts and sciences.

Several dynamics within the black higher education field combined to make the NAACP's claims on the state to provide graduate and professional education more plausible. As Figure 1.3 indicates, following World War II, enrollment at black colleges rebounded eventually surpassing its pre-war maximum of 38,000.

Due in large part to returning veterans taking advantage of the GI Bill of Rights, by 1948 black colleges enrolled more than seventy thousand students. This time period also marked an important shift among public and private black colleges. As Figure 1.4 illustrates, by 1949, the public colleges enrolled more than 50 percent of the students attending black colleges, confirming a trend that began in the late 1930s. First, surging enrollment at black colleges meant that in the long run more blacks would obtain the prerequisite qualifications to attend professional and graduate school. Second, the higher education of blacks was truly a public endeavor—the state had begun to play an active role in the college education of blacks. These factors increased the efficacy of the NAACP's argument that the state had a responsibility to provide graduate and professional education to blacks.[49]

The NAACP's emphasis on graduate and professional training met with some early success. As a result of a lawsuit initiated by the NAACP, the University of Maryland enrolled its first black law student in 1936.[50] However, when challenged, most states opted to erect separate graduate and professional schools or programs for black students. Two days after the Supreme Court ruled in January 1948 that the state of Oklahoma must provide Ada Lois Sipuel with access to legal education, the University of Oklahoma's regents opened a black law school and within a week had hired three faculty to teach there.[51] Such tactics resulted in the elaboration of graduate programs at black colleges, particularly at the publicly controlled ones. Between 1951 and 1971, the number of graduate programs at public black colleges increased from ten to nineteen.[52]

Figure 1.3 Total Black College Enrollment, 1945–1975

Figure 1.4 Percent of Enrollment by College Type, 1945–1975

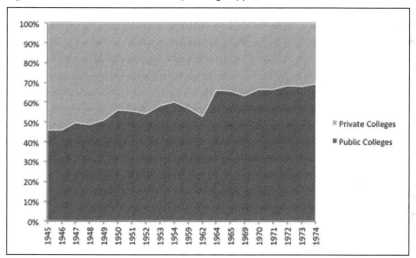

States did not confine their efforts to expand the curricular capabilities of black colleges to the graduate level. Fearing that the 1954 *Brown v. Board* ruling would provide increasing numbers of black children with the opportunity to gain adequate preparation for a college education, ensuring that the majority of black students would continue to attend black colleges became a priority.[53] This new goal conflicted with the reality that black colleges had been intentionally starved of critical resources, making them unattractive to better-prepared black students, particularly those now theoretically able to attend traditionally white colleges in the South.[54]

In response to this dilemma, Southern states sought to equalize the instructional capacities of schools designated for black students by bringing them up to par with those schools historically designated for white students. Historian James D. Anderson's case study of Mississippi provides a useful illustration of the region-wide pattern. A 1945 study of Mississippi higher education revealed that the state had deprived Alcorn, the black land grant institution, of the opportunity to become a "viable higher education institution."[55] Dilapidated buildings, an inadequate salary structure, and insufficient land for the purposes of an agricultural college ranked high among the concerns noted in the report. Despite this knowledge, the situation at Alcorn and the other black public colleges located within Mississippi did not change until the *Brown v. Board* ruling approached. In anticipation of the *Brown* decision, the state of Mississippi increased Alcorn's operating budget by $50,000, allocated $275,000 for additional buildings, and made a special appropriation of $77,000 in the 1950–51 academic year.[56] Mississippi's Board of Trustees of Institutions of Higher Learning planned to develop black public colleges as undergraduate institutions, concentrate graduate work at Jackson College, and when necessary channel black students to three traditionally white colleges—Ole Miss, Southern Mississippi, and Mississippi State University. Six months after the *Brown* ruling, a committee studying Mississippi higher education recommended: "The three institutions presently operated for Negro students should be maintained and developed further as part of the State program to meet the anticipated increases in college enrollment during the next decade."[57] This pattern of events led Anderson to conclude: "After more than eight decades of severely repressing the development of higher educational opportunities for blacks in Mississippi, the State Board was now making haste to enlarge undergraduate opportunities for black students at Jackson, Alcorn, and Mississippi Vocational, primarily as a strategy to preserve the state's tradition of racially segregated higher education."[58]

Though developing the black colleges can be seen as positive, it is still important to understand these changes as partial. The states elaborated the black colleges as a means of diverting black enrollment away from traditionally white colleges. These were not carefully thought out plans that conceived of black and white colleges as part of a unified system. As a result, the states duplicated programs across black and white colleges more often than not. Years later, when courts and legislatures began to conceive of black and white colleges as part of a unified system, program duplication became problematic. Black colleges no longer appeared unique. In a system still favoring traditionally white colleges, black colleges appeared redundant.

Nevertheless, enrollment figures indicate that these strategies met with success. Enrollment at black colleges increased sharply in the years after the *Brown* decision. Data from the U.S. Department of Education indicates the rate of high school graduation for blacks between twenty and twenty-four years old in the Southern states increased from 18 percent in 1950 to 57 percent in 1970.[59] Black college enrollment benefited from this trend. Yet, public colleges benefited most. As Figure 1.5 illustrates, private black college enrollment more than doubled during this period; however, enrollment at these schools steadied at around 55,000 students toward the 1970s. Comparatively, enrollment at public colleges more than tripled in this same time span, totaling more than 132,000 by the mid-1970s.

The federal government also directed more attention to black colleges in this period. Part of President Lyndon Johnson's Great Society, drafted by the U.S. Congress, the 1965 Higher Education Act intended to strengthen institutions of higher education and sought to raise the quality of financially struggling colleges. The act also contained an admission that the state and federal governments had participated in discriminatory allocation practices against black colleges. To remedy this, Congress developed a set of programs aimed at strengthening those schools that have

Figure 1.5 Black College Enrollment, 1950s–1970s

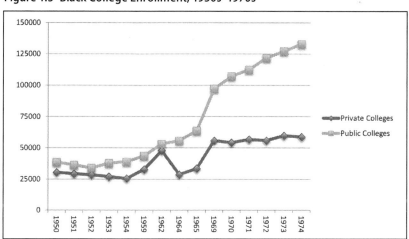

and had as their primary mission the education of black Americans prior to the year 1964. Congress referred to the schools that fit this criterion as Historically Black Colleges and Universities, thus bestowing an official title upon a group of schools that had existed for more than a century. The date 1964 had little to do with the history of these colleges. Congress chose a date that ensured the inclusion of the largest number of black colleges in existence prior to the act's implementation. Under Title III of the Higher Education Act, those colleges falling under the Historically Black College and University umbrella term (public and private) qualified for special funds that would allow these schools to improve their instructional capacity.

Despite expanding enrollment, curricular options, and budgets, some things remained constant within the black higher education field. Students continued to receive the majority of their degrees in education. Though the figure had declined since the early 1900s, education continued to account for 35 percent of the degrees awarded from black colleges in 1972. The pattern of degrees would not shift until the final time period. While degrees offer tangible evidence of continuity, the treatment of black public colleges in this period provides intangible evidence of the same.

Southern states continued to base their interest in black colleges on these schools' ability to help the state fulfill political objectives. The desire to maintain a dual system of education continued long after the *Brown* ruling. State-controlled black colleges enabled Southern governments to protect the traditionally white status of their flagship universities. As early as 1950, Mississippi officials conceded that some blacks would have to obtain education at state-run traditionally white universities. Yet, a 1975 lawsuit filed against the state claimed a dual system of higher education continued to persist. Once ignored, black colleges had become a linchpin in stemming the tide of black bodies on traditionally white college campuses.

Questioning Black Colleges, 1976–1999

In the immediate aftermath of the *Brown v. Board* ruling, prevailing wisdom held that black colleges would meet their demise. Upon learning of the Court's decision, John D. Rockefeller Jr., a longtime supporter of black colleges and chairman of the General Education Board, could see no further need for the schools.[60] The NAACP felt the continued existence of black colleges presented a barrier to black enrollment at traditionally white colleges. Walter White, the NAACP's executive director from 1931 to 1955, took things a step farther, declaring black colleges as inferior to their white counterparts.[61] As the previous section illustrates, these predictions rang false. Indeed, the immediate impact of *Brown* on black colleges resulted in a renaissance of sorts. State educational authorities and legislators who had long ignored the needs of black colleges suddenly took an active interest in promoting the well-being of these schools. Enrollments increased. Budgets expanded. Curricular choices multiplied.

Not until the 1970s did the long-anticipated signs of trouble emerge. During this period, traditionally white colleges began to actively recruit black students that performed well academically and those that excelled athletically.[62] Black colleges could not compete with the scholarships, curricular choices, or facilities of their traditionally white counterparts.[63] In the Southern states, black students' enrollment at traditionally white colleges increased from 4.3 percent in 1970 to 9.5 percent in 1976.[64]

As expected, the migration of black students toward traditionally white colleges was consequential for the growth and development of black colleges. Figure 1.6 illustrates that enrollment at black colleges decreased between the late 1970s and early 1980s.

Enrollment was not the only area of concern. School closures and mergers suggested the field had begun to contract in more ways than one. Daniel Payne (private, four-year) closed in 1977; The Virginia College (private, two-year) closed in 1980; Mississippi Industrial College (private, four-year) closed in 1982; Friendship College (private, two-year) closed in 1981; Natchez Junior College (private, two-year) closed in 1983; Clark College (private, four-year) and Atlanta University (private, graduate school) merged in 1988. These mergers and closures suggest that the environment could no longer sustain the number of black colleges that

Figure 1.6 Total Black College Enrollment, mid-1970s to mid-1980s

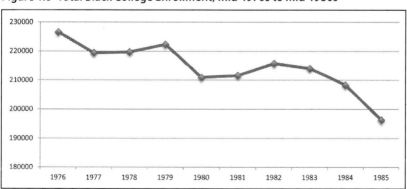

existed prior to the racial desegregation of higher education. Because resources are limited and finite, only a certain number of organizations can exist at any given time. That is, the environment's capacity to sustain organizations is fixed.

Black colleges closing or merging was not a phenomenon confined to this time period. New Orleans University and Straight College merged to form Dillard University in 1935. Leland College closed in 1960. Yet, higher education desegregation created new pressures. The terms of competition between historically black and traditionally white colleges shifted. Prior to higher education desegregation, it was quite common for foundations to maintain separate funding programs for Negro and White colleges. Southern states often maintained separate agents for Negro schools. Most obviously, traditionally white colleges did not seek out black students nor did black students enroll at these colleges. Black and white colleges did not operate as part of the same field. Distinct environments and subsequently discrete resource streams sustained the schools.

The racial desegregation of higher education eroded these distinctions. Particularly in the area of students, historically black and traditionally white colleges were now competing over an admittedly growing number of college-ready blacks, but still working with limited and finite resources. This competition was consequential for black colleges. Already smaller and more resource starved than the average traditionally white college, private black colleges were especially vulnerable in this period. In the year it closed, Virginia College had only $392,000.00 in its current revenue fund. Natchez Junior College fared even worse, with $72,000.00 that same year. In the 1976–77 academic year, private black colleges had $455,440,000 in current revenue compared to the $14,181,494,000 of their traditionally white counterparts.[65] Even among wealthy universities, income from endowment had declined from 30 to 16 percent of revenues between 1930 and 1950.[66] Income from student tuition and fees had become an important revenue stream. Black colleges favored keeping tuition low. The economic needs of their students dictated as much. Compared to students at traditionally white colleges, black college students came from lower-income families dependent upon federal aid to pay tuition.[67] By the 1970s, student tuition and fees at black colleges had not kept pace with inflation.[68] Couple this dynamic with declining enrollments and black colleges found themselves with fewer and fewer resources to operate their schools.

In addition to school mergers, closures, and the out-migration of black students, further analyzing enrollment highlights other critical developments among black colleges during this time period. As Figure 1.7 documents, black college enrollment increased in the mid-1980s eventually stabilizing at around 260,000.

However, demographic data suggest that a different type of student had matriculated to black college campuses.[69] In 1976, nonblack students made up 12 percent of the enrollment at black colleges. This figure increased to 18 percent by 1982. This trend affected the public black colleges more than their private counterparts. According to data from the U.S. Department of Education's 1982 report *The Traditionally Black Institutions of Higher Education*, less than 1 percent of the white students attending black colleges enrolled at private black colleges. By contrast, white enrollment at one-quarter of the public colleges exceeded 15 percent. Strikingly, white students at Kentucky State University, Lincoln University of Missouri, Bluefield State College of West Virginia, and West Virginia State College accounted for more than half of all students by 1982.

Black colleges continued to wrestle with the legalities of racial desegregation throughout this period. While not as widely known as the *Brown* ruling, the *Adams* case was directed specifically at the postsecondary level. In this class action suit filed against the U.S. Department of Health, Education, and Welfare (HEW) in 1970, the NAACP Legal Defense Fund argued that Southern states continued to practice segregation and discrimination within higher education. The NAACP Legal Defense Fund argued that the HEW had not done enough to enforce Title VI of the 1964 Civil Rights Act that prohibits the allocation of federal funds to segregated public schools. Ruling in favor of the NAACP Legal Defense Fund in 1972, the U.S. District Court for the District of Columbia decided that

Figure 1.7 Total Black College Enrollment, 1986–1996

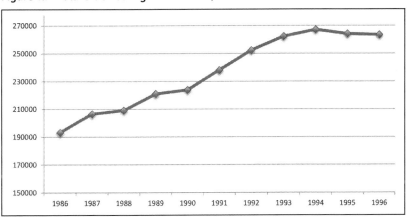

the HEW had to obtain acceptable desegregation plans from the states named in the lawsuit or begin to enforce Title VI by withholding funds from these schools.

Black primary and secondary schools did not fare well in the wake of the *Brown* ruling, and black educators worried that the district court's ruling would jeopardize black colleges. A 1973 ruling by the U.S. Court of Appeals stipulated that any plans to desegregate should preserve black colleges. Yet, at the state level, cases such as *Sanders v. Ellington* suggested that black colleges would not walk away from these battles unscathed. Plaintiffs in this 1968 case charged that the state of Tennessee continued to operate a dual system of higher education and that the funding formula for higher education favored traditionally white colleges and universities. The state's plan to expand the University of Tennessee's Nashville campus and its effect on historically black Tennessee Agricultural and Industrial State University played a central role in this case. Following a series of rulings, in 1977 the District Court of Middle District of Tennessee ordered the merger of the Nashville branch campus with the black college. This new entity known as Tennessee State University opened in 1979. Years later, following student protests, the state committed funds to a capital improvement plan for Tennessee State University in 1986.[70]

The Tennessee case offered a prelude of what would come when the *Adams* case was dismissed. Higher education desegregation became a state-by-state issue. Decades-long court cases led to further partial adaptations for black colleges. On the one hand, states deployed more resources to black colleges, enabling the schools to improve and expand facilities. Yet given the context in which these improvements occurred, the black colleges were not free to choose what types of changes they should undergo. These changes had to fit within court rulings and legislative actions that at times appeared antagonistic toward the continuation of black colleges altogether. A general pattern emerged wherein states first proposed to merge or close their historically black colleges as a means to achieve desegregation targets. When court intervention precluded such action, states then focused on making upgrades to black colleges so that these schools could in theory attract more white students and thus desegregate. However, the states did not compensate black colleges for the historic or cumulative effect of underfunding. This is important because without adequate funds to get up to speed with traditionally white colleges, black colleges would on average stand out as the comparatively weaker links in these unified systems of higher education. Chapter 4 further explores this moment giving particular attention to black college advocates' efforts to meet the challenges of this era.

Despite the declining black enrollment exhibited in this period, black colleges continued to play a pivotal role in the landscape of black higher education. Through the 1990s, black colleges accounted for 25 percent of all bachelor's degrees awarded to black students. Interestingly, the types of degrees awarded to black students diversified during the period. As early as 1982, a new pattern emerged. Education degrees accounted for 17 percent of all degrees at black colleges. At 26 percent, students attending black colleges now received the majority of their degrees in business. This marked a significant break in the historic degree pattern of black colleges that continued throughout the 1990s. Chapter 5 takes up this issue in depth.

Conclusion

They began in the nineteenth century as institutions dedicated to educating freed men and women. With their commitment to educating the descendants of these freed people intact, they concluded the twentieth century as more diverse entities than anyone might have imagined. They progressed in tandem with black Americans. When black Americans' educational opportunities increased through the GI Bill or desegregation at the primary and secondary levels, black colleges flourished. Yet, the interest and progress of these organizations at times diverged from that of the black Americans. The desegregation of higher education precipitated the out-migration of black students to traditionally white colleges. This counted as progress—black Americans could now attend any school of their choosing. Inevitably, this development challenged the black colleges, illustrating the necessity of understanding organizations as social actors unto themselves. The needs, desires, and responsibilities of the black colleges differed from those of their core constituents. As this chapter documents, social, legal, and economic inequities abounded. Each influenced the black colleges' ability to craft strategic responses. The remaining chapters of this book focus more intently on inequality as a barrier to adaptation.

2

Collective Action and Status Inequality

Operating a college is an expensive endeavor. Even for the smallest private black college, faculty salaries, building maintenance, administrative expenses, and lab equipment ran into the hundreds of thousands of dollars in the 1940s, and each year those in charge faced the challenging task of creating a budget. Tuition and student fees rarely, if ever, provided sufficient income to cover anticipated expenses. Benedict College, a small liberal arts school located in Columbia, South Carolina, expected less than $40,000 of income in student fees but budgeted for $111,170.98 in expenses during the 1944–45 academic year.[1] State-affiliated schools turn to legislatures to cover gaps of this kind. Private colleges depend on income from their endowments and gifts to make up such deficits. Many private black colleges lacked endowments altogether and even among those fortunate enough to be endowed, the income typically made little difference.

Private black colleges relied heavily on gifts from foundations, and college presidents spent much of their time cultivating relationships with foundation officers. Some, like Mary McLeod Bethune, were skilled fundraisers. Not only did foundation officers praise the work she did at Daytona Educational and Industrial Training School for Negro Girls, many, such as C. E. Lucas, felt they had no choice but to fund the school because they remained under her "hypnotic influence" after visits to Daytona.[2] Other college presidents were less skillful in their interactions with foundations. Accusing the General Education Board of donating to inferior schools won Wilberforce University's president W. S. Scarborough no fans.[3]

Regardless of college presidents' individual skill, foundations did not like to fund current operating expenses—precisely the type of funding the college presidents needed to balance their budgets. Foundations took a longer view. While there were programs designed to provide emergency aid for colleges, particularly during periods of widespread economic turmoil such as the 1930s, the leading foundations preferred to fund strategies aimed at putting the colleges on the path toward achieving sustainable solvency. Foundations wanted to encourage private black colleges to establish endowment funds and to expand their base of giving.

To make this happen, foundations appropriated money toward endowment on the condition that the colleges raise a matching sum from other sources. After completing its endowment campaign for $300,000 in 1945, Bennett College for Women of Greensboro, North Carolina, collected $200,000 from the Rockefeller family foundation, the General Education Board. Subsequently, Bennett amassed more than $800,000 in its endowment fund.[4] Encouraged by Bennett's efforts in 1946, the foundation agreed to appropriate $50,000 more if the college could secure another $150,000.[5]

It is difficult to argue with the leading foundations' logic regarding the importance of endowments. Relying on yearly gifts to make up budgetary deficits is not a feasible strategy. Charting a course toward sustainability was paramount. But building for the future did not help black college presidents meet their current obligations. In 1943, Frederick Patterson, president of Tuskegee Institute, proposed a compelling solution to this dilemma.

Patterson wrote an appeal in the *Pittsburgh Courier* highlighting the perpetual needs facing private black colleges and how the Depression and the ongoing war effort further exacerbated their difficulties. He challenged his fellow private black college presidents to make monetary appeals to a wider public than they typically had, and he suggested they do this collectively through a national fundraising campaign. The money raised would then be distributed among the schools on the basis of the amount of effort put into the campaign, school size, and need.[6] The result of Patterson's plea was the founding, in 1944, of the United Negro College Fund (UNCF).

Fundraising collectively broke the longstanding tradition of each school fundraising for itself. A cooperative effort of this sort was truly novel among colleges and universities. Private black colleges envisioned the UNCF as an educational philanthropy organization, but it was unlike any other model of black higher education philanthropy they had ever seen. The Rockefeller, Carnegie, and Rosenwald educational foundations were funded through family largesse. Each foundation owed its existence to an initial bequest from an industrialist. UNCF founders knew they could not count on a large donation to provide the seed money for their effort.

Community chests provided the best example of what the private black college presidents hoped to establish. In particular, the March of Dimes' campaigns provided a reference to how numerous individuals contributing small amounts of money could lead to a successful outcome.[7] The private black college presidents were determined to widen their donor base beyond foundations, and making appeals to a large number of individuals became a key component of their plan. With the March of Dimes' style of philanthropy in mind, the UNCF was created to conduct solicitations and campaigns for "colleges . . . predominantly . . . availed by members of the Negro people"[8] and to receive, hold, and administer any donations to those colleges.

Many colleges were prevented from participating in the UNCF initially. Other colleges, though invited to participate, lagged in organizational development. The organizational characteristics that factored into whether a college was invited to participate or made a good affiliate of the UNCF cannot be fully appreciated until we account for how the inequality regimes operating within the black higher education field made it difficult for particular kinds of black colleges to claim rewards, especially funding. Because they controlled the purse strings, foundations were able to construct preferences that disadvantaged many private black colleges. These preferences were reflective of and steeped in the larger racial project that continually undermined the work of the vast majority of black colleges, private or public.

Analyzing the UNCF's formation provides an opportunity to trace how partial adaptation arises. Confronted by inequality regimes, black colleges choose adaptive strategies that reinforce rather than challenge the practices, processes, and beliefs that do not benefit their schools. Theoretically, the UNCF's formation is a classic example of adapting to solve resource dependency issues. Relying on foundation aid tied the private black colleges together. In the years preceding the UNCF's formation, foundation aid withered. Fund values declined as a result of the economic depression and changing tax laws, and the GEB planned to dissolve itself in the 1950s.[9] These events heightened the sense of connection among private black colleges. Not only were the schools competing for rapidly decreasing sums of money, college presidents often bumped into one another during visits to foundation offices.[10]

Collective efforts like the UNCF emerge when organizational leaders recognize their mutual interdependence and decide cooperation is the best path forward.[11] Accordingly, collective action was a proper adaptive response to the resource dependence problem facing private black colleges. However, though a good idea, the possibilities of collective action in this scenario were determined by field-level dynamics other than resource dependence. Whether or not a college was able to take part in the UNCF had less to do with its dependence upon philanthropists and more to do with its status. The majority of private black colleges were resource dependent upon philanthropists.[12] Yet, eligibility for UNCF membership was restricted and eventual UNCF members were the most organizationally developed of all private black colleges. Consequently, the way the UNCF took shape—an organization consisting of the most developed private black colleges—can be understood as a form of partial adaptation because it claimed to be about solving the resource dependence problems confronting black colleges; however, the UNCF's formation ultimately reified the practices underlying the inequality regimes that made it difficult for the majority of black colleges to been seen as worthy of investment. The field's structure all but guaranteed this outcome.

Historically, a college's ability to access the resources and support promised by the UNCF was influenced by its prior level of development, which in turn was dependent upon foundation aid. By inviting those private black colleges that were the most developed already, the UNCF solidified distinctions between "worthy" and "less worthy" colleges, further undermining the work and achievements of private black colleges that fell short of foundation preferences. Even if those organizing the UNCF had wanted to include "less worthy" colleges in this fundraising venture, doing so was problematic. The UNCF needed the support of philanthropic foundations. This further reinforced the partialness of this adaptation. On the one hand, the UNCF's formation represented a potential counternarrative to the inequality regime that empowered claims that black colleges deserved less financial stability than similarly situated white colleges. On the other hand, because the UNCF did not challenge the criteria by which powerful groups such as philanthropic foundations judged private black colleges as worthy or unworthy of investment, the constraints of the inequality regime gripping the black higher education field remained intact.

Problematizing which colleges were invited to participate in the UNCF and in the end joined it necessitates an understanding of the field-level dynamics shaping status distinctions among private black colleges. Investigating which colleges were invited to participate and subsequently joined illuminates which field members had the power to decide what made a private black college "worthy" of financial investment and how the characteristics that marked "worthiness" contributed to the sustenance of the inequality regime within the black higher education field.

Status Distinctions as a Field-Level Process

Understanding an organization's status, or its rank, is essential to understanding its ability to control and gain resources, exert influence, and wield power.[13] Organizational scholars trace the concept of status to the writings of Max Weber and Thorstein Veblen. Defined as an "effective claim to social esteem in terms of positive or negative privileges"[14] by Weber, both he and Veblen viewed status as a positional concept manifesting itself in the relationships between actors. Status, then, as Veblen attests, captures the notion of relative value. A characteristic highly valued in one setting may yield no privilege in another. Said otherwise, an organizational characteristic valued by private black colleges may mean nothing to other field members.

Within the black higher education field, it is easy to comprehend the status differentials that existed between particular actors and black colleges. The money available to philanthropic foundations gave them power over the black colleges and thus a higher rank. The power to regulate higher education gave the state a higher rank than black colleges. Alternatively, the tendency to think about black colleges in monolithic terms makes it difficult to understand whether and how the colleges ranked against one another. Though they were subject to the same dynamics (e.g., racial segregation, philanthropic meddling), some black colleges still ranked higher than others. It is equally important to recognize the institutionally defined nature of the status system operating within the black higher education field that distinguished one college from another. That is, though a black college could rank higher than its counterparts, the characteristics determining this rank were not defined solely by black colleges.

Research on organizational status suggests this is not an uncommon situation. Third parties often play a crucial role in determining the value of particular organizational characteristics. Additionally, third parties tend to value different criteria than the subjects of their ranking would themselves use. A contemporary episode illustrates this process.[15] When it began to rank law schools, *U.S. News and World Report* valued peer and professional assessments of school quality, the selectivity of students, the placement success of schools, and the resources available to faculty above all other metrics. Notably, these were not the metrics or organizational characteristics that most law schools would have chosen. Most schools preferred to be judged according to idiosyncratic characteristics that set them apart from other schools as opposed to a generic set of characteristics that could be used to compare schools to one another. However, *U.S. News and World Report* occupied a powerful position within the field. Unlike the individual schools that could be seen as proffering organizational characteristics that worked in their favor, *U.S. News and World Report* was seen as using "objective" criteria by which all schools could be compared. Students in particular relied on *U.S. News and World Report* to gauge the quality of law schools. Accordingly, even if they preferred to use other criteria, the law schools could not ignore the organizational characteristics valued by this ranking system.

Likewise, third parties played a critical role in determining the organizational characteristics making up the status system for black colleges. The dynamics operating within the black higher education field were complicated by the resource differentials operating among the field members. Not only did field members, most notably philanthropies, have a say in what organizational characteristics would be valued, but philanthropies could withhold key resources, financial and political, from those colleges perceived as lower in status. In this way, it was at the level of the field that status inequities affecting black colleges' ability to gain resources, express rights, and develop distinctive capabilities, that is to say, adapt, first emerged. Communities of organizations do not operate that differently than communities of people. Within communities of people, some members possess more power, skill, and influence than others. The same types of inequities can be found within communities of organizations. One field member can construct a status system by which another is ultimately judged and rewarded, drawing attention to the inequities between actors within the field (e.g., black colleges and philanthropies), and to the inequities among the focal field members (e.g., black colleges).

Philanthropies did not finance every effort related to black higher education; thus, being deemed high status or worthy was all the more important.[16] In *Private Wealth and Public Life*, historian Judith Sealander argued that although it once had been an activity to fulfill the personal whims of the wealthy, in the twentieth century philanthropy was increasingly used to influence public opinion and decision making. Through foundation giving, philanthropists hoped to change the world. The relationship between philanthropies and private black colleges grew out of a larger interest to improve Southern education following the Civil War. Historically, Southern education lagged far behind education in other areas of the country on key indicators of progress. In 1860, the school term in the Southern states averaged forty-five fewer days than Northern and Western states combined.[17] While the gap between the three regions had closed by 1930, the Southern states continued to average thirty fewer days of school.[18]

Northern industrial philanthropists grew concerned over the state of education within the South, claiming that the region "has been so handicapped in many ways that its attempts to provide educational facilities for all its children, while courageous and praiseworthy, have not as yet succeeded in meeting the problem."[19] With an initial bequest from his father of $1 million, John D. Rockefeller Jr. led an effort to improve Southern education through his philanthropic fund, the General Education Board.[20]

Though it was established later than many foundations also concerned with improving Southern education, including the Peabody, Slater, and Carnegie Funds, the General Education Board or GEB as it was known, came to have the most prominent role in the realm of black higher education. Many funds began to act through the GEB, supporting projects endorsed by John D. Rockefeller Jr.[21] Additionally, GEB board members directed other education foundations, leading some to feel that the GEB had "virtual monopolistic control of educational philanthropy for the South and the Negro."[22]

In his biography, GEB officer Frederick T. Gates noted that the foundation wanted to promote a "comprehensive system of higher education."[23] In the foundation's estimation, if carefully "nourished," about one-fourth of the four hundred colleges and universities known to Gates could be formed into a system of higher education. Donations to the selected colleges represented an investment in the future of American higher education. That a college existed did not qualify it as a worthwhile investment. It had to contribute to the comprehensiveness of the overall system envisioned by GEB officers.

The ideal of developing a comprehensive system of higher education was not benign. Nor can this ideal be understood absent the presence of inequality regimes operating within the Southern political economy broadly or the black higher education field specifically. The preferences that foundation officers held were not random and they certainly were not inconsequential. For instance, foundation officers valued endowment and perceived schools with healthy endowments as more capable of fitting within their vision of a comprehensive system of higher education. Black colleges did not have extremely wealthy alumni making regular and hefty contributions. Most lacked a meaningful endowment fund, thus limiting their potential in the GEB's eyes. Still, black colleges could not ignore the importance the GEB placed on this organizational characteristic. Organizations cannot eschew the status system supported by powerful field members even if they fall outside its parameters. Quite the opposite, organizations must attempt to adapt so as to gain the legitimacy and approval accorded by being highly ranked within the status system. Thus, even if small or negligible, most black colleges chose to work to increase their endowment fund to partially adapt to a status marker prized by the GEB. Foundation officers developed their preferences in spite of, not in light of, the social milieu in which black colleges operated. That is the nature of power and inequality. Colleges hoping to gain philanthropic support had to attest to how their operations fulfilled foundation ideals and goals. Foundations did not have to shape the status system to suit the eccentricities of black colleges.

In the case of the UNCF, as the college presidents created an organization designed to expand their donor base, they continued to solicit the large foundations for support. They turned to the Carnegie Foundation, General Education Board, and Julius Rosenwald Fund to determine if the foundations were willing to support this new venture. To gain the support of foundations, those charged with organizing the UNCF would have to convince foundation officers that the UNCF furthered foundation goals. In this way, foundation officers continued to influence black college adaptation. The types of colleges favored by foundations made better affiliates for the UNCF than the ones foundations found questionable. Essentially, not all private black colleges were equally worthy of investment in philanthropists' opinions. The questions then become: "How did the colleges affiliating with the UNCF measure up against the characteristics foundations valued?"; and "What does this valuation tell us about the organizational characteristics distinguishing private black colleges from one another?"

Quantifying Foundation Preferences and Elaborating the Status System

In addition to inviting the three professional black colleges that enrolled graduate students, the UNCF's exploratory committee invited those four-year private black colleges that received an A or B rating by a regional accrediting agency to affiliate with the organization—thirty-six schools in total. The Southern Association of Colleges and Secondary Schools maintained an "Approved List of Colleges and Schools for Negro Youth." Approval from the Southern Association indicated that in general a black college met the same standards as a similarly situated white college and its graduates should be treated as such. Those receiving an A rating met in full the standards set up by the Southern Association. The quality of these schools meant that their graduates should be admitted to any institution requiring a bachelor's degree for entrance. While those receiving a B rating fell short on at least one standard, the quality of these schools too warranted that their graduates be admitted to any institution requiring a bachelor's degree for entrance.

In giving weight to a college's rating, the UNCF's exploratory committee barred many private black colleges from participating.[24] Despite their affiliation with other cooperative groups such as the Association of Colleges and Secondary Schools for Negroes,[25] the rating requirement prevented fourteen private black colleges from joining the UNCF.[26]

Correspondence records between black colleges and foundations suggest that while necessary, a school's rating or accreditation was not a sufficient condition to receive funding. Accreditation was more of a minimum requirement that colleges needed to meet before their application received further consideration. The statistical data included below provide a broader picture of what organizational characteristics mattered to foundations, why they mattered as well as how colleges invited to affiliate with the UNCF, those that helped organize the UNCF, and those that ultimately joined the UNCF fulfilled foundation preferences.

During the UNCF's planning phase, Patterson remained in close contact with foundation officers. He forwarded the list of colleges he hoped would affiliate with the UNCF and the list of colleges attending the planning meetings. Table 2.1 contains the results of the analyses comparing the colleges that did and did not attend planning meetings held in April and November 1943. The analyses compare organizational characteristics of the colleges that did and did not help organize the UNCF, and they focus on key organizational characteristics that foundation officers historically used as they tried to assess whether a college was a worthy investment.

Accordingly, the analyses provide a sense of what information foundation officers had available to base an opinion on whether donating to the UNCF advanced the development of a comprehensive system of higher education. Most importantly, the analyses provide insight into the organizational characteristics constituting the status system among black colleges.

Table 2.1. Comparisons of the Organizational Characteristics of UNCF Affiliates and Nonaffiliates

Foundation Preferences	April Meeting		November Meeting	
	Participants	Nonparticipants	Participants	Nonparticipants
College Enrollment (%)	91	95	98**	82
Total Enrollment	533.47*	363.95	459.88	377.10
School Income ($)	279,600.00**	114,190.50	215,320.00*	109,909.10
Black Trustees (%)	29**	59	47	82
N	15	21	25	11

One-sided test, **p < .05, *p < .10

Were the "Colleges" Actually Colleges?

Though it may seem obvious that any academic institution referring to itself as a college conducts its work at the postsecondary level, as chapter 1 highlighted, this was not the case. Because blacks in the South did not have access to publicly funded elementary and high schools, the majority of private black colleges offered their students training at the academy level, as it was known, in addition to collegiate courses.[27] Many private black colleges also maintained academy divisions so as to provide those majoring in education with opportunities to conduct their practice teaching with academy students.

While foundations were sensitive to the rationale for maintaining academies, they also questioned whether "colleges" that did so contributed to the comprehensive system of higher education. Foundation officers believed that large numbers of academy students on campus made it difficult to develop high quality postsecondary course work. Black colleges were long criticized by foundations because their teachers split time between college and academy teaching, thus dividing limited resources between the college and academy divisions.[28] Adding to these concerns, philanthropic donors felt it important that a school be able to differentiate between its academy and college expenses.[29] Yet, much to the foundations' dismay, few schools with significant enrollment at the academy levels were able to do this.[30]

When the UNCF was being organized, many colleges continued to enroll students at the academy level.[31] As foundation officers pondered the list of potential affiliates, things did not seem promising. According to Table 2.1, in April 1943, out of the thirty-six schools invited to do so, fifteen college presidents gathered to discuss the feasibility of collective fundraising. While the schools represented at this meeting enrolled 91 percent of their students at the postsecondary level, those private black colleges that were not represented at this meeting enrolled a higher percentage. If the UNCF were to establish itself as an organization that helped foundations promote a comprehensive system of *higher* education, it had some work to do.

Out of the thirty-six invited to join the UNCF, twenty-five schools attended a meeting in November 1943. This was an important moment in the UNCF's development. The organization had been in the process of forming since April and by November invited schools had to officially commit to the collective fundraising venture. The UNCF's status would largely hang on the schools represented at this meeting. Ninety-eight percent of the students at these schools were enrolled at the postsecondary level. This percentage fared well in comparison to the 84 percent college enrollment of those schools not represented at this meeting. As foundation officers weighed the list of affiliates after the November meeting, it was far clearer that donating to the UNCF would aid schools that concentrated their effort primarily at the higher levels of education and not the academy division.

Were the Colleges the Right Size?

Higher education and organizational scholars agree that enrollment is an important measure of a college's sustainability. Schools with unstable enrollments are at risk of merging or closing.[32] Even if a school's enrollment is small yet stable, problems still remain. Stakeholders interpret an organization's size as an outcome of its prior success and as a sign of its future dependability.[33] Smaller organizations have trouble obtaining the material resources needed to function, including but not limited to financial capital.[34] Large size, or in the case of a college, large enrollment, legitimates it.

Critics of black colleges routinely questioned the veracity of the population as a whole because many colleges had small enrollments. Holmes found that many black colleges had fewer than one hundred students enrolled and argued for reducing the number of colleges to fifty schools with approximately five hundred students enrolled in each. This idea echoed sentiments expressed by the federal government in its 1929 *Survey of Negro Colleges and Universities.*

Foundations were wary of small colleges, too. It was easier to understand how supporting large colleges helped create a comprehensive system of higher education. A large enrollment attested to a college's reach and influence. As the UNCF was being organized, Patterson's correspondence with the General Education Board suggests that he understood the importance foundation officers placed on enrollment. Patterson wanted to make sure that the largest colleges affiliated with the UNCF, so as to give the organization the appearance of having a national rather than a local character.[35] In Patterson's estimation, having the largest schools involved would drive the point home that these schools aided the cause of Negro education most.

Referring to Table 2.1, the average college represented at the April meeting had 533 students enrolled—a significantly higher proportion of students than those colleges not represented at the meeting. Though the difference no longer reached significance, those schools represented at the November meeting continued to outpace the enrollment of those not represented at the meeting. As the foundation officers pondered the list of potential affiliates, it was clear that the largest private black colleges were affiliating with the UNCF. This would suggest that donating to the UNCF meant investing in the colleges with the most reach and influence in black higher education.

Were the Colleges Financially Fit?

Foundations routinely used a college's financial standing as a sorting mechanism. Though it may seem counterintuitive, foundations preferred to support colleges with a promising financial outlook, often declining to fund schools perceived as financially insolvent. Such schools did not make good investments. Rufus Clement, president of Atlanta University, queried the GEB on behalf of Livingstone, another private black college, in his capacity as a trustee of that institution. The foundation informed Clement of their familiarity with Livingstone and its work, but advised that Livingstone should not approach the GEB until it cleared its debts.[36] In the GEB's estimation, donating to colleges such as this one would merely send good money chasing after bad.

A school's income was of particular concern to foundation officers. The amount of income a school had at its disposal bore directly upon the quality of courses, faculty, and facilities that it could develop. A measure of a college's vitality,[37] income played an important role in the accreditation process. Colleges had to provide evidence of "financial support sufficient in amount to promote achievement of the school's purpose."[38] In the ideal world, colleges used their endowment to demonstrate that sufficient financial support existed to fulfill the school's educational goals. In the absence of a significant endowment fund, as was the case for private black colleges, annual income received more weight in the determination of a school's ability to meet its objectives.[39]

On more than one occasion, black colleges received criticism because they had meager incomes. When it surveyed the schools in 1916, the federal government concluded that restricted incomes made it impossible for black colleges to provide adequate college-level facilities and faculties. Based on this assessment the government refused to recognize the majority of black colleges as postsecondary institutions. Twenty years later, Holmes continued to concur, arguing that black colleges with small incomes were incapable of offering a "standard grade of college work."[40]

Prior experience demonstrated that financial support would go to those colleges with the potential to add to the comprehensive system of higher education that foundations wanted to promote. This made income a bit of a double-edged sword for black colleges. The UNCF's existence was predicated on the fact that no private black college had sufficient income. Yet, because foundations used this figure to determine if a college had the capacity to offer high quality postsecondary work, income mattered. As foundation officers evaluated the list of potential affiliates, of the black colleges eligible to affiliate, those represented at the planning meetings had impressive incomes when compared to those not represented at the meeting. According to Table 2.1, colleges attending the April and November meetings had significantly more income than those not attending.

Did the Colleges Have the Right Leadership?

When a foundation donated money to a college it made an investment in that institution, not the individuals steering it. But the foundations certainly tried to ascertain whether those leading the college made good stewards of the donation. Several foundations believed that Meharry Medical College of Nashville, Tennessee, served an integral role in the higher education of blacks. Writing to William Graves, secretary to Julius Rosenwald, GEB officer Abraham Flexner, in March 1917, claimed

Meharry as the "most important school for the training of Negro physicians in the country."[41] After the GEB took a financial interest in Meharry, Flexner argued vehemently for the school's accreditation rating. Writing to Henry Pritchett of the Carnegie Foundation in April 1921, Flexner remained perplexed at the American Medical Association's refusal to give Meharry an "A" rating, suggesting that if medical schools for white students such as Baylor or Louisville received "A" ratings then Meharry should as well.[42]

In 1943, the GEB decided to transfer $4 million to Meharry for an endowment fund.[43] Before turning over such a large sum to the college, the GEB wanted assurance that the money would be properly invested. The GEB asked Charles Nelson, president of Nashville Trust Company and a Meharry trustee, to detail the school's current investment strategy. During this correspondence, the GEB made recommendations regarding the mix of stocks, bonds, and real estate investments, but also became skeptical of Nelson. Foundation officers felt that to date Nelson had made questionable investment decisions on Meharry's behalf and expressed concern about his ability to shepherd the forthcoming donation. Rockefeller family members and associates familiar with Nelson's work confirmed these worries.[44] To alleviate their worries, the GEB insisted upon the formation of a finance committee to oversee Meharry's investments. They also wanted to provide input on the committee's membership.[45]

Financial stewardship was not the only area that concerned foundation officers as they weighed the decision to support a college. Racial politics and etiquette were ever present in their minds. Foundations supported colleges in their quest to provide black Americans with higher education to the extent that doing so did not disrupt the South's culture of racial segregation.[46] Foundations tried to strike a delicate balance. On the one hand, foundations wanted to improve black colleges. On the other hand, foundations did not want to antagonize the white South. This often put foundations at odds with black college leaders, many of whom hoped to challenge Southern racial politics and etiquette.

Aware of foundations' stance on Southern racial politics, rumors emerged that the GEB favored schools that limited the presence of blacks on their trustee boards. On one occasion, J. F. Lane, president of Lane College, inquired whether the fact that his college's trustees were majority "colored men" would not "make impossible" a favorable decision regarding a grant application under consideration at the GEB.[47] Such concerns regarding the GEB's preferences for white leadership shed light on the reality that schools represented at UNCF organizational meetings had lower percentages of black trustees than those not represented, significantly so for the April meeting.

In response to Lane's query, GEB officer Leo Favrot responded that he would like to "disabuse" Lane's mind on one point—"it is not true that the policy of the General Education Board requires that a school be managed or controlled by a board of trustees the majority of whom are white men."[48] Favrot's protestation belied the reality that the GEB did at times express concern over the racial makeup of a college's leadership. Correspondence records suggest these concerns did not arise because the GEB preferred white to black leadership as a general principle, but instead because the racial politics of the time afforded white leaders greater autonomy.

When reflecting on the foundations' desire to create a cooperative center among private black colleges in Atlanta, Georgia, GEB officers expressed concern that Spelman College's president, Florence M. Read—a white woman—prevented this plan from coming to fruition. The officers suspected that though the other college presidents seemed amenable to working with one another, as black men they felt compelled to defer to the wishes of a white woman, even if her wishes ran counter to their institutions' interests and that of the GEB.[49]

According to Table 2.1, the racial demographics of the leadership among the colleges helping to organize the UNCF tilted toward white, significantly so at the time of the April planning meeting. Colleges had to get the approval of their trustee boards before they could affiliate with the UNCF, and trustees were crucial in the overall fundraising scheme.[50] Based on their experience overseeing previous cooperative endeavors among black colleges, foundation officers believed interracial dynamics thwarted coordination. As foundation officers contemplated supporting the UNCF, the presence of few blacks in leadership among affiliating colleges signaled to GEB officers that these colleges had the autonomy to carry out the foundation's vision of comprehensiveness.

Learning from the Nonaffiliates

After focusing on how the colleges that did affiliate with the UNCF stacked up against donor preferences, questions naturally emerge as to what those colleges that were eligible to do so but did not affiliate can tell us about the status system operating within the black higher education field. Three cases are used to explore this issue. While not dismissing any of the college leaders' reservations about the UNCF or their beliefs regarding the promise of cooperative fundraising more generally, it is important to understand the decision not to affiliate with the UNCF as being reflective of the social milieu in which these leaders operated. Understanding each schools' fundraising history sheds light on why leaders may have found fault with the idea of the UNCF. Moreover, analyzing these fundraising histories illuminates each school's position within the status system and what effect this may have had on the GEB's assessment of the UNCF had each school decided to affiliate. Essentially, these cases offer us the opportunity to contemplate how the absence of these schools from the UNCF's membership roll also reinforced status distinctions and foundation preferences.

Talladega College

Buel G. Gallagher, president of Talladega College, attended the April meeting, but expressed severe reservations about the UNCF's likelihood of meeting with success.[51] Talladega did not send a representative to the November meeting and the school did not participate in the UNCF's inaugural campaign.

The UNCF needed to establish its credibility. If a third party has difficulty discerning a new organization's status, then it will rely on its experience with and what it knows about any organizations affiliated with this new venture.[52] Accordingly, the UNCF would benefit from whatever social capital affiliated organizations had accrued with the foundations.[53] Likewise, the UNCF would suffer from whatever social capital affiliated organizations had allowed to dwindle with the foundations.

The GEB had a mixed experience with Talladega. In June 1926, the GEB approved a $500,000 conditional endowment appropriation for Talladega. This investment alone indicates that in the foundation's estimation, Talladega played an integral role in the comprehensive system of black higher education. In reporting on his visit to the college in December 1926, GEB officer Jackson Davis exclaimed, "Talladega is perhaps the best liberal arts college for Negroes in the South."[54] As the college attempted to meet the terms of the conditional appropriation, problems occurred.

Indebtedness plagued Talladega's finances to the point that when the college raised the matching sums toward the GEB's conditional appropriation, it could not collect. Wanting to make sure that its appropriations went toward the future, the GEB did not release its payments to Talladega. Correspondence in January 1932 between GEB officer William

Brierly and a Talladega representative states that because the school had accumulated $13,665 of debt, the GEB could not justify authorizing a payment to Talladega's endowment. Brierly expressed hope that the debt "may be paid in the near future in order the College may receive the benefit of the pro rata sum which would be due from the Board."[55]After receiving several extensions on the time in which Talladega had to raise its portion of the endowment, the GEB issued an ultimatum: "Any portion of the Board's pledge not claimed by April 1, 1936, will automatically lapse."[56] Talladega managed to secure the funds in 1936.

In October 1938, Talladega applied once again to the GEB for an endowment grant—a common practice among colleges. As stated earlier, the GEB was so impressed with Bennett's ability to meet its endowment campaign in 1945 that the foundation immediately appropriated more money in 1946. This time, the GEB denied Talladega's appropriation request. Since securing the endowment money from the GEB, Talladega had fallen into debt once more. Between 1938 and 1940, though it granted the college small sums of money for specific projects such as cataloging library books,[57] the GEB repeatedly denied Talladega's request for monetary aid toward the yearly budget and endowment.

As the foundation officers considered the list of colleges affiliating with the UNCF in November 1943, seeing Talladega on the list would not have inspired much confidence. The GEB had witnessed the trouble Talladega had with fundraising firsthand. While the GEB continued to think quite highly of the college, even recommending it for participation in the American Council on Education's survey in 1938,[58] Talladega's inability to remain debt-free even after completing its initial endowment campaign perplexed the foundation. Furthermore, throughout its interactions with Talladega, the GEB urged the school to do away with its academy division,[59] yet only half the students enrolled at the college were at the postsecondary level at the time of the UNCF's formation. Thus, even though the UNCF invited Talladega to affiliate, the fact that Talladega did not may have been a blessing in disguise. The absence of Talladega from the list of affiliates further reinforced the foundations' distinctions between schools with strong and weak financial stewardship and schools with high and low proportions of college enrollment.

Wilberforce University

Unlike Talladega College, though eligible to join, Wilberforce University never sent a representative to the UNCF's organizational meetings.

Located in Ohio, near Xenia, a prominent stop along the Underground Railroad, Wilberforce had a complicated and decidedly negative experience with the GEB. Correspondence records between the university and the foundation begin in 1905. Despite the support of the Carnegie Foundation, President Garfield's son James, and President Taft himself, the GEB did not take a financial interest in the university. This disinterest is even more curious in light of foundation officer Trevor Arnett's assessment that Wilberforce's academic work was above average for a colored institution in 1922.[60]

After years of denying Wilberforce's requests for aid, in March 1929 GEB officer Leo Favrot informed the university that the foundation had come to the conclusion that:

> Wilberforce lies outside our province for several reasons. I might mention only three here, as follows: 1. The location of Wilberforce University outside of the South. 2. Wilberforce College receives $10,000.00 a year from the State of Ohio in addition to the separate school maintained at Wilberforce by the State. 3. Wilberforce is greatly in debt and contributions by our Board are made only to institutions free of debt.[61]

Based on foundation records, two of these claims seem misleading at best and specious at worst. Several schools supported by the GEB including Tuskegee, Hampton, and Meharry received money from their respective states. In fact, the GEB played an active role in brokering a deal for Meharry in which the state of Tennessee reimbursed the school for each Negro resident enrolled at the medical college. Because Negro students could not enroll at any medical college of their choosing, the GEB felt it only fair that Meharry receive some kind of compensation for the work it was doing to provide Tennessee with well-trained Negro doctors. While the GEB did not like to, it did at times help colleges pay down their debts. During Talladega's endowment campaign, the GEB partnered with the American Missionary Association, the college's denominational sponsor, to relieve the school of debt in 1932.[62]

The real problem appears to be that because it was located in the North, Wilberforce did not fit within the GEB's comprehensive plan to promote black higher education. The GEB saw black higher education as a Southern problem. In January 1938, Favrot stated this point far more emphatically after Wilberforce president D. Ormonde Walker requested an in-person meeting with foundation officers:

Our Board's program in Negro Education is restricted to a group
of selected institutions mainly in the South. There is no inclina-
tion on the part of the officers to consider grants to other institutions. On the contrary, the tendency is to restrict the program
even further. We have had requests in the past to consider the
needs of Wilberforce University but have not seen fit to extend
the scope of our activities in Negro Education to include this institution. Under these circumstances, I fear it would be useless
for you to come to New York for a conference with us.[63]

As foundation officers perused the list of potential UNCF affiliates,
the absence of a school such as Wilberforce further replicated the status
distinctions between Southern and non-Southern black colleges.

Meharry Medical College

In an interesting twist of fate, it appears that one school did not affiliate
with the UNCF precisely because of its high status. The case of Meharry
Medical College demonstrates that foundation preferences shaped adaptation not only through expressed hostility toward a school, as in the case
of Wilberforce. By giving generously to Meharry, foundation preferences
created the conditions for maladaptive behaviors to take root. Meharry
leaders were not proactive fundraisers and as a result lacked the ability
to understand why joining the UNCF was potentially a good idea. The
case of Meharry Medical College provides insight into the perils of falsely
believing that philanthropic support would never cease.

As Meharry Medical College's leadership weighed the decision to affiliate with the UNCF they may have come to the conclusion that Meharry
did not need the type of help promised. After all, the GEB had invested
heavily in Meharry since the early 1900s, and in 1937 alone the GEB
contributed $140,000 toward the school's current operating expenses.
As stated earlier, in foundation officer Abraham Flexner's opinion from
March 1917, Meharry was "the most important school for the training of
Negro physicians in the country."[64] At this time, the GEB appropriated
$7,500 toward Meharry's fiscal year expenses and in March 1919 made a
conditional endowment appropriation of $150,000 to the college.[65]

Though the GEB's opinion of the college never soured, in the mid-
1940s the GEB's investment approach toward Meharry changed. The
GEB had committed itself to appropriating $3,700,000 toward Mehar-
ry's endowment. But the college faced extreme difficulty in raising the

matching sum of $1.7 million. Hoping to encourage action on the part of the trustees and help Meharry stabilize its financial situation, the GEB decided to transfer $4 million to the college's endowment fund in 1943.[66]

Though a good administrator, Dr. Edward L. Turner, president of Meharry, was not a good fundraiser. His lack of skill in this area was exacerbated by the fact that the college trustees were of little help. Because the Rockefeller family foundations had given so generously to Meharry through the years, the trustees had become accustomed to doing nothing to help the school make ends meet. Why learn how to cultivate support elsewhere when the Rockefeller-related foundations had assured the college's survival for nearly forty years?

Robert A. Lambert, associate director of medical sciences at the Rockefeller Foundation, argued that turning over the endowment would "put on the trustees a responsibility which they have never assumed."[67] Though a large sum, the endowment would not yield enough income to enable Meharry to cover its yearly operating expenses. The foundation officers believed this reality would force the college trustees to take on a more active role in securing the college's financial position.

Because foundations had so generously supported the college, Meharry's leaders were not accustomed to taking a proactive stance toward fundraising. Because of their history with the school, as foundation officers looked over the list of colleges affiliating with the UNCF, the absence of Meharry probably surprised few. Affiliating with the UNCF was precisely the type of adaptation the foundation officers would have liked Meharry to undertake. And given the GEB's plans, there was no better time for Meharry to adapt by affiliating with an organization promising to raise funds for current operating expenses. Foundation officers recognized the role they played in retarding the college's fundraising capabilities and hoped the decision to place more responsibility on the school would set Meharry on the right course. The absence of this school from the list of affiliates further reinforced the distinctions between schools that took a proactive versus reactive stance to fundraising.

Conclusion

The irony of the UNCF is that for an organization formed to provide funding for financially insecure private black colleges, it ended up supporting only the most privileged. Black colleges were never independent actors and each faced the challenge that the resources for funding were concentrated in a few large foundations. This concentration of donors shaped the capacity of development among black colleges. Donors' decisions about which schools to fund and which not to fund over time resulted in a status hierarchy among the colleges in facilities, curriculum, faculty, and staff. This status hierarchy was then reproduced among UNCF affiliates. The colleges affiliating with the UNCF were more developed with regard to their postsecondary capacity, enrollment, and income. This outcome was not random.

A college's ability to achieve development in such areas historically depended on whether foundation officers felt the college added to the comprehensive system of (black) higher education. Those colleges that were already privileged via past donor funding and related expansion possessed the organizational markers that became crucial for attracting investment from foundations as the UNCF came to fruition. As the UNCF emerged, the status distinctions within the field solidified further. Collective fundraising promised to reduce financial inequities facing the colleges while at the same time bolstering the status inequities among them.

The UNCF's formation reaffirmed the existing inequality regimes in important ways. First, by turning to an organization such as the GEB, the UNCF did not fundamentally challenge foundation ideals regarding the types of colleges that added to the comprehensiveness of the American higher education system. This is not to suggest that organizational characteristics such as accreditation, income, and college enrollment are inaccurate means to judge a college's fitness in and of themselves. At the same time, it is important to recognize that at no point were foundations forced to interrogate the structure of white racial domination in which they formed preferences for these particular organizational characteristics.

By inviting schools that were either accredited or rated, the UNCF affirmed foundation beliefs about the importance of this distinction despite the historic difficulties that black colleges confronted when they sought this distinction from all white accrediting agencies. Even Meharry Medical College, a school foundations widely respected, could not get rated, while the medical schools at white colleges such as Baylor, which foundations thought less highly of, were able to attain accreditation. Though the UNCF created a membership pathway for all private four-year colleges that became accredited at a later date, the message was clear: unaccredited private black colleges did not add the same value to the higher education landscape as the accredited or rated ones. In a higher education system where all was equal, that is, where accrediting boards had always seen it as their goal to rate black colleges and where accrediting boards respected the work of black colleges as much as that of white colleges, this would have been fair. But black colleges did not operate in a world of equality. Furthermore, by not inviting two-year colleges the UNCF also reinforced the preference for four-year colleges, suggesting that two-year schools did not add to the comprehensiveness of American higher education. This occurred despite the real difficulties that many black students faced when trying to pay for four years of college. Including two-year colleges in the UNCF potentially represented a strategy that recognized the need and perhaps desire of some blacks to attain some college if nothing else.

By making the choices that it did, the UNCF set the stage for future adaptation among private black colleges. Throughout the UNCF's existence, all private four-year black colleges have affiliated at one point or another. Thus, all private four-year black colleges have had to seek accreditation and rise to the preferences touted by philanthropies. Given accreditation's importance, most schools would have sought it. But there was no countervailing force within the black higher education field to challenge the importance of the organizational characteristics philanthropists' preferred, given the circumstances under which black colleges operated. Engaging the philanthropists ensured that the preferences and inequalities structuring the black higher education field would continue to reign.

3

Advocacy and Racial Inequality

Twenty-seven schools joined the United Negro College Fund as the organization embarked on its first fundraising campaign in 1944. Status differences aside, these schools would work together to broaden the donor base of private black colleges. In addition to soliciting foundations, a traditional source of support, the UNCF also sought donations from the general public, a group the black colleges had yet to cultivate. The UNCF had to tell foundations and the public why it was worthwhile to financially support private black colleges. Particularly for the general public, who had little experience with supporting black colleges, the reasoning for doing so would not have been immediately obvious. The inequality regimes operating with America made it evident why black organizations deserved less, not more support. Raising money for private black colleges required constructing a narrative that would legitimate the schools themselves as actors worthy of support and the activity of donating to the schools.

Unlike the previous chapter, where adaptation resulted in the creation of a new structure or physical entity, adaptation in this instance was focused on cultural transformation. Convincing people to financially support private black colleges required altering the assumption that starving black colleges of critical resources was the best way to maintain white racial dominance. The UNCF had to articulate the value of black colleges to a field of actors guided by inequality regimes that to date had made it difficult, indeed impossible at times, for black colleges to claim financial rewards.

In the early years, the UNCF's leadership team worked in conjunction with the John Price Jones Corporation, the firm responsible for the University of Chicago's fundraising, to develop campaign strategy and material.[1] Direct solicitations played a key role in the UNCF's effort to create a new understanding about the role and value of black colleges within Southern and American society. Each year, the UNCF distributed a report entitled "A Memorandum Concerning the United Negro College Fund, Inc." to foundations. In these reports the UNCF provided philanthropic foundations, such as the General Education Board, Carnegie Corporation, and the Phelps-Stokes Fund, with a history of private black colleges. This narrative included information on the beginnings of the colleges, the educational work that the colleges had done throughout the years, the colleges' connection to their surrounding communities, profiles of selected students, as well as enrollment and financial information of the member colleges. The UNCF often drew attention to the historical connection between philanthropy and the livelihood of member colleges and attempted to make the case for the continuation of this relationship.

For individual givers, the UNCF also produced and distributed glossy brochures as a part of its cultural transformation project. These brochures were intended for "potential large givers, mass distribution at meetings, as follow-up pieces, and as mail enclosures."[2] The UNCF advised that these brochures "help dramatize the argument through pictures or printed text, and generally give additional information to help translate the impulse to give into action."[3] For example, during the 1947 campaign cycle the UNCF printed 235,000 brochures for distribution. At the time, the UNCF was courting Laurance S. Rockefeller's participation. As part of his solicitation he received one of these brochures entitled "Hope to all, A Statement of Purpose from the United Negro College Fund."[4] Prospective donors were to receive these brochures whenever possible. For instance, three thousand potential contributors were identified by the New York City fundraising committee and the UNCF provided the committee with brochures for these individuals.[5] Among other topics, the brochures contained descriptions of the students attending the colleges, the campuses, the state of black higher education, the ways in which potential donors could help, and how the UNCF distributed money.

At the time of its founding, less than 1 percent of the thirteen million blacks living in America attended college.[6] Therefore, the UNCF had to introduce the wider public to the fact that blacks attended college, the difficulties blacks faced when seeking a higher education, and the organizations responsible for providing this education to the majority of black students. As such, these brochures represented more than a means to raise money. Through these brochures, the UNCF framed the issue of black higher education for potential donors and observers alike. Frames are an important part of any attempt at cultural adaptation. Frameworks enable organizations to order the experiences of those attempting to understand their activities.[7] Frames condense the "world out there" by selectively punctuating and encoding objects, situations, events, and experiences of actions within one's present or past environment.[8] Frames or "definitions of a situation . . . which govern events . . . and our subjective involvement in them" represent an important component in any adaptive strategy.[9] Through the process of framing an organization can articulate its purpose, explain why it is necessary to adapt and gain support for the proposed way of doing things.

As it attempts to engage in cultural transformation, an organization must construct frames that are comprehensible to the field of actors with which they hope to engage. Fields produce particular political and discursive opportunities that limit the frames available to an organization. Political opportunities refer to the constellation of relationships among the actors within the field. The relative (in)stability within the political environment affects whether an organization can or cannot use frames to exploit cleavages among allies.[10] Comparatively, discursive opportunities refer to the meaning-making institutions of society and have a direct effect on the words that an organization can or cannot use as it constructs a frame.[11] A frame has to be understandable, thus an organization must be careful of the words it chooses. At the time of the UNCF's formation, the field simultaneously provided an opening and limited the organization's frame construction process. American society continued to operate under state-sanctioned racial inequality; yet, the institutions supporting state-sanctioned racial inequality faced increasing scrutiny and legal challenge. Though some within the black higher education field welcomed the end of state-sanctioned racial inequality, many, including large donors, did not. Consequently, the UNCF's attempt to create a shared understanding about the value of black colleges and the legitimacy of donating to these schools reflected the tensions of a society wrestling with the real possibility that state-sanctioned racially segregated higher education might meet its end.

Still living under the "separate but equal" system of education when the UNCF began in 1944, Americans by and large had yet to dedicate their collective efforts to improving access to or the quality of education for blacks. Prior to the 1954 Supreme Court ruling in *Brown*, most Americans remained unaware of or apathetic to the gross inequities in the educational system that hindered the progress of black students. During the first ten years of its existence, the UNCF operated in a legal and cultural environment that viewed the problems facing black Americans as the problems of the South and not the country as a whole. Focusing on these first ten years highlights how inequality regimes once again lead to partial adaptation. The political and discursive opportunities within the black higher education field did not allow for the UNCF to frame the role of black colleges outside the context of racially segregated education. This occurred despite the reality that many of the cases that laid the groundwork for the *Brown* ruling were decided in this ten-year period. These legal precedents steadily chipped away at the state's ability to segregate. However, the alliances within the black higher education field had yet to fracture. Southern state educational authorities desperately wanted to maintain segregation. Foundations still preferred to remain agnostic. Though not in favor of segregation, black college leaders also recognized that absent this system many including the leaders of civil rights organizations questioned the need for their schools. Hence, while the UNCF advocates that black colleges deserve more financial support, the organization does not attack the broader inequality regimes responsible for black colleges' financially precarious position. Though inequality regimes constrain the schools' ability to garner resources, the regimes also provide a raison d'être for the schools' existence.

The UNCF embarked upon a cultural transformation project that intended to frame the black college experience for the wider public. Operating under the grip of racism was part of the black colleges' experience. Nevertheless, the untoward effects of existing within a system that privileged whiteness and white higher education organizations remained curiously absent from the frames. The theme emerging from these documents indicates that the UNCF viewed the attacks on and responses to racial segregation as an opportunity to frame a message that spoke to the desire to maintain racial segregation. Operating within a discursive structure that depicted blacks as unruly and in need of control, the UNCF highlighted the need for a talented tenth to contain the black community. The black colleges were framed as bulwarks of segregated education, focused on providing apolitical social and economic leaders for black communities.

Adaptation, then, is partial on two fronts. First, the UNCF did not narrate the entire, and perhaps the most crucial, component of the black college experience—racism. The frames themselves were partial or incomplete. Second, by arguing that the value of black colleges was best understood in relation to segregated society, the UNCF did not develop a rationale for supporting black colleges that could easily translate to a post-*Brown* world. The cultural transformation project did not adequately account for the shifting legal landscape that would forever alter society's understanding and valuation of single-race entities. Casting donations to black colleges as an activity that strengthened the system of segregation was consequential far beyond the campaigns.

To understand how racial inequality structured the words the UNCF used to articulate a rationale for the financial support of black higher education requires setting the campaign narrative against the backdrop of the cultural and political machinations of the time. Only then is it possible to understand how and why the UNCF constructed its argument for broad-based support of private black colleges.[12]

Education as Uplift

Within America, blacks were depicted as dangerous and unruly.[13] These characterizations emanated from beliefs that a hierarchy of races existed, beginning with the savage and ending with the civilized being.[15] The theories supporting these views affirmed the "association of black with evil, savagery, and brutishness."[15] These theories stoked the fears of white Americans by claiming that blacks represented inept, yet menacing figures in need of control.[16] Blacks were thought to disdain work, to maintain a passion for "rum and tobacco," and, in particular, black men were thought to hold a perpetual lust for white women.[17]

During legal segregation, black leaders sought to redefine the framework of ideas surrounding blacks by claiming that as a whole the race could assimilate and adopt the behaviors of white Americans. Through education, service, and moral living, black leaders believed "the race" could uplift itself to the position of whites.[18] Within this uplift discourse, college-educated blacks were seen as necessary for the functioning of the black community. Educated blacks provided much-needed leadership and stewardship to the dangerous, unruly masses incapable of self-control.

The UNCF framed its ideas to fit within the prevailing discourse that depicted blacks as problematic figures and played upon the fear that many white Americans associated with the black community. The UNCF did so by articulating the experience of all blacks regardless of their intention to attend college, in essence providing a vivid depiction of the masses in need of support. According to the UNCF, the black community did not have access to proper medical care: "Right now, for example—there are only 4,000 Negro doctors in the whole United States—and only 1,600 dentists—12,000 nurses."[19] Moreover, blacks did not have qualified educators at their disposal: "There are still needs to be met. . . . They are reflected . . . in the lack of qualified teachers."[20] Furthermore, the economic outlook for blacks was bleak: "[M]any new and formidable problems will face us. . . . High on the list undoubtedly will be the question of a sound economic position for the Negro."[21] And all of this meant that blacks did not have the monetary resources necessary to better their circumstances: "But certain hard facts must be faced if this urgent need for more college-trained Negroes is to be met. Among them is the dollar barrier to education that remains for large numbers of Negro youth."[22] This also caused blacks to lack adequate numbers of professionals working within their communities: "A great many more Negro social workers, clergymen, engineers and agricultural experts are needed."[23] In the final analysis, these factors amounted to the following:

> Take any standard by which we judge a civilization—health, years of life ahead for a new-born baby, the chance for jobs—each one shows Negroes have fewer than average opportunities. Put these, and all other comparisons of opportunity between whites and Negroes together, and you have the "Negro problem."[24]

The UNCF delved further into the discourse that depicted blacks as unruly by suggesting that the problems plaguing the black community were unlikely to stay contained within it. When referring to the "Negro problem," the UNCF framed it as having the potential to affect people outside the black community: "It is an issue that bears on virtually every problem we shall face in the post-war days ahead . . . not only because of its vast size . . . but because of its tremendous potential influence upon every other group."[25]

After detailing the shortage of black professionals, the UNCF offered three chilling points: First, "unless something can be done to untie some of the knots for so large a segment of our [Negro] population, to make this increasingly a better America, a deep unrest may cloud and shadow not only our post-war world but the whole of America for many years to come."[26] Second, "A nation . . . climbs to greatness only when all of its people move upward at the same pace. If some have poor health, or too little education, they hold back all the rest."[27] Third, "Everyone must have the chance to develop the best that is in him, not only for his own sake, but for the nation's."[28]

To emphasize the "Negro problem" was no longer contained to the South, the UNCF discussed the migratory patterns of black Americans: "The tremendous migration of Negroes from the Southern states into other parts of the country makes the need for well-educated, qualified Negroes the concern of every community in the land, not just of the South."[29] Such statements made it easier for the UNCF to connect the progress of blacks to the progress of the entire nation: "These figures underline the urgency of the task ahead. Each of us has an important stake in that task, for if the Negro tenth of the nation does not have equal opportunity for advancement, the progress of the remaining ninety per cent will be slowed. For clearly what affects so large a segment of our population affects us all."[30]

The "Negro problem" as characterized by the UNCF could be solved via education:

> Only out of education, on its higher levels, can come the needed stream of trained Negro teachers, ministers, doctors, dentists, agriculturalists, business men, professional men, social workers and many others who will provide the race with its leadership and guide and lead it upward and forward in the days ahead.[31]
>
> More trained Negros are needed for positions of leadership and responsibility.[32]
>
> This tragic disparity in educational opportunity has created an acute shortage of college-trained Negroes in business and industry and in the professions.[33]

The UNCF argued that donating to black higher education would stem the tide of an impending crisis. By supporting the colleges, the number of trained professionals able to solve the black community's daunting problems would increase:

> Workers trained in agriculture are spreading over the south and working on the fundamental problems of raising the economic level of living among Negro farmers. . . . They are aiding the adjustment of rural migrants to urban living and helping with the problems of modern living.[34]
>
> In large cities and small towns in every section of the nation, these graduates are numbered among the Negro teachers, doctors, religious leaders, lawyers, businessmen, social workers, engineers and skilled technicians in industry and agriculture. Wherever they live and serve they are helping to raise the level of education, improving health and living conditions, and contributing to the economic progress of the community.[35]

Furthermore, contributions to the UNCF were seen as an effort to "[t]each hope to all . . . assure justice and opportunity to our Negro minority . . . a tangible contribution toward greater stability and understanding in our country."[36]

By claiming that "only out of education" would the skills, leadership, and service needed within the black community come, the UNCF utilized the uplift discourse to argue against the historical sentiment that limiting blacks' access to education was a proven mechanism for securing social and economic stability within America.[37] At the same time, by relying so heavily upon the "unruly black" trope to make its case, the UNCF did not challenge the belief system supporting racial inequality. The UNCF did not address the historical injustices that resulted in the crises they sought to address within the black community. As such, someone unfamiliar with American racial politics could have read a campaign brochure and come away with the impression that the black community suffered from awfully bad luck, as opposed to understanding the situation as being reflective of intentional policy decisions on the part of the nation and the regions in which most blacks lived. Focusing on how the UNCF discussed black graduates further illustrates how the organization's framing perpetuated the beliefs and practices associated with racial inequality.

Black College Graduates

The success of a framing strategy is dependent upon the divisions and opportunities for action within a field.[38] As discussed in chapter 1, though mass protest had yet to occur, legal challenges to racially segregated education increased in the 1940s, culminating with the 1954 *Brown* decision. During the ten-year period prior to *Brown*, the UNCF emphasized the constructive role that black college graduates could play within a society debating the merits of racial segregation. The UNCF incorporated the fears of white society regarding the seeming end of racial segregation in their framing of black college graduates. Above all else, the UNCF framed the graduates as people who operated mainly within their own communities, people who sought to increase understanding and goodwill between whites and blacks, and people who desired to work within the system of segregation, not challenge it.

When the UNCF talked about its graduates as leaders, it made sure that readers knew these graduates were holding leadership positions in the black community. For instance, when extolling the graduates, the

UNCF indicated the relationship between their work and the black community with the following: "Negro people have chosen sound leadership. The Negro graduates, who by nature of their training in the private Negro Colleges move into positions of leadership, have given expression to the wants and aspirations of their people."[39] When referring to the work of professionals trained at their colleges, the UNCF connected these graduates' activities to the black community: "In discussing Negro college education, one thinks first of the training of those professional leaders—the doctors, nurses, social workers, teachers, ministers, lawyers and others—needed by our 16,000,000 Negro citizens."[40]

The consistent references to the role that black college graduates played within black communities reinforced segregationist ideals because the black college graduates shouldered the responsibility of providing needed services to other blacks throughout the country: "Theirs is a major responsibility for the advancement of nearly 15,000,000 Negro citizens."[41] "When they graduate, they move about the country in response to economic opportunity and in response to situations calling for leadership and service. What they do and where they do it is tied in closely with the mobility of the Negro population."[42]

When the graduates were described as being in a position of leadership that involved people of other races, the graduates focused on bridging the gap between blacks and those people to increase goodwill and cooperation. For example:

> Both in the region of their homes and in all the rest of the country therefore will be found the graduates of the colleges—earning a livelihood, taking active interest in community affairs, and offering quiet dignified sound leadership in working out the complex problems of race relations and social adjustment.[43]
>
> And while black graduates give expression to the aspirations of their people, it is also they who work untiringly with other groups in the [Negro] community to solve problems.[44]

To calm fears regarding struggles over segregation, the UNCF framed black college graduates as though their desire to serve preceded any drive to challenge the political circumstances of the time. This graduate was presented as being a responsible individual, a leader in the black community, and one dedicated to service. For example, the 1947 general brochure included several profiles of black college graduates. Cleo W. Blackburn, one of the profiled graduates, ran a neighborhood center in Indianapolis. The vignette explained that the migration of Negroes to Indianapolis had created a "city of potentially taut race relations." Blackburn helped the migrant Negro "to understand his new environment" with services including industrial job training and healthcare. The UNCF carefully constructed an image of a college graduate that did not confront the political structure that made it difficult for blacks to obtain jobs and healthcare. The UNCF chose to highlight Blackburn's efforts to work within the system instead of any efforts that could have been construed as outright challenges to the system. Furthermore, to drive home the idea that graduates eased interracial interactions, when concluding Blackburn's profile, the UNCF claimed that racial cleavages still existed, but thanks to Blackburn's efforts "something negative, even hostile, is giving way to something positive, friendly, and significant."

Time and again, the campaign brochures provided scenarios that resonated with white Americans concerned about maintaining a racially segregated society premised upon denying blacks the opportunities available to whites. The system of racial segregation held out the promise that, while barred from using the facilities and services available to whites, blacks had access to separate and equal services of their own. However, a system whose foundation is built upon "separate, but equal" can survive only if adequate numbers of blacks receive the proper training necessary to provide service and stewardship to their fellow community members.[45] Otherwise, black Americans might venture into white communities and neighborhoods demanding access to the services not available closer to home.

By incorporating elements of segregationist discourse the UNCF made it possible for potential donors to view a contribution as part of the larger project of shoring up a racially segregated society and as a means to ensure that service-oriented, not politically minded, blacks took on leadership roles: "These [Negro colleges] were the sources from which had come nearly ninety percent of America's outstanding Negro leadership, including the majority of the professionally trained teachers, doctors, ministers, lawyers, social service workers—and the skilled technicians of industry and agriculture."[46]

Black Colleges and the American Experience

Beyond framing the "black experience," the UNCF also articulated why black colleges, as social actors themselves, were important to the American landscape. In many ways, the UNCF used the campaign documents to dissuade any fear that postwar America could function without the black colleges. Of particular concern was the National Association for the Advancement of Colored People's (NAACP) integrationist strategy. The NAACP sought to solve the "Negro problem" by advocating for the integration of blacks into larger society.[47] Beginning in the mid-1930s, the NAACP's legal staff focused on developing strategies aimed at the desegregation of public graduate and professional schools in the Southern states. Charles Hamilton Houston, an architect of the NAACP's legal strategy, felt such cases "were essential to the development of the leadership of the race."[48] The emphasis on graduate training yielded success. In 1936, the University of Maryland was required to admit a black student to its law school as a result of a suit initiated by the NAACP two years earlier.[49]

While such achievements represented progress for "the race," these cases undermined the position of black colleges. The NAACP vowed to eliminate segregation and therefore rejected the strategy of adding graduate or professional programs to black colleges. Instead, the NAACP sought to have black students admitted to established programs at historically white state-controlled institutions.[50] While the NAACP's lawsuit was successful, it appeared as though those directly affected by integration efforts were not receptive. Survey results indicated a high level of hostility among white students enrolled at the University of Maryland's law school following the court's ruling.[51] Such sentiments bolstered the position of segregated institutions of higher education, as a 1951 speech by Charles Dollard to UNCF supporters indicates:

> There are encouraging signs of improvement in this situation [segregation], but the change must necessarily be a slow one. . . . Given these facts, it requires no very profound analysis to determine that if in the next several decades Negroes are to have any reasonable opportunity for higher education, that opportunity must be provided by Negro colleges and universities located in the South. . . . Negro boys and girls now of college age or who will arrive at college age within the next twenty-five years will not have a reasonable opportunity for higher education unless the Negro colleges in the South continue to operate.[52]

On the heels of the *Brown* decision, the UNCF further emphasized the role of the private black colleges: "The growth of higher educational opportunities for Negroes has been tremendous, both in quantity and quality. But there remains an urgent need to strengthen and secure those institutions which have provided the major share of these opportunities—the private Negro colleges. The majority of America's outstanding Negro leadership has come from the private Negro colleges."[53]

By emphasizing the slow pace of integration, the UNCF articulated why supporting the black colleges was even more important now that racial segregation was near its end. From the campaign pledge, "For increased educational opportunity for American youth, and better race relations, I hereby subscribe" to the claim, "The tremendous migration of Negroes from the Southern states into other parts of the country makes the need for well-educated, qualified Negroes the concern of every community in the land, not just of the South," the UNCF appealed to the desire of many to maintain the racial structure of postwar America in which blacks would remain segregated from whites in all realms.

Racial Inequality and Financing Black Education

Sociologist Jeffrey Haydu encourages observers of history to identify the connections between events that span time to demonstrate how earlier outcomes shape later ones as actors continue to grapple with more or less the same set of issues. In agreement with Haydu, organization theorists Paul Hirsch and Y. Sekou Bermiss argue that even if actors want to do something new, the past has a way of structuring and at times limiting the possibilities. Old ways of thinking inform present day decision making. In the case at hand, as had occurred in the past, racial inequality continued to structure the adaptive capacity of black colleges, particularly their ability to mobilize resources.

During the first fifty years of the black higher education field, the question of the role of an educated black citizenry in the United States was largely understood in its connections to the curricular emphasis of black colleges: If blacks were going to receive an education, what kind should it be? Much has been said and written about the debates between Booker T. Washington and W. E. B. Du Bois. Both men held firm to their beliefs regarding the proper path that black education should follow. Yet, the historical representations of these two men and their positions mask the nuances of a black educational philosophy that advocated combining the best elements of vocational and classical studies within a unified curriculum.

Black leaders understood the importance of both types of training. Vocational education in the skilled trades, artisanship, and agriculture would promote the development of a black business class independent of white communities and was necessary if blacks were to find employment outside of poorly paid occupations such as domestic service and farm labor.[54] Notwithstanding the benefits of vocational education, few black leaders argued that it should be the only type of education available to black college students. Instead, black educational leaders wanted vocational education to occur alongside that which focused on the liberal arts. It was important that the most "intellectually able" black students receive the same kind of education available to the most advanced white college and university students.

The need for financial support from educational philanthropies complicated the desire of black communities to intertwine the best of vocational and liberal education within black colleges. Foundations tried to achieve two incompatible goals—promote black educational advancement while pacifying Southern white opposition. Achieving the former goal often conflicted with the latter. To promote black education, foundations established building, salary, curriculum, and endowment programs to stimulate the growth and development of black colleges. To placate Southern whites, foundations did little to directly confront segregation and cooperated with Southern whites to promote particular forms of black education, namely vocational education.

By the 1940s, the debates between Washington and Du Bois were long settled. Yet, the legacy of this era remained, for the debates over curriculum served as a proxy for a larger question: "What is the role of an educated black citizenry in the United States?" An important lesson learned from the curricular debates was that the advocates of vocational education articulated a vision of education that did not challenge racial inequality. The state of affairs in post–World War II America only exacerbated the need to reexamine the role of educated blacks. The resulting effect of this examination on black colleges' ability to mobilize resources was strikingly similar to what had occurred earlier. Those advocating for black colleges continued to find it necessary to demonstrate how black higher education fit into the larger Southern and American narrative of race relations.

The rhetoric used to justify black higher education represents a connective string holding time together for black colleges. As the UNCF developed rationales for the role of an educated black citizenry and black colleges in this process, their outlook and understanding was greatly influenced by the rationales developed when the black higher education field began during the late nineteenth and early twentieth centuries.

Conclusion

Showing how white Americans—the beneficiaries of racial inequality— would profit was crucial to any effort on the part of black colleges to mobilize financial resources. Inequality regimes make it necessary to demonstrate how uplifting the oppressed will benefit the oppressors. This reality results in partial (cultural) adaptations that do not fully narrate the conditions confronting oppressed communities. Through framing, the UNCF provided a compelling case that documented the necessity for black colleges and how the graduates of these schools could play a vital role in society without disrupting the system of racial segregation. Supporting black higher education was key to ensuring that blacks in need of social services would be able to turn to qualified blacks within their communities. Underserved and undereducated blacks had no reason to venture into white communities for help or to demand improved conditions. When necessary, whites could interface with educated blacks versed in interracial cooperation, not the blacks on the verge of destruction or pushing for revolution. Supporting black colleges guaranteed the reproduction of black leaders amenable to racial inequality—the kind of leaders that focused on working within the system, not challenging it.

The decision to incorporate segregationist ideologies into frames limited the UNCF's ability to adapt in important ways. The UNCF hoped to expand the private black college donor base. Strengthening ties to the black community, particularly college alumni, was a key goal. Yet, this goal proved difficult. When reporting on the 1946 campaign and specifically the claims that more Negro professionals were needed to serve the wider Negro population, the UNCF publicity director noted:

> The fact that the need for more professionally trained Negroes to serve was shown appears to have been a sound point among whites.... Under the circumstances, the idea of helping Negroes to help themselves seemed fair and equitable to whites.... There seems to be handicaps to such an argument among Negroes.... First, the appeal for more professional Negroes merely to serve Negroes is not one that would ordinarily induce many Negroes. ... Such an approach would seem to constrict the natural desire of Negroes to be of service to everyone on a basis of equality. Any

distinction that is drawn on this score would tend to challenge what he has come to believe is the democratic way of serving.[55]

If the goal had been to build stronger ties to the black community, why use frames that alienated this audience? One explanation stems from Kevin Gaines's book *Uplifting the Race*. Gaines argues that many educated blacks held paternalistic beliefs toward uneducated blacks. The analysis of the 1946 campaign speculated that fewer blacks donated to the UNCF because "professional Negroes have too often set themselves apart from" the less educated, contributing to the contempt of the "masses of Negroes" for the professionals in their communities.[56] If true, then including frames that alienated black audiences was another way for black leaders to express their attitudes toward the less educated.

Another explanation builds off the work of historian Marybeth Gasman in *Envisioning Black Colleges*. Gasman concludes that in its early days, the black leaders involved in the UNCF had less control over the organization than did white leaders. This would suggest that the final decision regarding the inclusion of frames that alienated blacks rested with the more powerful white members of the organization.[57]

While both explanations illuminate possibilities, each places too much weight on the role of individuals and not enough on the context in which individuals act. For instance, yes, white leaders were powerful influences in the UNCF's early years; nevertheless, black leaders were also involved in the construction of the campaign message. Correspondence files indicate that the college presidents engaged in hotly contested debates over phrasing, such as when the phraseology "of a national cause" was changed to "of national concern."[58] The limited involvement of black leaders cannot fully account for the framing choices. Nor can these leaders' antipathy toward uneducated blacks.

It is crucial to understand that the UNCF's decision to frame the benefits of black higher education in a way that did not challenge racial inequality was necessary given the social milieu of the time. Despite recognition that positioning Negro college graduates as the rightful leaders of their community had little sway on the majority of blacks, the UNCF continued to utilize this framing throughout its first ten years. Campaign analyses had shown that it was whites, not blacks "who represent the largest area of contributors."[59] It made no difference that these frames did not resonate with blacks or that these frames may have deepened class divisions within the black community. To mobilize resources from whites at this moment in history necessitated the inclusion of frames that perpetuated racial inequality.

As a result, the value of black colleges was largely understood in relation to state-sanctioned racial segregation—a system that was facing its greatest challenges. Between 1944 and 1954, the UNCF averaged $450,000.00 in donations from individual donors.[60] Each time these donors opened a campaign brochure the message was clear. Indeed, supporting black colleges helped black Americans. But supporting black colleges helped maintain the system of racial segregation; thus, doing so also helped to strengthen the white racial project. These donors and all others familiar with the UNCF's work had reason to link the value of black colleges to their role in making segregation a reality. Though the UNCF's frames were intended to raise money for private black colleges, much of what the UNCF said was generic enough that it applied to public black colleges as well. Thus, given the UNCF's reach and influence, the framing choices were relevant to all black colleges. The chapter that follows will demonstrate the consequence of black colleges being ideologically linked to segregation. Black colleges, public and private, found it increasingly difficult to narrate a new rationale for the political, moral, and financial support of black colleges after a series of court rulings made it illegal to maintain racially segregated systems of higher education.

4

Adapting to a World without State-Sanctioned Racial Inequality

State-sanctioned racial inequality defined and structured the black higher education field. Public black colleges might have never come to fruition if not for this institution. Private black colleges could not raise funds without acknowledging it. Like all institutions, state-sanctioned racial inequality had regulative, normative, and cultural-cognitive aspects. State and municipal laws in Southern locales regulated the separation of blacks and whites. The norms supporting state-sanctioned racial inequality dictated that whites should remain separate from blacks and were obliged to use both legal and extralegal means to guarantee this outcome. The taken-for-granted nature of state-sanctioned racial inequality made it so that whites especially found it difficult to imagine a world in which blacks had equal rights.

The regulative, normative, and cultural-cognitive elements of an institution reinforce one another. The Supreme Court's ruling that blacks had no rights that whites were bound to respect (*Plessy v. Ferguson*) gave credence to the norms guiding interpersonal interactions with blacks. For a cultural-cognitive structure to take hold and perpetuate itself, it must have a cadre of supporters that will enact the institution's principles, myths, and rituals on a regular basis.[1] The regulations and norms supporting state-sanctioned racial inequality created a series of rituals that had to be enacted to maintain the system. Someone had to post the "Whites Only" sign. Someone had to ensure that blacks were not admitted to schools designated for whites. Enacting these rituals strengthened this inequality regime as it became a routine way of life.

For better or for worse, the institutions supporting state-sanctioned racial segregation provided a framework in which to understand the purpose and role of black colleges. State-sanctioned racial inequality gave reasons for both blacks and whites to remain invested in these schools. Blacks wanted to ensure access to higher education. Whites wanted to maintain a racially separate education system. The black colleges fulfilled each group's goal. The *Brown* ruling called all of this into question. Suddenly, the institutions that gave meaning to black colleges had been undermined. What did it mean to be a black college going forward? Without question, *Brown* represented a historic victory in the fight for civil rights. It removed centuries-long constraints on the educational choices of individual black Americans. *Brown,* however, posed specific challenges for black colleges as organizations. It laid the groundwork for questions pertaining to the usefulness and value of race-specific educational entities altogether.

The historical and legal record provides ample evidence with which to trace how the institutions supporting the black higher education field changed following *Brown,* and how black colleges adapted to these events. The racial desegregation of higher education challenged the regulative, normative, and cultural-cognitive elements of the inequality regimes operating within the South in important ways. Many actors within the black higher education field concluded that black colleges were an impediment to achieving a racially integrated higher education system. For black college leaders and advocates, these challenges made it necessary to once again embark upon a cultural transformation project, this time to carve out a new understanding of what it meant to be a black college in a post-*Brown* world. In particular, black college advocates took actions aimed at repairing and recreating the regulative, normative, and cultural-cognitive elements of the institutions supporting the black higher education field. They performed institutional work[2] in hopes of reestablishing the legitimacy of single-race educational spaces in an environment that increasingly favored, if only in theory rather than practice, racially integrated ones.

Black college advocates were not entirely successful in their efforts. Within the field of actors, a theory of race neutrality that left little space to convey the value of primarily black educational spaces prevailed. Regardless of this outcome, focusing on the institutional work black college advocates performed provides a way to understand how proponents articulated the role and necessity of black colleges in a racially integrated higher education system. Furthermore, focusing on institutional work will again show how partial adaptation arises in response to the field of actors. Black college advocates were not the only field members recalibrating in light of the *Brown* ruling. Initial court rulings focused on ensuring that individuals had the right to attend any school. In response to *Brown*, Southern state authorities intensified their efforts to maintain traditionally white and historically black educational spaces. No longer able to deny blacks admission to traditionally white colleges outright, Southern state educational authorities used creative means to guarantee that black and white students continued to choose separate schools. The state claimed that blacks were not denied the right to attend traditionally white colleges, but instead chose to attend historically black ones.

The stalemate might have remained had the field of actors continued to emphasize individual access to colleges and universities. However, the judiciary began to focus more and more on systemic solutions to integrating higher education and to adopt color-blind legal ideologies. To fully adapt to the federal court system's demands for integrated systems of higher education meant that Southern colleges had to lose their racial identifiability. The colleges could be neither white nor black. Within this color-blind ideology black colleges were construed as obstacles to integration. Their very existence prevented black students from integrating traditionally white colleges of the South. To fully adapt, then, would require black colleges to abandon their "blackness" and their advocates to yield the position that there was value inherent in maintaining black colleges in light of the reality that black students still found it difficult to gain access to white colleges.

Limited or partial adaptation to the institutional norms supporting race neutrality and color-blind legal ideology represented the only feasible solution for black colleges in this period. Black colleges did look to integrate their campuses. Nevertheless, black college advocates rejected the tenets of color-blind ideology. Black college advocates argued that the end of state-sanctioned racially segregated higher education was not just cause for society to disinvest from the perpetuation of black colleges as racially identifiable entities. They continued to argue for the legitimacy of educational spaces that were dedicated to meeting the specific needs of black Americans.

Institutional Logics, Desegregation, and Black Colleges

In May 1954, the United States Supreme Court ruled against racially segregated public education at the primary and secondary levels. Arguing that "in the field of public education, the doctrine of 'separate, but equal' has no place,"[3] *Brown* became the law of the land. The initial legal environment following *Brown* focused on individual rights and access. In arguing the case, the NAACP claimed that the Supreme Court's *Plessy* ruling "was wrong because it allowed states to use race as the rationale for denying black Americans certain constitutional rights that were freely exercised by other Americans."[4] Despite the fact that the legal precedents for *Brown* were set at the graduate and professional level, the ruling itself was about K-12 schools. It remained unclear whether and how this ruling should be applied to higher education or whether the ruling impinged on black colleges' right to exist.

The *Journal of Negro Education* published a series of special issues on desegregation in the years following the *Brown* ruling. In the summer of 1958 the journal dedicated an entire issue to "Desegregation and the Negro College." The tenor of the papers in this volume did not suggest that those studying or affiliated with black colleges felt the institutions supporting these schools were in jeopardy. Martin Jenkins summarized the situation as follows: "What are the prospects of the Negro college? All of the contributors . . . are of the opinion that most of these institutions will survive and that in the immediate future they will continue to serve a predominantly Negro clientele, although some recognition is given to the probability of varying degrees of desegregation in particular institutions."[5] Jenkins himself was slightly more skeptical, arguing that "it is inevitable that eventually the Negro college, as a *Negro* college will disappear."[6] While Jenkins called for black colleges to integrate their campuses, he saw few reasons why the *Brown* ruling in and of itself should threaten the longevity of these schools.

Like other contributors, Jenkins saw desegregation as just one of the many factors, not the defining factor, that would affect black colleges following *Brown*. Guy Johnson, another contributor to the 1958 issue, argued that desegregation, the demand for college education, the economic outlook, and ideological factors would each influence the vitality of black colleges in a post-*Brown* world. To the extent that few colleges, public or private, within the Southern states had undergone any real desegregation, Johnson could not see why black colleges would suffer. Add to this the recalcitrant position that most Southerners held toward integration, the growing demand among blacks and whites for college education, and the improved economic conditions, and Johnson felt that enrollment at black colleges would fare quite well: "Very few colleges will be eliminated completely as a result of desegregation per se. However, there are several marginal Negro institutions which are likely candidates for elimination in the normal course of events. Desegregation, by raising the level of competition, might be a contributing factor in their demise."[7]

Thus, in the years immediately following *Brown*, while black college advocates recognized that things had shifted, few felt that the ruling completely undermined the institutions supporting the field of black higher education. In their estimation, *Brown* primarily affected the legal elements of the institution. Blacks as individuals were no longer confined to black colleges. Nor were whites limited in their options. In fact, the evidence available at the time suggested that black colleges had done a far better job integrating their campuses than had traditionally white colleges. As early as 1958, black colleges located in border states such as West Virginia had effectively desegregated.

Given the rampant resistance to desegregation, black college advocates did not see why or how the *Brown* ruling had shifted the normative or cultural-cognitive elements of the institutions supporting the field. Southern politicians' and educational authorities' position on racial inequality's righteousness hardened during *Brown*'s immediate aftermath. To keep their traditionally white colleges from integrating, these authorities enacted more elaborate rituals than had existed in the pre-*Brown* era. Knowing that few alumni from white universities would endorse a black applicant, the state of Georgia required applicants to submit certificates from alumni of the college or university they wanted to attend.[8] After passing a law that permitted the firing of any principal, teacher, or state employee that advocated for integration, the state of Louisiana then required applicants to public universities to submit a character certificate signed by their local school officials.[9] Realizing that, on average, black students had lower ACT scores, the state of Mississippi required higher scores to gain admission to the traditionally white universities than to the black ones.[10] The regulatory environment surrounding black colleges may have been fragmented, but the normative and cultural-cognitive dimensions that mandated whites to protect their spaces from blacks had not receded.

Not until a decade later did the implications of desegregation begin to fracture the institutions supporting black colleges. The 1968 Supreme Court decision in *Green v. School Board of New Kent County* (*Green*) stipulated that school boards were not merely required to "cease unconstitutional actions . . . rather, they had a proactive responsibility to enact policies and procedures that would transform segregated schools into integrated ones."[11] From here on, desegregation plans would be judged "on their effectiveness in eliminating the vestiges of segregation."[12] One year later, the U.S. Department of Health, Education, and Welfare (HEW) found ten states in violation of Title VI of the Civil Rights Act of 1964 because each continued to maintain dual systems of higher education.[13] It became clear that the meanings attached to desegregation extended beyond the individual to include schools as social actors. As the judiciary began to apply the *Green* ruling to higher education, black colleges, not black individuals, took center stage in this new phase of desegregation.

Black college advocates understood that the Southern states' efforts to maintain segregation made it difficult for black colleges to integrate their campuses. Given the new responsibility placed upon schools to integrate, black colleges sought relief in the court system. In *Norris v. State Council of Higher Education* (*Norris*), black plaintiffs sought to prohibit state officials from engaging in tactics that threatened a black college's ability to attract white students. Here the plaintiffs argued that the state of Virginia's planned expansion of all-white Richard Bland College, located in Richmond, would make Virginia State College, also located in Richmond, less attractive to white students.[14] The district court used *Green* to argue that Virginia had to do more than ensure the use of nondiscriminatory admission and hiring practices. Expanding Richard Bland College would stifle desegregation efforts. On the one hand, black college advocates got what they wanted. Southern state efforts to forestall black colleges from recruiting white students were put in check. However, in making its ruling in *Norris*, the court further stipulated that states were responsible for converting their "white colleges and black colleges to just colleges."[15] The norms within the field were shifting such that it was now seen as appropriate to pursue the desegregation target by removing the racial identity of schools. The field was beginning to move toward a theory of race neutrality. This was not a move black college advocates welcomed.

Black college advocates wanted to maintain a space for schools dedicated to facilitating the needs of black Americans. Sure, the advocates wanted the ability to attract white students. But not at the expense of maintaining spaces catering to the unique educational needs of blacks. The situation facing black colleges worsened when in *Swann v. Charlotte-Mecklenburg Board of Education*, the Supreme Court ruled "a school's identity should not be reflected in the racial composition of the faculty, the quality of its facilities and equipment, or the sports activities of the school," leading to a situation in which the "continued racial identifiability of public schools—and by extension, colleges—created the presumption of a constitutional violation."[16] According to this ruling, as long as black colleges remained "black" they could be interpreted as impediments to desegregation.

Here again, we see how the field of actors produced a situation that encouraged black colleges to pursue strategies that were most likely to lead to partial adaptation. Because the courts began to argue that promoting integration within higher education required schools to be racially androgynous entities, black college advocates now had to argue against the *Norris* ruling, despite its more useful aspects. Black college advocates knew that Southern state policies undercut the ability of black colleges to recruit white students. Relying on individuals to opt into black colleges had not led to integrated campuses. Yet, black colleges could hardly fully adapt within an institutional framework that argued schools should lose their racial identification.

Institutions are not uniform spaces, but instead contain within them "ambiguities, multiple layers, potentially decomposable components, or competing logics which actors can use as vehicles for experimentation, conversion, or recombination, and transformation."[17] Within the black higher education field, multiple interpretations of the state's obligation to desegregate existed. The interpretation of the state's role beginning to take hold did not benefit black colleges. As such, black college advocates looked to advance another position, for which there was also legal precedent.

In *Alabama State Teachers Association v. Alabama Public School and College Authority*, "a black teachers' organization at Alabama State College in Montgomery challenged the constitutionality of an act of the Alabama legislature creating a branch of Auburn University in Montgomery."[18] The teachers' association held that the branch campus would weaken Alabama State's ability to recruit white students and further perpetuate the dual system of higher education. In its ruling, the district court argued that the nature of postsecondary education differed substantially from that which occurred at the K-12 levels. In the court's view, states did not have the same duty to eliminate dual systems of education at the postsecondary level as states did at the presecondary levels. As long as states enacted nondiscriminatory admission and hiring practices then according to this district court states had met the standard set in the *Green* ruling.

Institutional logics refer to the "material practices and symbolic constructions" that act as "organizing principles" and are available to "organizations and individuals to elaborate."[19] For example, the institutional logic guiding capitalism "is the accumulation and the commodification of human activity."[20] Conflicting court rulings provided alternative bases upon which to elaborate the role of black colleges in a post-*Brown* world.

In one account, though the state had a more limited role, the position of black colleges as racially identifiable schools remained intact. If the institutional logic stemming from the Alabama case reigned, as long as the hiring and admission policies at black colleges did not prevent students of a particular racial category from attending, then black colleges could more easily carve out a space within this landscape. In this scenario, the logics guiding the field would by and large remain race conscious, as they had been pre-*Brown*. Alternatively, if the institutional logic stemming from the Virginia and Charlotte cases reigned, then the black colleges were at risk of being converted to "just colleges," with no special emphasis or dedication to black students.[21]

An institutional logic guided by a theory of race neutrality did not appeal to black college advocates. Absent state-sanctioned racially segregated education, black college advocates engaged the regulative, normative, and cultural-cognitive dimensions of the institutional environment to maintain a role for the schools within an environment now privileging integrated education and non–racially identifiable colleges. At the regulative level, advocates, through the appeals process especially, called for the courts to interpret desegregation statutes such as *Green* in a way that favored the continuation of race-conscious public policy. Gaining momentum for this position was difficult given the efforts underway within the field to dismantle the dual system of higher education operating within the South.

In 1970, for instance, the NAACP Legal Defense Fund filed suit (*Adams v. Richardson*) against HEW arguing that the agency had failed to enforce Title VI of the Civil Rights Act of 1964. Despite citing ten states for operating dual systems of education, HEW did not cut off federal aid as Title VI required. Instead of pursuing a school-by-school strategy as it had done in the cases leading up to *Brown*, with this lawsuit the NAACP Legal Defense Fund combined all levels of education—a move that "recognized the increasingly systemic organizations of higher education and the need for *systemic* solutions to the problems of racial discrimination."[22] After all, despite the increasing number of black students attending college, ten years after *Brown*, 65 percent were still enrolled in black colleges.[23] The slow pace of integrating white colleges suggested that relying upon blacks to opt into white colleges, or whites to opt into black colleges, was not a promising solution. The NAACP Legal Defense Fund prevailed and HEW was ordered to enforce the law.

With the increasing focus on removing the racial identifiability of schools, black college advocates grew concerned that if *Adams* were upheld, a legal basis for eliminating black colleges would exist. Working together through the National Association for Equal Opportunity in Higher Education (NAFEO), in 1973 public and private black college presidents filed an amicus brief with the Court of Appeals for the District of Columbia, where the *Adams* case was now located. Though the *Adams* ruling had more of a direct impact on black public colleges, black private colleges were affected by this situation as well. The state could not force black private colleges to close or integrate. Yet, black private colleges could not escape the emerging sentiment that it was racially identifiable colleges, not the states, that were the true impediments to integration.[24]

Black college advocates used the amicus brief to argue against the logic of applying legal standards developed at the K-12 level to postsecondary schools. By doing so, the advocates attempted to resurrect the precedents set at the higher education level prior to *Brown*. In those cases, the courts had ruled in favor of individual choice and held that states could not bar blacks from attending white institutions. The racial identifiability of a school and hence, black colleges, hardly factored into these cases at all. Only recently had higher education desegregation been framed as a systemic issue that could not be remedied by ensuring individual access. It was under the systemic framework that black colleges entered into the debates regarding desegregating higher education. If courts continued to focus on individual access, black colleges could more easily adapt. Black colleges were willing to admit white students and had no plans to make it more difficult for white students to attend. If courts continued to focus on ensuring individual access, then admitting white students did not necessitate abandoning the preference for emphasizing the educational needs of black Americans.

Black college advocates also used the amicus brief to insist that black colleges should not be conceptualized as organizations responsible for perpetuating discrimination. After all, it was the traditionally white colleges that had intentionally denied black students admission and had benefited from discriminatory funding allocation schemes. This represented an attempt to counter the cultural-cognitive framework that situated all single-race entities as affronts to integration. Indeed, in the advocates' eyes black colleges were themselves victims of discrimination. As Leland Ware argued, viewing black colleges as barriers to integration is "ironic because the long-neglected and drastically under-funded black schools will, in effect, be penalized, while institutions which engaged in discriminatory practices will benefit."[25]

Black college advocates also objected to the notion that "eliminating the racial identity of state colleges promised to enhance educational opportunities for black students."[26] It was black colleges who had continued to "serve as a bridge between a crippling and debilitating elementary and secondary educational system" for black students.[27] The argument put forth in the amicus brief resonated with one being deployed by black college advocates in *Hunnicut v. Burge*, a case focused on Fort Valley State College, a black public college in Georgia. In this case, the United States District Court for the Middle District of Georgia accused Fort Valley of being "little more than a "diploma mill" for marginal students."[28] Similar to the *Adams* case, black college advocates in *Hunnicut* pointed to Fort Valley's role in serving "a population of students who were academically under-prepared by Georgia's still-segregated elementary and high schools."[29]

While the Court of Appeals did not overturn the *Adams* case, black college advocates did gain some ground. The court of appeals directed states to consider the positive role of black colleges in Southern higher education; going so far as to direct states that "[t]he process of desegregation must not place a greater burden on Black institutions. . . . The desegregation process should take into account the unequal status of the Black colleges and the real danger that desegregation will diminish higher educational opportunities for Blacks."[30] It is difficult to see how this recognition would have come to light absent the NAFEO amicus brief.[31]

Thus, their attempts to maintain a space for black colleges within an institutional framework privileging race neutrality were partly successful. Black college advocates were able to argue that protecting individual choice meant ensuring that those who wanted to attend black colleges could do so. This would only happen if black colleges were not "sacrificed on the altar of integration."[32] Furthermore, through the appeals process, black college advocates got the courts to endorse the shared understanding that the role of black colleges in Southern education could be positive even absent state-sanctioned racially segregated education. However, the matter of higher education desegregation was far from settled.

Even with the *Adams* ruling, Southern states continued to neglect the needs of black colleges, and underfunding persisted. In Mississippi, for example, when combined, traditionally white University of Mississippi and Mississippi State University averaged more than $38 million in state appropriations between 1970 and 1974. Meanwhile, not one historically black college within the state totaled more than $20 million over the same time period.[33] As a result, relative to their white counterparts, black colleges had worse facilities, lower salaries, and faced greater difficulty upgrading curricula. Southern political authorities appeared to take little interest in providing a context in which black colleges could flourish. Southern legislatures established branch campuses of their traditionally white colleges in close proximity to black colleges, effectively siphoning off resources and students that might have otherwise gone to black colleges.[34] Black colleges lacked the political and financial resources necessary to fully adapt. Once again, advocates sought relief from the court systems. Just as before, advocates' attempt to make it easier for black colleges to adapt resulted in legal precedents that all but ensured partial adaptation.

In a lawsuit first filed against the state of Mississippi in 1975, known as *Ayers v. Fordice* and later *United States v. Fordice*, black college advocates argued that increasing access to Mississippi's "all-white universities should supplement, not replace, the academic opportunities afforded to black Mississippians by black colleges."[35] To make this possible, advocates believed any statewide desegregation plan had to ensure significant enhancements to black colleges. Black college advocates stipulated that guaranteeing the equal protection of blacks as individuals necessitated protection of the educational organizations that blacks might choose.

This argument sits well within organization theory for it recognizes the reality that within American society, life-chances are largely determined by one's access to organizations. Black college advocates' arguments that "individuals can only receive higher education from institutions. Hence, if state policies unconstitutionally discriminate against certain institutions, such actions would abridge the rights of individuals receiving an education in such settings,"[36] further highlighted the reach of state-sanctioned racial segregation. It was not just the state's failure to protect individual rights that damaged black Americans, it was also the state's failure to recognize and protect the right of organizations trying to serve these individuals that compounded the system's effects. Black college advocates argued that the state's past history toward these schools had created a ""cumulative deficit" that the state was now obliged to remedy."[37]

By the time the *Ayers* case came to trial[38] in 1987, integration remained stagnant among Mississippi's public colleges and universities—more than 99 percent of white undergraduates still attended traditionally white colleges and more than 70 percent of black undergraduates attended black colleges.[39] Nonetheless, the district court agreed with the state of Mississippi's argument that such outcomes no longer represented intentional efforts on the part of the state to prevent blacks from attending formerly all-white colleges and universities, but instead were reflective of individual choice. The court also agreed with the state of Mississippi's argument that remediating black colleges went beyond the scope of desegregation law and policy. In making its conclusion, the court relied on the precedent set by the *Alabama State Teachers Association* case that focused on ensuring the removal of non-race-neutral policies.[40]

Black college advocates called for racially conscious, not racially neutral remedies. Given the South's history, this made sense. Black colleges had not been conceived of nor did they currently operate within a racially neutral environment. It was impossible for black colleges to fully adapt in a context that assumed racial neutrality. It was the very "blackness" of these organizations that made it difficult for the schools to claim rewards relative to traditionally white colleges. Black colleges could never overcome the cumulative effects of state-sanctioned racial inequality if Southern states were not forced to enact racially conscious remedies. If the courts did not direct Southern states to institute racially conscious financial and political solutions to address the organizational deficiencies plaguing black colleges, partial adaptation was the only realistic outcome. Black colleges would continue to lack the resources necessary to meet the challenges of an increasingly complex and competitive higher education landscape.

As the *Ayers* case worked its way through the appeals process, various courts debated whether the correct legal standard had been applied. In its first ruling, the United States Fifth Circuit of Appeals disagreed with the district court's interpretation of *Green*. The Fifth Circuit relied on an interpretation of *Green* from a case decided upon by the Sixth Circuit that held that states had an "affirmative duty to eliminate all 'vestiges' or effects of segregation, 'root and branch,' in a university setting."[41] As if the situation were not confusing enough, when the Fifth Circuit granted a rehearing of the case some months later, it "reinstated the trial court's decision" which had focused on the existence of race-neutral policies as evidence that Mississippi was making good-faith efforts to eradicate the vestiges of segregation.[42] The *Ayers* plaintiffs and the U.S. Justice Department in its role as plaintiff-interveners appealed the case to the Supreme Court.

Notably, even in its role as an ally, the U.S. Justice Department's position in this litigation diverged from that of the *Ayers* plaintiffs (black college advocates) at times. When the Justice Department filed an initial brief with the Supreme Court in 1991, it reversed its position from arguments made at the lower courts. In the Supreme Court brief, the Justice Department countered the *Ayers* plaintiffs' core argument that the state of Mississippi needed to financially compensate black public colleges "to remedy a century of underfunding and lack of support."[43] Perhaps the federal government feared the implications of this ruling, for it too had participated in discriminatory funding against black colleges.

As the more powerful actors (i.e., states, Justice Department officials, courts) within the black higher education field divested from racially conscious institutional rules that had once sustained black colleges' right to exist, black college advocates were left to perform the work of maintaining this logic on their own. Now black college advocates had to engage in extra work to ensure that the Supreme Court would receive a unified message from all those advocating on behalf of black colleges. Black college advocates were able to reiterate the core points of their argument to President George H. W. Bush.[44] If states were not required to address funding disparities between their white and black postsecondary schools then "states would be provided with a legal justification for the continuation of the practice of underfunding" black colleges.[45] At the president's insistence, the Justice Department "reversed its position when it filed its reply brief before the Supreme Court."[46]

When the Supreme Court issued its *Fordice* ruling in 1992, it was not entirely clear which side prevailed. The Supreme Court argued that the state of Mississippi had not done enough to desegregate its institutions of higher education. Still, the Court's provision that a "state does not discharge its constitutional obligations until it eradicates policies and practices traceable to its prior de jure dual system that continue to foster segregation"[47] confused matters. Whereas traditionally white colleges had particular admission or hiring policies traceable to de jure segregation, few thought of the colleges themselves as practices traceable to the system. Alternatively, black colleges—the organizations themselves—are seen in this way. Accordingly, the *Fordice* ruling provided a legal framework for claiming that as practices traceable to de jure educational systems, black colleges were impediments to integration. Furthermore, the ruling specified that practices traceable to de jure racial segregation could "be sustained for only two reasons: if said policies cannot be practically eliminated, or if the elimination of said policies or programs would violate sound educational practices."[48]

The Supreme Court did not require states to rectify past or current funding disparities between white and black colleges and even held that doing so could be interpreted as an effort to further subvert the *Brown* mandate. Getting the states to meet their financial obligations to the colleges was the reason the case was filed. Nevertheless, the Supreme Court reasoned that the state could not meet its "burden under *Brown* to take affirmative steps to dismantle its prior de jure system when it perpetuates a separate but 'more equal' one."[49] Thus, states were obligated to do more than erect race-neutral admission policies to bring about desegregation. But states could not implement race-conscious policies either, for fear that doing so would perpetuate a more equal, yet still separate system of higher education within the South.

After analyzing the *Fordice* ruling, political scientist Albert Samuels argued that the Supreme Court did not fully comprehend what the *Ayers* plaintiffs wanted. While the *Ayers* plaintiffs felt that equalizing the funding between the state's white and black schools was key to achieving desegregation, the Court saw this as a separate issue. The Court even suggested the possibility that increasing funding at the black colleges might go a long way toward enabling the state of Mississippi to desegregate its institutions. After all, if the black colleges were more equal to the traditionally white counterparts, more white students might choose to attend them. This would eventually eliminate the racial identifiability of black colleges, the legal and social standard advanced by the Supreme Court's decision.[50] Not understanding that this was the crux of the *Ayers* plaintiffs' argument, the Court instead saw this as an issue that would have to be addressed in the future.[51]

That such confusion remained after years of engaging the regulative, normative, and cultural-cognitive pillars illustrates the difficulty inherent in institutional work, particularly when multiple groups with unequal power are involved. When several groups engage in parallel institutional work, there can be "significant disagreement among field constituents as to which arrangements should be adopted."[52] Not surprisingly, the institutional arrangement that prevails "strongly reflects the key values and interests of the dominant players"[53] within the field.

The Justice Department's arguments regarding whether the state of Mississippi had met the *Green* standards of desegregation, which called for "some level of racial mixture in formerly segregated schools,"[54] drowned out the *Ayers* plaintiffs' central concern about Mississippi's duty to redress discriminatory practices that rendered black colleges unequal. Similar "schisms between private [b]lack plaintiffs and the United States as intervener developed in Louisiana, Alabama, and Tennessee."[55] In each situation, black plaintiffs' concerns about the past effect of segregation on black colleges were overshadowed by Justice Department or other federal bureau concerns about dismantling the remnants of segregation. More often than not, the private black plaintiffs wanted to improve the very schools the federal government targeted when it called for the higher education systems of formerly de jure states to be desegregated. Consequentially, the *Fordice* ruling's implicit requirement of racial integration and suspicion of single-race entities signified that, "as it stands, a prior de jure state's continued maintenance of public HBCUs that remain predominantly African-American is apparently illegal unless the court accepts a constitutional theory under which those institutions may continue to survive."[56]

Despite the Supreme Court's ruling that the state had to do more than erect race-neutral admission policies to desegregate its colleges and universities, on the whole the *Fordice* case both reflected and strengthened the inequality regime operating within the South and America. Inequality regimes make it possible for the field of actors to construct claims that disadvantage the black colleges. As the Court saw it, strengthening black colleges by rectifying past funding discrepancies risked perpetuating a dual system of higher education. If black colleges were able to claim the financial rewards owed to them by the state, this would produce negative consequences. The Court placed little credence in the argument that strengthening black colleges might actually hasten desegregation, instead claiming that this was a matter for a later date. By failing to direct the states to strengthen black colleges, the Supreme Court further empowered the Southern states to starve the colleges of resources necessary to adapt in this postsegregation historical moment. In fact, pouring too many resources into black colleges could be seen as a concerted effort to thwart desegregation. Yet, the Court did not suggest that pouring resources into traditionally white colleges would produce the same result. Black colleges entered the *Fordice* case with the intent of challenging the inequality regime but were still unable to claim rewards relative to traditionally white colleges following the case.

Furthermore, black colleges now confronted an environment in which the very existence of black colleges could be interpreted as unconstitutional. Thus, to some extent, the inequality regime was stronger than it had ever been. Prior to *Brown*, the inequality regime necessitated the perpetuation of black colleges. Without black colleges the state could not claim that it was fulfilling its duty to provide educational facilities for both blacks and whites. After *Brown*, the state no longer had to prove that it provided separate educational facilities. In fact, the state had to prove quite the opposite. Southern state officials no longer had to champion the existence of black colleges. Officials could use the *Fordice* ruling to call for the closure or merger of state-affiliated black colleges. Though no longer tied to state-sanctioned racial inequality, the institutions supporting the black higher education field continued to allow those supporting white racial projects to disadvantage black colleges.

In the wake of *Fordice*, legal scholars concerned with the fate of black colleges proceeded by questioning the ruling's integrity and articulating other legal precedents the Supreme Court could have used to provide better legal grounding for black colleges. Tarvald Smith argued that the Supreme Court made the wrong decision in *Fordice* and should have relied on the precedent established in *Bazemore v. Friday*, which held that "if a state has discontinued its prior discriminatory policies and has adopted and implemented good-faith, race-neutral policies and procedures, then it has met its constitutional obligations to eradicate segregation."[57] Applying the *Bazemore* standard, Smith argues, would have enabled the Supreme Court to further scrutinize whether Mississippi's efforts to eradicate segregation in its system of higher education were in fact "good-faith." As legal scholar Thomas McKenzie points out, even Justice Scalia, the lone dissenter in *Fordice*, argued that "under the *Bazemore* standard, given the fact that Mississippi originally adopted ACT admission requirements as an effective way of excluding blacks, the district court should have required Mississippi to prove"[58] that its continued use was not racially exclusionary.

Applying *Bazemore*, Smith argues, better reflects and respects the element of choice as an essential component of the pathway to college that *Green* is not equipped to handle. According to Smith, *Green* was developed at the K-12 level, where freedom of choice had been shown to further segregation—parents continued to choose to send their children to racially segregated schools. By forcing school districts to eradicate segregation via busing and mandatory assignment, the Supreme Court had essentially limited a student's ability to choose to attend a racially segregated school. Smith argues that higher education remedies should differ from those developed at the K-12 level:

> When students graduate from high school they are not required to attend college. Those who decide to attend college are free to choose any college, provided they meet that institution's admission requirements. Student choices are then made to reflect their interests in an institution's academic programs, location, tuition, and school tradition. Therefore, remedies should be fashioned to

remove barriers which might interfere with their choices without lowering an institution's academic standards.[59]

Smith felt applying *Green* to higher education interfered with student choice and stood to restrict it even further because the *Fordice* ruling gave District Courts the "power to approve remedies fashioned by school governing boards which eliminate programs and merge institutions."[60] Both justices Thomas and Scalia argued that the *Fordice* ruling all but guaranteed the "elimination of predominantly black institutions."[61] Scalia felt that states would "have an exceedingly difficult time proving that programs which foster the continued existence of historically black institutions serve a sound educational justification."[62] The Supreme Court claimed "sound educational policy" as the standard by which courts should judge whether the racial identifiability of a school "helps or hinders the achievement of equality in education."[63] As Smith concluded:

> The practicability of maintaining all eight institutions [of higher education in Mississippi] will probably be the most considered factor. . . . *Fordice* gives district courts the authority to remedy segregation and racial identity in higher education by determining whether the continued existence of all institutions in the former *de jure* states continue to foster segregation. If the courts determine that the existence does promote segregation, then they may remedy the problem by closing or merging institutions. Such a remedy threatens the existence of smaller institutions in former segregated states, especially the historically black institutions. Closures and mergers of institutions will be considered by the courts as a means of ending the dual educational systems which were created during segregation.[64]

Wendy Brown-Scott goes beyond the *Fordice* decision to offer a metacritique of the post–civil rights atmosphere itself, calling for focus to shift toward "the other governing constitutional principle announced in Brown—the provision of equal educational opportunity."[65] Like Smith and McKenzie, Brown-Scott also disagrees with the Court's decision in *Fordice*. However, instead of arguing for the application of one legal precedent over another, Brown-Scott contends that the courts have construed the *Brown* ruling too narrowly, thus focusing on desegregation as the only possible solution to achieving educational equality. Whether education occurred in an integrated or predominantly black setting, what matters, Brown-Scott holds, is that the courts guarantee that black students have equal opportunities. Brown-Scott urged the legal community to interrogate its unquestioned faith in the notion that segregation, particularly when it is not state mandated, "represents inherent inequality."[66] Focusing on providing equality of opportunity, as opposed to integrating blacks into traditionally white schools, better matched the civil rights imperatives of empowerment and self-determination that prevailed at the time of the *Fordice* ruling. As Brown-Scott stipulated:

> In the 1990s, full inclusion in American society remains the predominant civil rights goal of African-Americans. The term "inclusion," however, connotes cultural pluralism and self-determination, rather than integration or assimilation. This evolving change in ideology, from a narrow vision of assimilating African-Americans into white society to a broader notion of cultural pluralism, illustrates the point that legal ideology must fit the current social and political context.

Still, other scholars have sought to explicate how black colleges can be justified within the *Fordice* framework. To this aim, Frank Adams Jr.'s legal analysis traces two constitutional theories under which the continued existence and funding of black colleges is justified. *Brown* and cases that had come before it (*Sweatt v. Painter, McLaurin v. Oklahoma*) relied on the intangible qualities (e.g., rich traditions, prestige, intellectual heritage) that "hastily created" de jure schools lacked and the negative effects of de jure segregation on black student self-perception as the reasons why legally segregated education violated constitutional principles of equality. Alternatively, Adams Jr. argues that "[f]or over a century, these institutions [black colleges] have been the cornerstone of the African-American university student's intellectual experience" and that black colleges "possess those qualities which *Sweatt* and *McLaurin* deemed as indicia of greatness in institutions, including . . . reputation in community . . . faculty committed to the nurturing and development of eager minds . . . experienced administrators and influential alumni."[67] Though many may have started as part of a haphazard attempt to thwart racial integration, public black colleges had evolved from there into something more substantial. For instance, Texas State University for Negroes began as an effort on the part of state officials to stall law school integration. Nevertheless, within a short time, the school had an updated library, a liberal arts college, a graduate school, and a school of pharmacy.[68] Moreover, Adams Jr. argues that black colleges do not impose a stigma of inferiority but "because of their rich legacy and commitment to excellence," black colleges "actually help meliorate the self-perception of their students, creating an environment which nurtures the learning process."[69]

While legal scholars question whether the Supreme Court applied the correct precedents in *Fordice* and whether a constitutional imperative for black colleges remains, a sociological analysis instead focuses on whether and how lawsuits such as *Fordice* provide a space for defeated movements and institutional projects to reemerge.[70] In isolation, it appears that the legal battles following *Brown* represent a concerted effort by the judicial system to apply constitutional imperatives to a specific type of case—how best to guarantee equal protection and due process in the realm of higher education. As in any legal case, plaintiffs and defendants will disagree but both perspectives will have merit. Furthermore, "law" itself is open to many interpretations. For instance, despite belonging to the eight-justice majority in *Fordice*, Justices O'Connor and Thomas wrote concurring opinions offering a different analysis of the state of Mississippi's culpability and of the future role of black colleges respectively. Though *Fordice* created more ambiguities than clarity, particularly with regard to black colleges, in isolation this too suggests that the ruling reflects nothing more than the nature of the American governing system. Courts rule, but do not implement. Law in theory may be clear; law in practice is rarely ever.

If, instead, one views the legal battles following *Brown* as another piece of evidence in the long chain of events in the overall struggle for black higher education, then it becomes easier to see how institutional orders from the pre-*Brown* period became "resources or platforms for organizing alternatives"[71] in the post-*Brown* era. It is crucial to understand that the debates over how to apply desegregation precedents to higher education created a space for those who continued to remain antagonistic toward black colleges to further undermine the schools' legal and political standing. The post-*Brown* period provided those still committed to a white racial project with an opportunity to develop the principles that would guide the inequality regimes going forward.

For a moment, Southern state authorities had resolved to care about black colleges because doing so enabled them to maintain predominantly white flagship schools. For these authorities, black colleges remained an instrument that enabled the state to fulfill its desegregation objectives without having to actually desegregate. The goals of the white racial project remained unchanged. Keeping the traditionally white colleges predominantly white was extremely important to Southern political leaders. The means of achieving this goal shifted. Keeping the traditionally white colleges white required investing some political and financial resources in black colleges. However, black college advocates wanted more than what Southern officials had in mind. Black college advocates wanted remuneration for the past. Black college advocates wanted the capacity to do more than partially adapt. Black college advocates wanted to attack the cumulative organizational deficiencies that made it difficult for black colleges to compare well to traditionally white colleges. This was not a part of the white racial project post *Brown.*

In the midst of the *Fordice* lawsuit, only 7 percent of black students within Mississippi were enrolled at the state's traditionally white universities.[72] Meanwhile, black enrollment at Mississippi Valley State, the black college, was 99.3 percent.[73] Yet, Mississippi's Republican governor, Kirk Fordice, was quoted as saying that, "if a court ordered him to raise taxes to equalize spending between historically black colleges and white institutions, he might call out the national guard."[74] Given that black students continued to receive the bulk of their higher education opportunities from black colleges, not equalizing the spending between these organizations and their white counterparts meant that black higher education suffered statewide.

Southern politicians were not the sole actors within the black higher education field committed to the white racial project. Only in the years leading up to the *Brown* ruling had the judiciary reversed its long-term neglect of black Americans and the organizations serving this constituency. Like Southern state educational authorities, the post-*Brown* desegregation hearings afforded the judiciary an opportunity to give voice to the underlying hostility that remained toward black colleges. As Brown-Scott posits, the judiciary viewed pleas to upgrade the black colleges "as expressing a preference for Jim Crow–style segregation." The Supreme Court refused to adopt a legislative stance that would have allowed the black colleges to flourish by drawing a parallel between the work of black colleges and the "harmful discrimination practiced by white segregationists."[75] Not to mince words, in *Knight v. Alabama*, another higher education desegregation case, the Supreme Court stated:

> The Constitution does not teach that because a historically black institution has suffered discrimination that it is entitled to an elevated academic mission. The danger of creating parallel universities in mission . . . cuts too close to the doctrine repudiated

by Brown v. Board of Education, when the only reason for doing
so is the racial discrimination suffered by the historically black
institutions.[76]

As *Fordice* and other higher education desegregation cases worked
their way through the courts, the American political center had swung
to the right. Albert Samuels argues that "the Mississippi case was one
battlefront in a larger national debate over the meaning of the civil rights
revolution of the 1960s."[77] With arguments regarding the separation of
the races no longer in vogue, constituencies who had once supported this
position began to instead argue against "race consciousness in the determination of public policy," claiming that it "constituted a prima facie
violation of the American principle that citizens be judged based on their
individual merits."[78] As defendants in higher education desegregation
cases, Southern states adopted this philosophy. The state of Mississippi
alleged that since the Constitution protected individual rights, the *Ayers*
plaintiffs and the black community more generally did not have "a constitutional right to educational institutions with equal resources as white
institutions."[79] According to the state of Mississippi, advocating for group
rather than individual rights "fundamentally violated the American
Creed."[80] Hence, complying with *Brown* "required the implementation of
race-neutral, color-blind policies in higher education."[81]

Not only did Southern states advance this more conservative approach to civil rights, courts did too. The precedents debated in *Fordice*
were established in a moment when the Supreme Court rulings had "expanded the court's ability to foster desegregation."[82] Initially filed in 1975,
by the time *Fordice* arrived at the Supreme Court in the 1990s the winds
had changed. In more recent years, the Supreme Court had struck down
desegregation plans that involved busing between districts and plans
that would have ensured a racial balance between majority and minority
students. By the time *Fordice* was decided, "the belief that race was an
inherently illegitimate basis with which to ground public policy"[83] had
emerged within the Supreme Court.

Situating black college advocates' efforts to maintain a space in the
post-*Brown* environment in the context of institutional work illuminates
the challenges facing black colleges in the broadest sense possible. Though
not handed down until 1992, because it consolidated the rebranded conservative position toward black higher education, in essence the *Fordice*
case had been long decided. Thus, black colleges did not end up on shaky
constitutional ground as a result of this case because the Court applied

the wrong legal precedent. Black colleges ended up in the position that they did because the *Fordice* ruling codified the growing preference for an allegedly race-neutral institutional landscape in which colleges whose core mission remained the education of black students could not easily adapt. As Wendy Brown-Scott argued, "rather than accepting them as appropriate remedies for racial discrimination" an overwhelmingly white (liberal and conservative) judiciary perceived enhancing black colleges as racism.[84]

Situating black college advocates' efforts against the growing wave of conservatism toward civil rights draws attention to the reality that multiple parties performed institutional work aimed at maintaining a space in the post-*Brown* era. *Brown* not only loosened the institutional underpinning that once supported black colleges, it also altered that undergirding traditionally white spaces. By the 1970s, those who argued against integration in public education under any circumstance were seen as racists and out of touch with the nation's core principles. Yet, these groups did not recede from the institutional landscape altogether. Like the black college advocates, conservative groups worked to repair and re-create their political perspectives' framework.

Paramount on the agenda for those advocating a conservative approach to civil rights was pushing back on the *Brown* decision and more specifically federal oversight of *Brown*'s implementation at the state and local level. The development of a color-blind policy perspective resulted from these groups' efforts. If a school put a good-faith effort into overhauling its policies so that they were no longer racially conscious, what more could federal authorities want? As courts adjudicated cases, the Supreme Court especially gave credence at first to a more liberal interpretation of the court's reach and of states' responsibility to desegregate. During the 1950s and 1960s, the Supreme Court upheld lower court rulings that required states to actively dismantle policies and procedures that promoted racial segregation. These initial decisions rarely differentiated between those instances when a policy had a segregative intent or outcome. During the 1970s, the court system scaled back its efforts to ensure that desegregation occurred. The Supreme Court split hairs, requiring plaintiffs to prove that state policies were enacted with a discriminatory intent. Moreover, "Plaintiffs had to prove how racial discrimination unconstitutionally abridged their liberties"[85] in the present. States could not be punished for past discrimination.

While black college advocates engaged in institutional work to solidify a place for their schools in the post-*Brown* landscape, conservative forces regrouped, calling for the use of race-neutral and color-blind leg-islation. Latching on to the conservative position, state officials in *Ford-ice* argued that "requiring the state to make massive investments at the historically black colleges to compensate for past discriminatory policies would unconstitutionally punish the state for *past,* as opposed to present, discrimination."[86] The sum total of the conservative efforts post-*Brown* affected black college advocates' ability to maintain an institutional logic that was inherently grounded in a race-conscious philosophy and cumu-lative effects.

Without this logic, partial adaptation is all that could be expected of black colleges. In *Fordice*, advocates held that the state of Mississippi needed to compensate black colleges for past funding disparities. Unless the state remediated black colleges, the schools would face the daunting task of updating their facilities, salary structures, and curricula without adequate funding. Through *Fordice*, advocates pushed for the courts and the state to acknowledge the particular educational needs of black stu-dents and the expertise of black colleges in this process. Creating a shared understanding of the value of black colleges, as organizations open to integrating yet primarily focused on black education, was key. Absent this understanding, black colleges could only partially adapt normatively and culturally to an environment that questioned the relevance of primarily black spaces. Fully adapting to such an environment would have required black colleges to abandon their historical connections to the black expe-rience and become "just colleges."

In addition to the changing tenor of political discourse, black col-leges continued to struggle against the power imbalances within the field. To fight the charges leveled against it in *Fordice*, the state of Mississippi financed its defense by assessing the state universities.[87] Thus, while black college advocates worked to prove the state had discriminated against black colleges, the black colleges helped the state argue against correcting these discrepancies.[88] This situation paralleled the double taxation that plagued black communities in the pre-*Brown* era. Yet again, blacks took on the responsibility to secure educational access for their own commu-nity while being simultaneously compelled through the taxation powers of the state to contribute to a system that went against their interests.[89] Though black college advocates attempted to maintain an institutional space for black colleges grounded in race-conscious ideology following *Brown,* the advocates were less successful than the conservative forces ar-guing against them. The higher education desegregation struggles made it clear that "[t]he American judicial system that once sponsored the practice of legally excluding ethnic minorities from White institutions of higher education now disallows placing an "undue" burden on Whites in order to remedy past injustices."[90]

As educational scholar M. Christopher Brown notes, when "'higher education systems initiate desegregation plans, public black schools are merged or closed."[91] The *Fordice* ruling did not explicitly call for this type of action as a remedy to segregation. While the Supreme Court speculated that closing colleges was a possibility, the Court also specified that they were "unable to say whether or not such action is constitutionally required."[92] Alternatively, the Court held that eliminating program duplication between black and white colleges and revising admission criteria could make "institutional closure unnecessary."[93] Despite the sentiment among black college advocates that if states followed the spirit of the Supreme Court's decision that *Fordice* "could result in additional resources being given to black colleges to improve facilities,"[94] a widespread interpretation of the ruling is that black colleges are a problem to be dealt with, not resources worth cultivating.[95] That most observers and commentators have interpreted the Supreme Court's *Fordice* ruling in a way that places black colleges in peril represents a major achievement for those working against black college advocates. The institutions giving meaning and structure to the black higher education field make it possible to question the constitutionality of the very existence of black colleges.

Without a unified approach to higher education desegregation, district courts were charged with the responsibility of developing desegregation plans on a state-by-state basis following the *Fordice* ruling. In 2002, a federal judge approved a desegregation plan for the state of Mississippi. The $503 million dollar settlement plan required the state to "pay for new academic programs, constructions projects, and endowments at the state's three historically black institutions over 17 years."[96] However, the settlement also required the black colleges to maintain at least 10 percent nonblack enrollment for three consecutive years before the schools could control certain portions of their share of the principal from the endowment funds.[97]

Remarkably, the traditionally white colleges in the state had no such stipulations levied against them regarding the enrollment of nonwhite students. *Ayers* plaintiffs and other black college advocates have noted the "irony of the federal government's prohibiting admissions based on quantifiable 'affirmative action' (designed to increase black participation at historically white schools), yet requiring public black universities to spend public money to recruit a preset number of non-black students."[98] One advocate even labeled the requirement a "one-way racially offensive remedial process."[99] While African American enrollment at Mississippi's traditionally white colleges was slightly above 20 percent at the time the settlement was negotiated, it remained unclear if this was a result of university-led efforts or the efforts of "students who insisted on their right to attend."[100]

The focus placed on black colleges goes to show how far the institutional landscape had shifted since the years following the *Brown* ruling. After *Brown*, traditionally white colleges and state agencies "were subjects of scrutiny,"[101] yet fifty years later black colleges are "asked to find ways to diversify student enrollments." By 2008, Jackson State University and Mississippi Valley State University had failed to meet the enrollment requirement and subsequently had not received their portion of the endowment. More striking, once received, the endowment funds must be used to recruit nonblack students and personnel.[102] Black college advocates continued to express their discontent. The *Ayers* plaintiffs challenged the settlement, however, and when the Supreme Court refused to hear their appeal the settlement went into effect. Alvin O. Chambliss Jr., the lawyer representing the advocates, claimed that "[g]iving half a billion dollars to Mississippi's historically black colleges" would be helpful, but that doing so would not "ensure a level playing field for black students."[103] For instance, the settlement did not prevent Mississippi governor Haley Barbour from proposing in 2009 to consolidate the state's three black colleges into one.[104] Given the high proportion of black Mississippians enrolled at the black colleges, merging these schools would have effectively consolidated and limited the higher educational opportunities statewide—the schools were not geographically proximate and had different educational missions.

The state of Maryland offers another example of the post-*Fordice* landscape. Unlike Mississippi, when it was notified that its operation of a dual system of higher education violated federal law, the state of Maryland reached an agreement with the federal government in 1985. When the *Fordice* ruling was issued in 1992, the Office of Civil Rights applied the new standards to the state. In 2000, this resulted in a new desegregation plan in which Maryland agreed to improve educational opportunities for blacks attending black colleges, enhance black colleges, eliminate unnecessary program duplication between black and traditionally white colleges, improve the campus climate for blacks attending traditionally white colleges, and provide need-based financial assistance for blacks trying to access and complete graduate and professional school.[105] When state officials claimed they had fulfilled their commitment to the desegregation plan in 2006, black college advocates voiced their skepticism.

Of particular concern was whether the state had done enough to make the black colleges comparable to the state's traditionally white colleges.[106] Black college leaders charged that "[e]fforts to enhance Maryland's Black institutions have been slow and exceedingly limited."[107] Black college advocates also charged that the state had failed to "prevent unreasonable program duplication between Black and White institutions," citing an instance when a joint MBA program between two traditionally white colleges was proposed when Morgan State University, a black college in close proximity, already had one.[108] Program duplication, black college advocates held, was "pervasive" and had led to the state's black colleges being "far more segregated now than they were forty years ago. In 1972, 43% of graduate enrollment . . . was White, and a year later . . . 53 percent. In 2006, it was 14 percent."[109] Such practices on the part of Maryland's educational authorities led black college leaders and advocates to doubt whether the state would continue to invest in its black colleges if the federal government ruled that Maryland had met the terms of its desegregation agreement.[110]

Conclusion

The institutions supporting the black higher education field shifted from being grounded in a race-conscious to a race-neutral logic following *Brown*. Yet, both logics produced a similar result. Black colleges were starved of the political and financial resources necessary to fully adapt. Prior to *Brown*, the inequality regimes disadvantaged black colleges. Ensuring that black students attended poorly equipped and underfunded schools was an essential facet of the decidedly race-conscious institutional framework. Following *Brown*, though allegedly race-neutral and color-blind, the reconstituted institutional framework continued to disadvantage black colleges. This logic was deployed to support a white racial project now situating black colleges as the true impediments to integrating Southern higher education. Allowing black colleges to make claims for greater political and financial rewards risked furthering segregationist goals. Thus, even when the schools were able to reach remediation settlements with the state, as the case of Mississippi showed, the colleges were not able to claim the monies until white enrollment reached a certain threshold lest the state be seen as supporting segregation.

Just as the reconstituted institutional framework of race neutrality continued to disadvantage black colleges it also produced partial adaptation, though perhaps a more complicated form of it. As chapter 3 demonstrated, prior to *Brown*, black college advocates used the segregationist, race-conscious framework to their benefit. The UNCF essentially argued that donating to black colleges was a way to maintain an effective segregated higher education system. Yet, it was nearly impossible for black college advocates to utilize the race-neutral, color-blind framework whatsoever. Black colleges could not adapt to or accept this institutional framework without abandoning their core mission.

As problematic as the system of state-sanctioned racial segregation was, its regulative, normative, and cultural-cognitive dimensions better supported the role of black colleges. This institutional configuration produced partial adaptation, but in a sense it may have been easier for black colleges to handle. Yes, black colleges found it difficult to express their rights, develop their distinctive capabilities, and grow their resources relative to traditionally white colleges within the pre-*Brown* institutional landscape. Then again, law and custom supported the schools' right to exist. Alternatively, the logics guiding the racial integration of higher education could be used to argue against the very presence of black colleges. Within the regulatory space, the emphasis upon the "justifiability" of single-race entities placed the black colleges in a position of having to defend the schools' educational contribution. Unless the educational contribution of such an entity was made clear, it violated constitutional principles. The normative space stipulated that educational organizations should not maintain a missionary focus on the education of black students in particular. Schools that continued to do so were viewed with suspicion. Finally, the cultural-cognitive space provided scripts that not only situated single-race entities as poor alternatives to mixed-raced settings, but also as impediments to integration regardless of the state's role in guaranteeing this outcome.

As chapter 5 demonstrates, this institutional environment laid the groundwork for isomorphism to occur. The organizational processes and outcomes of colleges could not be racially identifiable. The institutional environment encouraged black colleges to abandon practices that made them distinct and potentially identifiable relative to traditionally white colleges. The idiosyncrasies between black and white colleges eroded throughout the last decades of the twentieth century. The final empirical chapter takes up this matter in full.

Despite the institutional work performed by their advocates, to many the value of black colleges following the *Brown* ruling remains unclear and perhaps negligible. What constellation of the field of actors might have enabled black college advocates' institutional work to yield more promising results in the post-*Brown* world? Black college advocates would have been more successful in their calls for states to rectify their past discriminatory actions against black colleges had the judiciary recognized "the pedagogic value of an all-Black learning environment."[111] Instead, black college advocates confronted an environment that located "the source of the problem in the African-American individual and the institutions that they operate, rather than in those institutions operated and maintained by the dominant white group and the attitude of white supremacy propagated in society."[112]

To make education systems work for black Americans, Brown-Scott argues, requires those charged with crafting solutions to

> [c]ross the border into the cultural realm of the Black community and accept those assumptions that have allowed African-Americans to survive the ravages of racial subordination. One of those assumptions has been that subordination, based on white supremacy, is unacceptable. Another is that African-Americans have the inherent ability, given the material resources, to develop solutions to the problems that plague the African-American community.[113]

Absent this type of environment, advocates were left to demonstrate the educational value of black colleges. Meanwhile, the value of traditionally white colleges, organizations who had intentionally denied access to American citizens solely based on their race, went unquestioned and remained taken for granted. Because black college advocates did not control the parameters of the debate, the measures used to prove their educational value, and more importantly the fact that the schools do not act as impediments to integration, can work against them. Because the student bodies remain primarily black, enrollment trends at black colleges "are typically framed as problematic when placed against desegregation expectations."[114]

In light of this, scholars have called for black college advocates to engage in forms of institutional work that account for the "limitations of the law relative to desegregation and the correction of past injustices."[115]

Higher education desegregation cases were intended to eradicate dual systems of higher education yet, more than fifty years following *Brown*, a dual system of higher education within the South remains. Throughout the twentieth century, the majority of blacks continued to receive their higher education in the South.[116] Blacks had not reached equity in enrollment and degree completion across the former slaveholding states, regardless of the type of federal oversight in place.[117] In Mississippi, where *Fordice* originated, more than half of African Americans continued to enroll at black colleges in the first decade of the twenty-first century.[118] Black education remains a Southern problem for which the law has provided little relief.

Black college scholars and advocates must rely less on institutional work aimed at the regulatory pillar of the environment to create a space for black colleges. Robert Palmer, Ryan Davis, and Marybeth Gasman recommend that black college advocates highlight the changing state-level demographics that favor black colleges to advance arguments about why the schools are an integral part of Southern higher education systems.[119] Since black colleges serve racial and ethnic minority students, as these groups continue to increase relative to whites, black colleges will play a key role in producing the citizens that will make Southern states economically prosperous and competitive. Alternatively, Minor recommends that black college advocates "capture the discourse on race" and work to define its meaning relative to higher education.[120] Until advocates articulate to the public and policymakers why race still matters and its effect on issues related to higher education, including "student choice, enrollment, policy decisions, board appointments, or fundraising successes,"[121] then it will not be clear why black colleges are still a necessary part of the higher education system. As this chapter has shown, capturing the discourse on race is difficult to do when confronting a field of actors invested in maintaining the dominance of traditionally white spaces and willing to reconstitute the inequality regimes so as to guarantee this outcome.

5

Building Legitimacy amid Inequality

The institutional environment privileging non–racially identifiable colleges and universities was at odds with black colleges. The battles over higher education desegregation depicted black colleges as inferior substitutes for better-resourced, more prestigious, and racially neutral traditionally white colleges. Because they were traceable to de jure segregation, black colleges had to justify their continued existence. This was hardly fair. After all, traditionally white colleges were themselves birthed in a segregationist moment and benefited greatly from state-sanctioned racial inequality. Time and again, the growth and development of black colleges had been intentionally stunted so as to maintain the superiority of the colleges and universities serving white Americans.

Much of the debate about the role of black colleges post-*Brown* stemmed from arguments situating these organizations as relics of America's racially segregated past that behave fundamentally different than traditionally white colleges. Yes, in some ways black colleges did and continue to behave differently from their traditionally white counterparts. Their mission to educate black students separated historically black and traditionally white colleges from the start. That they continue to emphasize the educational needs of black students means that even contemporarily, black colleges maintain a different political alignment than traditionally white colleges.

In other areas, black colleges did change their orientation following *Brown*. The emergence of an institutional environment penalizing schools if they could be racially identified by their organizational outcomes all but guaranteed this. Black colleges prepared students for a wider range of professional opportunities post-*Brown* than they did during the era of state-sanctioned racial segregation. Debates regarding the necessity of schools that continued a missionary focus on students from one racial group overlook the meaning of this particular transformation. Thus, it is critical to consider what black colleges actually do, as opposed to whom they educate or why they began to adequately gauge the extent to which black colleges changed following *Brown* and more importantly to estimate how similar black and traditionally white colleges actually are.

Colleges are credentialing institutions, primarily responsible for providing students with access to degrees. Focusing on the outcome of this credentialing process—the earned degree—makes it possible to compare the behavior of black and traditionally white colleges. Treating the black colleges as one part of a larger whole draws attention the way in which the field structured organizational outcomes that diverged and then converged with traditionally white colleges. We can trace the effect of the shift from a race-conscious to a race-neutral institutional environment on black colleges.[1]

When the federal government began to routinely collect and distribute organizational statistics for historically black and traditionally white colleges, the schools exhibited racially distinct earned degree patterns. Over time, black colleges went from having curricula primarily focused on teacher training to more comprehensive ones. This points toward two trends in the black higher education field. At the individual level, black students moved away from majoring in education. At the organizational level, black and traditionally white colleges became homogeneous during the last decades of the twentieth century. One trend tells the story of how individual choice at black colleges changed in the last decades of the twentieth century. The other tells the story of how the distinctive capabilities of black colleges shifted in response to the field of actors.

During state-sanctioned segregation, earned degrees at black colleges reflected the racially conscious institutional constraints facing college-educated blacks. While the progress was slow, previously closed labor markets opened to college-educated blacks following the 1964 Civil Rights Act. Occupational inequality for college-educated blacks declined. Earned degrees at black colleges began to reflect this new reality. The profile of earned degrees diversified, becoming more similar to that of traditionally white colleges.

Focusing on homogeneity between black and traditionally white colleges is important. Organizational field scholarship contends that institutionalized organizations gain legitimacy through the process of incorporating practices and procedures that are collectively valued. As multiple organizations incorporate these practices and procedures they become alike or isomorphic. Unlike production organizations whose success is tied to efficiency, schools depend on the "confidence and good faith of their internal participants and external constituents."[2] For institutionalized organizations, becoming isomorphic demonstrates adherence to and a willingness to engage in collectively valued behavior. Following *Brown*, to gain legitimacy, theory suggests that black colleges would become isomorphic with an institutional environment that included traditionally white colleges, placed value upon facilitating student access to a wide range of degree programs, and stipulated that schools could not have racially identifiable outcomes. Black colleges did just this.

Here is where the paradox of inequality comes into play. Contrary to theoretical propositions, the continued legal debates over the racial identifiability of black colleges (see chapter 4) suggests that the schools gained few positive benefits from institutional isomorphism. The field of actors continued to focus on the students attending the schools as the primary means of arguing that black colleges are racially identifiable entities traceable to de jure segregation. Organizational scholars hold that legitimacy, that is, "a generalized perception or assumption that the actions of an entity are desirable, proper, or appropriate within some socially constructed system of norms, values, beliefs, and definitions,"[3] should come to organizations that become isomorphic to the demands of the institutional environment. Despite the fact that by the 1980s, black colleges facilitated student access to as diverse a range of degrees as traditionally white colleges, the schools were not able to reap the rewards and lay claim to the title "legitimate."

Prior to *Brown*, black colleges focused their curriculum on teacher training. Black college graduates could always find work as teachers. In fact, training black teachers for segregated Southern schools was a specialty that black colleges were best suited to fulfill. Black colleges were able to exploit the limitations inherent to operating under state-sanctioned racial inequality. Black colleges molded curricula so as to train students in occupations the black community needed and in which students could always find work.

Following *Brown*, inequality regimes foreclosed potentially beneficial alternatives to isomorphism. The reconstituted institutional environment left little space for black colleges to continue to exploit niche opportunities as they once had. Exploiting niches particular to the black community risked producing racially identifiable organizational outcomes. Yet, exploiting such niches, that is, resisting isomorphism would have made it clear that black colleges were more than replicas of traditionally white colleges.[4]

Adaptation toward isomorphism reified the inequality between black and traditionally white colleges and can once again be understood as partial. *Brown*, *Adams*, *Fordice*, and other desegregation cases created the impression that the traditionally white colleges were superior academic institutions. In becoming isomorphic with traditionally white colleges, black colleges lost their niche focus. Few black colleges offered students access to majors not available or emphasized at traditionally white colleges. This made it more difficult to discern the schools' distinctive competence in relation to traditionally white colleges and universities, furthering concerns that black colleges were no longer needed.

The Historical Relationship between Black and Traditionally White Colleges

Higher education consists of multiple organizational populations that share the common goal of providing students with a postsecondary education while differing in areas such as organizational form, programmatic emphasis, and their interdependence upon one another. Within the organization studies literature, understanding the level of similarity or homogeneity present within a given population has been the subject of many studies. Scholars hold that organizational fields provide a "context in which individual efforts to deal rationally with uncertainty and constraint often lead, in the aggregate, to homogeneity in structure, culture, and output."[5] Institutional pressures force one unit in a population to resemble other units facing the same environmental constraints.[6] As a result, dominant patterns emerge.

During the black higher education field's development, college leaders incorporated existing organizational templates to develop their educational program structure. Using existing templates of organization is a way for new schools to demonstrate their acceptance and compliance with culturally valued approaches to education.[7] Incorporating accepted educational archetypes made it easier to gain acceptance for the black higher education field's activities. It may have been a novel ideal to educate blacks but the fact that those looking to do so avoided using novel educational models added to the acceptance of their efforts.

Private black college leaders used the northeastern liberal arts model of education as a template for organization. This was important because training that focused on humanistic development was institutionally accepted as the best way to prepare students for civic engagement in a democratic society, a key goal of the black liberal arts college. At the behest of Southern state educational authorities, black public colleges were to serve as the organizational counterpart to the white-only state-run universities. Mimicking this institutionally accepted form of education was important because doing so enabled the states to claim that blacks had access to separate, yet equal educational facilities.

Despite the emulation of particular organizational templates, the institutional environment surrounding the populations of northeastern liberal arts colleges and traditionally white public colleges of the South did not restrict student occupational mobility in the same way that it did for black colleges.[8] This led to racially identifiable variations in organizational outcomes across the populations of black and traditionally white colleges. While students at black colleges overwhelmingly focused on education, students elsewhere did not. In *Black Elite: The New Market for Highly Educated Black Americans*, Richard Freeman reports that when asked about their prospective occupations in 1961, nonblack males had much more variety in their choices than black males. The majority of nonblack males (23.7 percent) aspired to work in business, with teaching ranking second (15.9 percent) and engineering ranking third (13.9 percent). By comparison, most black males (46.3 percent) aspired to work as teachers and no other occupation was selected by at least 8 percent of the respondents. Overall, in the former slaveholding states, on average 55 percent of college-educated blacks held employment in teaching-related occupations according to the 1960 census.[9]

In the aggregate, this resulted in racially distinct earned degree patterns between black and traditionally white colleges. Data from the Earned Degree series of the Higher Education General Information Survey illustrates this point. Beginning in the late 1960s, colleges and universities submitted detailed data on the number of degrees granted across their educational program offerings to the U.S. Department of Education. I used this data to determine the percentage of degrees earned from particular educational programs at the bachelor's level for the private black colleges, public black colleges, private northeastern colleges, and traditionally white Southern public colleges in the 1968–69 academic year.[10]

The data in Table 5.1 make clear that in the 1968–69 academic year, black colleges awarded the largest percentage of degrees in education while schools that traditionally served white students had more varied outcomes. Education degrees accounted for nearly one-half of all earned degrees at black public colleges. By comparison, white public colleges awarded equal percentages of their degrees from programs such as business administration, the social sciences, and education. White private

Table 5.1 Degree Distributions, 1968–1969

Program Name	White Public Colleges	Black Public Colleges	Black Private Colleges	White Private Colleges
Business	16%	9%	9%	16%
Education	17%	45%	28%	9%
Social Science	16%	18%	26%	27%

See Appendix 4 for full listing of degree categories

colleges awarded similar percentages of business degrees as their public counterparts, but more social science degrees.

Using the public colleges as comparison points, data from the 1969–1970 College Blue Book detail the organizational differences between black and white colleges further.

Alabama Agricultural and Mechanical College, a black college, offered students access to bachelor's degrees in forty-eight educational programs. Alabama State College, another black college, with eleven educational programs leading to a bachelor's degree, provided their students with access to even fewer programs. By comparison, students attending the traditionally white flagship school, the University of Alabama, had access to 103 educational programs leading to a bachelor's degree. On average, the black public colleges facilitated access to thirty-two bachelor's degrees, whereas the traditionally white public colleges in the South facilitated access to more than one hundred.[11]

While the data in Tables 5.1 and 5.2 suggest that the black and white colleges differed in their capacity or in their internal ability to facilitate student access to a wide variety of educational programs,[12] it is important to understand the significance of this. It is easy to look at these data and assume that because students attending traditionally white colleges had access to more majors these schools had a better organizational capacity than their black college counterparts. However, such an analysis misses the critical point of understanding whether or not a particular capacity was appropriate or legitimate given the institutional pressures to which black or traditionally white colleges were subjected. These data do not indicate that one organizational configuration or one population's capacity was better or worse.

The data in Tables 5.1 and 5.2 suggest that given the institutional constraints confronting black and white colleges, the organizational capacities of both types of schools were indeed legitimate. Their diverging

Table 5.2 Number of Bachelor Degrees Available at Public Black and Traditionally White Colleges, 1969–1970

No. of Black College Programs		No. of White College Programs	
Alabama Agriculture and Mechanical College	48	University of Alabama	103
Alabama State University	11	University of Arkansas	140
University of Arkansas at Pine Bluff	36	University of Delaware	81
Delaware State College	21	University of Florida	234
University of the District of Columbia	14	University of Georgia	129
Florida Agricultural and Mechanical University	48	University of Kentucky	158
Albany State College	29	Louisiana State University - Baton Rouge	115
Fort Valley State College	34	University of Maryland	122
Savannah State College	27	University of Mississippi	68
Kentucky State College	17	University of Missouri	199
Grambling State University	33	University of North Carolina	60
Southern University - Baton Rouge	71	University of Oklahoma	111
Southern University - New Orleans	16	University of South Carolina	74
Bowie State College	20	University of Tennessee	119
Coppin State College	17	University of Texas	91
Morgan State University	19	University of Virginia	66
University of Maryland Eastern Shore	23	University of West Virginia	53
Alcorn State University	26	Average No. of Programs	113
Jackson State University	42		
Mississippi Valley State University	39		
Lincoln University - MO	108		
Elizabeth City State University	22		
Fayetteville State University	8		
North Carolina A&T	37		
North Carolina Central University	46		
Winston-Salem State University	9		
Central State University	52		
Langston University	31		
Cheyney State College	9		
Lincoln University - PA	22		
South Carolina State College	53		
Tennessee State University	28		
Prairie View A&M	27		
Texas Southern University	43		
Norfolk State University	25		
Virginia State University	66		
Bluefield State University	29		
West Virginia State College	27		
Average No. of Programs	32		

institutional environments meant that black and traditionally white colleges should structure earned degree opportunities in a racially distinct fashion. Yes, students in the traditionally white context had greater opportunities to earn degrees in a more diverse range of programs than did those attending black colleges, but this made sense in the context of the larger opportunity structure.

As the 1970s approached, the black higher education field existed in a fundamentally different institutional environment. First, opportunities in the teaching profession for college-educated blacks declined sharply. In what has been described as the "wholesale dismissal of Black educators,"[13] a professional opportunity that many college-educated blacks aspired to and relied upon evaporated following the *Brown* ruling. As Gary Orfield documents in *The Reconstruction of Southern Education*, a pattern of firing black teachers following school integration in Southern states had emerged by the mid-1960s. In 1954, the U.S. teaching force included approximately 82,000 black teachers. Between 1954 and 1972, the number of black teachers and administrators located within Southern and border states declined by more than 38,000. Federal, state, and local school integration efforts included plans to integrate student bodies, yet rarely addressed faculties. Implicit within most integration plans was the understanding that black teachers would not teach white children, and as a result, black teachers found themselves without jobs.[14]

A typical college student might wonder, "If I receive a degree in X, can I find employment?" While all students faced this dilemma, state-sanctioned racial segregation exacerbated the situation for black students. A black student pursuing a career in business administration during racial segregation was unlikely to find a corporate job upon graduation.[15] This same student could more easily find employment as a teacher. Racial segregation ensured the demand for black educators remained high. In 1900 alone, there were approximately 27,000 black teachers for the more than two million black elementary and high school students in the former slaveholding states.[16] Segregation precluded white teachers from filling this void. The supply of teachers for black children had to come from other black people.

Brown changed this. Despite the NAACP Legal Defense Fund's insistence that the court rulings and 1964 Civil Rights Act permitted the U.S. Office of Education to forbid such actions, the firing of black teachers continued. In 1979, a U.S. Department of Health, Education, and Welfare attorney was quoted as saying. "In a war there must be some casualties,

Figure 5.1 Earned Degrees in Education at Black Colleges

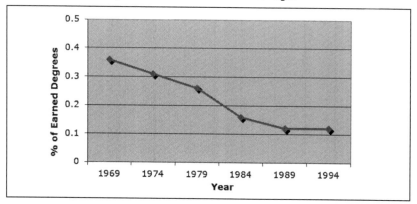

and perhaps the Black teachers will be the casualties in the fight for equal education of Black students."[17]

The loss of teaching jobs reverberated throughout the entire black community, particularly among college-going students. Between 1975 and 1985, the number of black students majoring in education decreased by 66 percent.[18] By 1975, only 8 percent of the black males surveyed chose education as a major.[19] Earned degrees at black colleges confirm this shift was long lasting. Figure 5.1 documents that among black colleges, the average school's percentage of earned degrees in education steadily declined from 36 percent to 12 percent between the late 1960s and the mid-1990s.

Second, competition for students from traditionally white colleges also added to the institutional environment's uncertainty. Never before had black colleges lost significant numbers of students to traditionally white schools, however, between 1970 and 1978, black college freshmen from the top quartile of their high school class more frequently attended traditionally white colleges than black ones.[20] Traditionally white colleges benefited from their reputation as superior academic institutions. This, coupled with their ability to offer students a greater range of degree programs, made it increasingly difficult for black colleges to remain the first choice for many black students. During state-sanctioned racial segregation, organizational and reputational differences mattered little, as traditionally white and black colleges drew distinct sets of students. Limited or not, these were the opportunities available to black students.

In light of these two factors, the black colleges' racially distinct degree pattern could be construed as illegitimate and not in line with the reconstituted institutional environment. Black colleges had to adapt. Specifically, black colleges had to erase the racially specific distinctions that differentiated them from traditionally white colleges. Doing so would allow black colleges to remain in step with the demands of the new institutional context. As this quote from a 1966 United Negro College Fund brochure illustrates, black college leaders recognized this:

> The Negro's quest for higher education can no longer be satisfied by institutions which train young men and women for a narrow range of vocations. . . . The Fund's member institutions are therefore reconstructing their educational programs in a concerted effort to train thousands of students for the many areas of professional employment formerly closed to Negroes.

Training black students for the professional areas formerly closed to them did not have to result in black colleges losing their racial identifiability in and of itself. Black colleges could have ventured down a path of expanding their organizational capacity in a way that still enabled the schools to exploit niche opportunities. Black colleges could have focused on majors once closed to black students, yet still not present at traditionally white colleges. This did not occur because exploiting strategic differences between black and traditionally white colleges could lead to racially distinct degree patterns. Such distinctions could then be used to argue that black colleges were refusing to become "just colleges," the legal standard adopted by the courts. Black colleges could not choose from a large repertoire of strategies in this period. Losing their distinctiveness was the only way forward. Field-level forces all but ensured this outcome.

The Field of Actors

Students and Labor Markets

One function colleges perform is connecting students and labor markets to one another.[21] For most of their history, black colleges linked their graduates to a labor market severely constrained by racial inequality. Black college graduates faced intense employment discrimination. Changes to employment laws slowly opened a number of formerly closed careers to black college graduates. Within the private sector, few firms had administrative mechanisms in place to increase the representation of blacks within their ranks. Nevertheless, over time, administrative

Figure 5.2 Occupations of Southern College-Educated Blacks

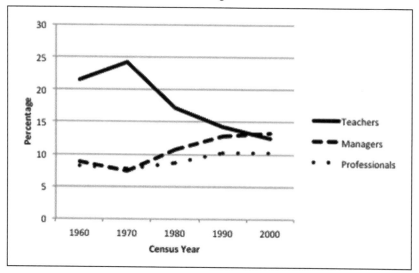

policies and routines designed to redress discriminatory hiring practices coupled with federal oversight of the hiring process did lead to greater representation of black workers.[22] Between 1966 and 1972, black male and female employment increased more than 40 and 100 percent respectively among all workplaces.[23] Thus, as opportunities in the teaching profession declined in the decades after *Brown*, opportunities in other occupations increased. Using census data, Figure 5.2 highlights the shifting career choices of college-educated blacks living in the Southern United States in decades following the *Brown* ruling.

In 1960, 22 percent of blacks with four or more years of college reported their occupations as teachers. In this same year, fewer than 10 percent of college-educated blacks reported working as managers or professionals. As the twentieth century came to a close, however, the occupational trends had reversed. By the year 2000, the percentages of college-educated blacks reporting their occupations as managers or professionals continued to increase. Alternatively, at 12.5 percent, the percentage of college-educated blacks reporting their occupations as teachers had reached its lowest point during the forty-year period.[24]

Shifting labor market opportunities for Southern college-educated blacks were of consequence to black colleges. Colleges located in the South continued to be the primary credentialing organizations for black students. For instance, thirty years following *Brown*, with 8.6 percent black enrollment, Maryland's flagship traditionally white campus ranked higher than those of Mississippi, Georgia, Alabama, Tennessee, North Carolina, Florida, and Texas.[25] By comparison, black enrollment at Morgan State, a publicly supported black college in Maryland, exceeded 90 percent.[26] In 2000, the nineteen Southern and border states accounted for 59 percent of black students attending degree-granting universities nationwide.[27] Black colleges, particularly the public ones, draw a large proportion of their students from within the same state and region. In 2000, the public black colleges in Virginia were the only ones to draw fewer than 70 percent of their students from within the region.[28]

Given the role of black colleges in the overall landscape of Southern education, occupational trends would influence earned degree patterns within the black higher education field. To illustrate, correlational analyses identified a statistically significant relationship between the percentage of education degrees granted by black colleges and the percentage of blacks reporting their occupation as teachers. Moreover, the analyses also indicated a relationship between the percentage of business degrees granted and the percentage of blacks reporting their occupations as managers and professionals.[29] Accordingly, there was a feedback loop between trends in the labor markets for Southern college-educated blacks and degrees at the institutions primarily responsible for credentialing these individuals.

Foundations

The General Education Board, once perceived as monopolizing black education, made its last appropriation in 1964; however, by the 1950s funds were nearly exhausted.[30] With the board no longer serving as a clearinghouse for projects related to black higher education, the role of foundations became more fragmented.[31] While the Rockefeller Foundation took oversight of the board's remaining activities, it focused more on international higher education. Instead of a Rockefeller-led effort, new players came to prominence within the black higher education field. The Ford, Kresge, Kellogg, Mellon, and Mott Foundations as well as the Pew Charitable Trust made grants to black colleges totaling more than $60 million.[32] The Ford Foundation, the largest American philanthropy in terms of endowment and expenditures at the time,[33] contributed almost 80 percent of this total.[34] The Ford Foundation's efforts to promote black colleges deserves further attention, particularly because the foundation became the single largest contributor to black colleges in the 1970s.[35]

Spelman and Morehouse Colleges of Atlanta, Georgia, sought funding from Ford in 1966 for a course of study leading to a Bachelor of Fine Arts degree. The grant narrative laid out the history of fine arts at black colleges, noting: "One of the anomalies of the situation is that for some years the predominantly Negro colleges have maintained a reputation for achievement in the arts, on a generally extra-curricular basis."[36] Racial segregation discouraged formal investments in the fine arts at black colleges. For example, theatre students faced professional barriers: "[T]here were practically no roles written for him," and "[I]n the production and technical levels the situation for the Negro was even worse."[37] Like most black college students, "serious students of the theatre . . . pursued positions which were open to them. Many went into high school teaching. Having participated in and been exposed to theatre, they were assigned or accepted the extra-curricular duty of supervising dramatic activities."[38] Given recent changes, the leaders of Spelman and Morehouse now felt it was time to formalize their focus on fine arts, stating that

> Civil Rights legislation, the formation of state Arts Councils, and governmental acknowledgement of the importance of cultural activities and willingness to subsidize them with limited funds, added to the fact that the performing arts and associated industries now appear willing to hire artists and technicians on a basis of ability and training and not because of artificial barriers such as color or race, require that a re-definition of the aims and objectives of the department of drama at Spelman take place if it is to continue its effective role. . . . [T]he drama department must further intensify its course of study for the purpose of adequately preparing students for positions in the professional world as actors, technicians, theatre managers and theatre historians.

Fine arts was not the only area in which Morehouse and Spelman wished to expand. Looking to capitalize on a Ford grant from 1960 for the Public and International Affairs Program, the schools approached the foundation again in 1964 to fund the non-Western component. The grant proposal made specific connections between training in international affairs and future job prospects. The International Affairs Program would assist in training for "careers in public affairs and for the leadership in those areas of public life where major policies are made and executed"[39] and the non-Western focus was particularly crucial because "[t]he more Negroes are prepared to serve the United States in other lands and the more Negroes are used in the Foreign Service of our government, the faster we can get the message across that the race problem is being solved in America. . . . A Non-Western Studies Program . . . will encourage an increasing number of our students to prepare for foreign service."[40]

Talladega College of Alabama also received support from Ford in July 1970 to strengthen its "faculty, course offerings, and library resources in the social sciences."[41] An October 1977 self-study submitted to the foundation detailed the progress made possible by the grant. In writing about the history program, Talladega officials noted:

> [T]en years ago, the history curriculum consisted of an amazingly catholic selection of eight history and two political science courses. In 1968, the American and European offerings were greatly expanded into period courses, but non-Western courses were virtually excluded. Significantly, however, "Topics in Negro History" surfaced that year. Also interesting was the fact that, while the U.S. surveys continued, there were no European surveys, because there was a two-semester Western Civilizations course required of all freshmen. This pattern remained unchanged until 1971, when two European history surveys were added. In 1972 nine new politics courses emerged with the advent of a full-time political scientist. And in 1974, three new African courses replaced other non-Western offerings. . . . Over the ten-year period, only three courses remain unchanged . . . nineteen have been added . . . covering essentially all of the major periods in United States, European and African history.[42]

The Ford grant files reveal that black colleges used this time period to expand their organizational capacity. Understanding the diminishing opportunities in the teaching profession, students attending black colleges naturally would have sought new majors. At the organizational level, the key to facilitating these shifts lay in black colleges' ability to offer students access to majors other than education. Ford grants facilitated the development of programs in politics and social work at Talladega. Similarly, a three-year Ford grant (1968–1971) enabled Tuskegee Institute to develop its division of humanities. Howard University of Washington D.C., sought support for an African Studies program (1968) and to strengthen its urban planning program (1969). Tennessee State University sought Ford funding for courses in engineering (1967) and to develop a school of business administration (1971). Notably, grant files document efforts to expand the range of opportunities available to students attending black colleges.

The Southern States

Discriminatory funding patterns by state officials created gaps in the curricular range of black colleges.[43] For instance, data from the *National Survey of the Higher Education of Negroes* indicate that in comparison to the eight fields of specialization available in education, the median black college offered four fields of specialization in trades and two fields of specialization in commerce, both business-related disciplines. By the time the U.S. government began to systematically survey colleges and universities in the late 1960s, roughly 20 percent of black colleges did not offer a business degree. A key reason that students at black colleges did not earn a significant number of degrees in programs other than education is that many black colleges offered few alternatives.

As discussed in chapters 1 and 4, to prolong racial segregation, Southern states enhanced public black colleges. Though black leaders knew these investments were tied to a segregationist philosophy, they welcomed them nonetheless.[44] By the 1970s, black college leaders, especially the public ones, connected the goals of desegregation with their ability to fully develop their institutions.[45] Duplicating programs available at traditionally white colleges was key if states hoped to ensure that black students would continue to select black colleges. Desegregation lawsuits indicate that states were quite successful in pursuing this strategy. Suits filed against Alabama, Louisiana, and Mississippi all cite the level of program duplication across black and traditionally white colleges as an impediment to desegregation. Mississippi, for instance, duplicated more than 30 percent of their educational programs across the state's three black and five white institutions of higher education.[46]

Earned Degrees at Black and Traditionally White Colleges in the Last Decades of the Twentieth Century

The end of state-sanctioned racial segregation caused the boundaries between black and white postsecondary institutions to blur. A new, larger field coalesced. The worlds of black and white higher education were no longer distinct. As this more expansive field took shape, black and traditionally white colleges exhibited racially distinct organizational patterns. Eighty-five percent of black college administrators, both public and private, identified their organizations as teacher training institutions in 1965.[47] Black colleges granted degrees in a narrower set of educational programs than did their traditionally white counterparts. Once structured into a field, however, organizations tend to become similar. Data on earned degrees illuminates the pattern of isomorphism that occurred among black and traditionally white colleges in the last decades of the twentieth century.

Focusing on the amount of variation or lack thereof in the degree distributions contextualizes the level of isomorphism or similarity between the earned degree distributions of black and traditionally white colleges. In particular, incorporating the index of diversity, a statistical measure of qualitative variation, sheds light on the implications of isomorphism in earned degrees at black and traditionally white colleges as well as for the racial identifiability of these schools.[48] We will see whether or not students across these organizational contexts began to have the same opportunities or not. Like equality of means tests in which two or more sample means are compared to one another to determine if they significantly differ, these inference procedures center on testing the proposition that the ability of students across these organizational contexts to earn degrees in a wide range of programs differs.[49] In essence, these inference procedures will track the decline in racially distinct organizational outcomes across the schools. We will see how it became impossible to identify historically black and traditionally white colleges by their earned degree distributions.

Figure 5.3 depicts the diversity indices for black private colleges, black public colleges, traditionally white Southern public, and Northeastern private colleges in five-year increments between the late 1960s and the late 1980s. Replicating the diversity indices in five-year increments reveals that by the 1980s, students attending black and traditionally white colleges had similar chances of earning degrees in a diverse set of educational programs. As the degree diversity of black public and private colleges increased, these institutions became more like traditionally white public colleges of the South and private liberal arts colleges located in the Northeast. Using public black colleges as the comparison point, the inference tests indicate that in the 1968–69 academic year, the degree diversity of public black colleges significantly differed from the

Figure 5.3 Degree Diversity of All Populations, 1969–1989

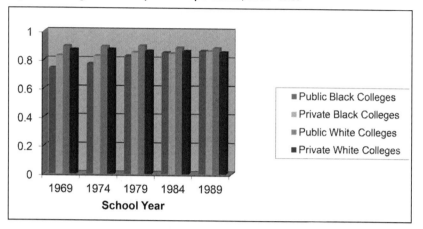

degree diversity of public white colleges (z = 2.34, one-tailed, α = 0.05) and private white colleges (z = 1.92, one-tailed, α = 0.05), but not the private black colleges.

In the 1968–69 academic year, degrees at black public colleges were the least widely dispersed. Students attending these colleges had a 74 percent chance of earning degrees in a distinct or diverse set of educational programs. Students at black private colleges fared slightly better, with an 83 percent chance of earning degrees in a diverse set of educational programs, however those attending traditionally white colleges of the Northeast and public colleges of the South had better chances of earning degrees in a diverse set of programs, significantly so. Comparisons between black and white colleges emphasize this point most clearly.

Figure 5.4 depicts the diversity indices for black (public and private) and traditionally white (Southern and Northeastern) colleges in the 1968–69 academic year. Degrees at traditionally white colleges were more widely dispersed across educational programs than those at black colleges. Two students, one attending a black college, the other attending a traditionally white college, had different probabilities of earning a degree in a diverse set of educational programs. Students attending black colleges had an 80 percent chance of earning degrees in diverse set of programs while students attending traditionally white colleges had an 88 percent chance. Attending a black college all but guaranteed that students would earn their degrees from a narrower range of educational programs than those attending a traditionally white college. The comparison

Figure 5.4 Black and Traditionally White Degree Diversity, 1968–1969

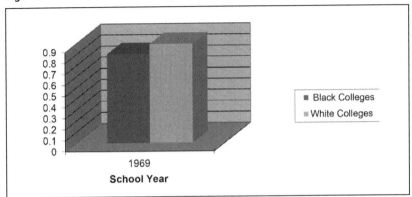

tests of these indices in the 1968–69 academic year indicate that the organizational capacity of black colleges significantly differed from that of traditionally white colleges.[50] Furthermore, the comparison tests stress the racial identifiability of these degree distributions. Again, this makes sense given the separate worlds of black and white higher education. Black colleges were isomorphic with other black colleges, not with traditionally white ones.

As the distinctions between black and white higher education eroded, however, a new pattern should emerge. Returning to the diversity indices (Figure 5.3), twenty years later things had changed quite noticeably. Using public black colleges as the comparison point, inference tests using the 1988–89 data reveal no significant differences between public white colleges ($z = 0.51$) or private white colleges ($z = 0.33$). By the final period, the degree diversity at these schools had become similar or isomorphic. Students attending each type of college had a similar chance of earning a degree in a distinct program. Once again, focusing on the black colleges as a group in comparison to the traditionally white colleges adds additional insight.

By the 1988–89 academic year, black colleges' diversity index reached .87, while white colleges' diversity index remained at .88, the same as it was in 1968–69. Thus, within a twenty-year span, two students—one attending a black college and the other attending a white college—had the same chance of earning degrees from a diverse set of educational programs.[51] Black and traditionally white colleges had become isomorphic with one another. You could no longer tell which degree distribution belonged to a white or black college.

Figure 5.5 Black and Traditionally White Degree Diversity, 1988–1989

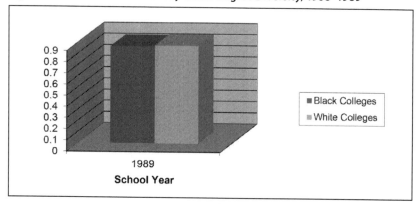

The degree distributions contained within Table 5.3 provide further detail. Referring to data presented earlier, in the 1968–69 academic year, black and white colleges had very different degree distributions. Students attending traditionally white public colleges of the South earned approximately equal proportions of degrees in business, education, and the social sciences. Alternatively, students at black public colleges received the overwhelming majority of their degrees from one field—education. Students attending white Northeastern private colleges received approximately 26 percent of their degrees in the program that ranked first—social science. Yet, these schools still had a higher amount of degree diversity than their black private college counterparts, because of the wider degree dispersal among the remaining programs. Overall, very little similarity existed in the proportion of students earning degrees across the educational programs.

As Table 5.3 indicates, by the 1988–89 academic year, the situation was different. Earned degrees at all four types of schools were dispersed in a similar manner and students within each population received the majority of their degrees in business administration. Comparing the amount of deviation between the proportion of students receiving degrees from a particular degree program at white and black public colleges, white public and black private colleges, white and black private colleges, and white private and black public colleges provides further information. Table 5.4 presents the results for these analyses.

The data indicate that the total deviation between the proportions of students receiving degrees from a particular program was significantly higher in the 1968–69 academic year than it was in the 1988–89 academic

Table 5.3 Degree Distributions, 1988–1989

Program Name	White Public Colleges	Black Public Colleges	Black Private Colleges	White Private Colleges
Business	24%	27%	29%	26%
Education	9%	13%	7%	3%
Social Science	13%	15%	15%	23%

See Appendix 4 for full listing of degree categories

year. The similarities in the proportion of students receiving degrees from a particular educational category had increased among black and white colleges. The reduction in the deviation scores over time indicates that black and traditionally white colleges began to shift and sort students into the same types of academic programs. Thus, on some level, it no longer mattered whether a student attended a black or traditionally white college. Students in both organizational settings were earning their degrees in similar educational programs. One could not look at the distribution of earned degrees and differentiate the population of black colleges from their white counterpart. Black colleges' capacity to facilitate student access to a diverse range of degree programs had homogenized with traditionally white colleges.

Conclusion

Once seen as an integral part of the educational landscape, higher education desegregation challenged black colleges' position. Suddenly, the legitimacy of black colleges was understood in relation to their ability to become non-racially specific. The limited range of earned degrees at black colleges stood as evidence to the contrary. As racially neutral outcomes became the standard by which Southern colleges and universities were supposed to be judged, black colleges' unique emphasis on education made them vulnerable to claims that their schools were "negligent, irrational, or unnecessary."[52]

As the black higher education field came to include traditionally white colleges, homogenization ensued. Black colleges adapted so as to have virtually indistinguishable earned degree distributions from traditionally white colleges. By the late 1980s, the schools were isomorphic with the institutional demands to facilitate student access to a wide range

Table 5.4 Deviation among Degree Distributions

Academic Year Ending	White and Black Public Schools	White Public and Black Private Schools	White and Black Private Schools	White Private and Black Public Schools
	σ	σ	σ	σ
1969	0.0697	0.0439	0.0505	0.0882
1974	0.0545	0.0375	0.0464	0.0724
1979	0.0454	0.0373	0.0394	0.0597
1984	0.0283	0.0375	0.0293	0.0379
1989	0.0263	0.029	0.0266	0.0357
F	7.02*	2.29*	3.60*	6.10*

*$\alpha = 0.05$, one-tailed, dfn = 19, dfd = 19

See Appendix 4 for related calculations

of degree programs and to have race-neutral outcomes. In important respects, the schools were homogenous to their better-resourced and more prestigious traditionally white counterparts. Black colleges did not have racially specific degree patterns. Black colleges adapted to the demands of an institutional environment privileging color-blindness and race neutrality of organizational outcomes.

This all seems positive. So, then, why do I argue that this is partial adaptation? Organizations adapt to improve their situation. In particular, institutionalized organizations engage in culturally valued practices to gain legitimacy. Still, black colleges gained very little with this transformation toward racially neutral organizational outcomes. If isomorphism of organizational outcomes is used as a framework for assessing legitimacy, then black colleges should have obtained it without question. However, the legitimacy of these schools continues to be understood in terms of their mission to educate black students. Because their mission did not change, the field of actors continued to cast the schools as vestiges of America's racially segregated past. Consequently, I argue that becoming isomorphic represented a partial form of adaptation because black colleges sacrificed their racially distinct outcomes for naught.

Becoming isomorphic with the institutional environment can be costly. This is especially true for stigmatized actors such as black colleges. Inequality regimes prevent stigmatized actors from laying claim to rewards. Hence, institutions do not reward actors equally for adherence to the rules. Because they will be excluded from the rewards, low-status, stigmatized, peripheral actors should diverge from institutional rules.[53] Avoiding conformity with institutionalized rules offers the best chance at something other than partial adaptation.

Following state-sanctioned racial segregation, black colleges remain stigmatized, perhaps even more so than when operating within the system. So instead of working "feverishly to solidify their social standing by demonstrating their conformity with accepted practice,"[54] it would have been better for black colleges to further solidify their niche status as organizations specializing in the development of black social and political leadership.[55] After all, it was black colleges that had prepared the leaders of the civil rights movement, not the traditionally white ones. Had black colleges emphasized majors connected to social and political leadership in the midst of higher education desegregation, their degree patterns would have highlighted how different and unique these schools were in comparison to "mainstream" colleges. Further capitalizing upon their peripheral position within American higher education is an adaptive strategy that accounts for the reality that stigmatized actors are often not rewarded for conformity. Thus, why pursue an adaptive strategy for which you may reap no benefits and one that ultimately leads to the loss of "features that distinguish the organization from others with which it may be compared."[56]

Yet the field of actors precluded an adaptive strategy that would have enabled the black colleges to maintain a unique identity. As a result of how desegregation played out in American higher education, the racial identifiability of black colleges took center stage. Had the field of actors remained focused on ensuring that blacks could attend traditionally white colleges, black colleges might have had the space to pursue a niche strategy. But once the field of actors switched its focus to ensuring that black college became "just colleges," adaptation had to fit within this framework.

What is interesting, then, about black colleges is that during the last decades of the twentieth century, the schools benefited neither from their position as peripheral actors nor from their institutional isomorphism. Black colleges had undergone true change. Despite fewer resources, black colleges had managed to facilitate student access to earn degrees in a manner comparable to traditionally white colleges. Even though they were able to credential their students in as diverse a range of programs as traditionally white colleges, as chapter 4 discussed, black colleges continued to be conceptualized as exotic and peculiar academic entities by the courts, state educational authorities, and other opponents that increasingly sought to consolidate or close these schools.

Despite eroding the racial identifiability of key organizational outcomes such as earned degrees, judgments about black colleges were based upon their student bodies' racial identifiability. The state of Mississippi refused to give black colleges access to endowment funds because their student bodies had not reached an acceptable threshold of nonblack enrollment. Consequently, regardless of what the schools did in other areas, the student bodies' racial composition provided fodder for those invested in claiming that black colleges had failed to sufficiently adapt. The inequality regimes not only prevents stigmatized organizations from pursuing the most beneficial adaptive strategies, it also prevents stigmatized organizations from gaining recognition when they successfully pursue nonoptimal ones.

6

The Story of Organizational Adaptation

Black colleges were not free to adapt in any manner of their choosing. When attempting to grow their resources, express their rights, and capitalize upon their distinctive capabilities, black colleges confronted an inequality regime designed to keep black organizations inferior. The field of actors provided a context for this state of affairs to flourish. Even when it appeared as though the black colleges were doing something radical, through further reflection the foregoing chapters have demonstrated how the field produced partial adaptation.

On the surface, the UNCF's formation and advocacy represent novel organizational solutions to a resource dependency problem. Fundraising collectively and making pleas to the American public were part of a larger plan to expand the black college donor base. Yet, once the long-standing status and racial inequalities that structured the organization's formation and advocacy are accounted for, the UNCF appears less pathbreaking. For a brief moment, enrollments and resources surged at black colleges post-*Brown.* Many leaders and advocates believed higher education desegregation would benefit black colleges. Both black and white students would be able to attend black colleges. In time, however, black colleges were cast as obstacles to racially integrating higher education. Investments in black colleges were tied to the enrollment and recruitment of white students. Regardless of their efforts to erode racially distinct organizational outcomes, because their student bodies remained predominantly black, few field members recognized the changes black colleges made in the post-*Brown* era.

Even with their constant effort to grow and develop, adaptations undertaken by black colleges did not produce the desired effect that organization theory imagines. Collective fundraising did not fundamentally alter the black colleges' relationship with foundations, as resource dependence theory would predict. Yes, donations from other groups increased, but, industrial philanthropies continued to account for roughly 20 percent of the UNCF's annual donations and more importantly, maintained an active involvement in UNCF's operations.[1] Black colleges could not cut ties with this group or effectively shield themselves from philanthropies. Moreover, including segregationist ideology in their campaign material, despite its appeal to whites, alienated the black community.

In the last decades of the twentieth century, black and traditionally white colleges had indistinguishable organizational outcomes with respect to earned degrees. Becoming isomorphic with the environment did not lead observers to see black colleges as legitimate, as institutional theory would predict. Engaging in institutional work did not result in regulative, normative, or cultural-cognitive institutional structures favorable to black colleges. Advocate efforts certainly helped black colleges maintain a space, albeit a tenuous one at best, within the post-*Brown* higher education landscape. Still, the field shifted toward a theory of race neutrality and color-blind legal ideology that painted black colleges as problematic.

Reflecting on the cases presented heretofore provides an opportunity to contemplate the similarities that made black college adaptation possible, but also the factors that made these adaptations partial and likely to reify the inequality regimes operating within the black higher education field. How could collective action within the black higher education field have been a real possibility, yet not reshape dependencies? How could there be space to frame the issue of black higher education, yet not space to problematize racially segregated education? How could black college advocates use institutional work to mount a defense of the schools post-*Brown*, yet fail to maintain a space for color-conscious educational policy? How could black colleges become isomorphic with the institutional environment, yet be characterized as illegitimate organizational forms?

Within the organizational field paradigm, scholars agree that external events are the primary impetus for change.[2] Crises in particular offer field members the chance to break from institutional norms, for doing as you've always done is futile if the environment has dramatically changed. The black higher education field certainly had its share of externally driven crises. The Great Depression decreased philanthropic fund values. Changing tax laws also hampered fund values. Furthermore, the General Education Board, a consistent contributor to black colleges, was a spend-down philanthropy set to expire sometime in the 1950s. These factors combined to make a collective fundraising effort such as the UNCF plausible within the black higher education field circa 1944. The timing for black colleges to initiate a new fundraising scheme was right. The traditional funding methods on which black colleges had relied were evaporating for one reason or another.

While economic perils laid the path for the UNCF's emergence, socio-legal crises created space for the black college advocates to articulate the role of black colleges in both the pre- and post-*Brown* eras. By 1944, the NAACP had made headway at the higher education level. State-sanctioned racially segregated education was near its end. By 1968, *Brown* was the law of the land and courts began to grapple with how to apply this decision to higher education. Prior to 1954, advocates adapted to the socio-legal environment by arguing that black colleges were a crucial element in the maintenance of a racially segregated higher education system. Society's preference for single-race institutions lent credibility to this argument. Following 1968, advocates tried a similar tactic. Here, advocates insisted that because many black students would still choose to go to black colleges, then black colleges should be protected. Advocates attempted to adapt to the post-*Brown* socio-legal environment by arguing that black colleges were an important element in the maintenance of a racially integrated system of higher education. Contrary to the earlier period, society's unease about single-race institutions made this argument suspect.

Multiple crises set the stage for black colleges to adapt their organizational capacity to facilitate degrees to a wider variety of majors in the last decades of the twentieth century. Teaching was no longer a viable occupation for black college graduates. Southern state educational authorities wanted to keep the number of black students attending traditionally white colleges low. Either factor on its own would have been enough to induce change among black colleges. That they existed simultaneously helps explain the rapid shift in earned degree patterns among black colleges.

As the chapters of this book have shown, the impetus for change is not enough to overcome the recalcitrant nature of the field. In each adaptive episode, inequality regimes constrained organizational choice to strategies that only marginally improved black colleges' ability to lay claim to rewards, particularly in relation to traditionally white colleges. More troubling, these partial adaptations did not loosen the inequality regimes operating within the field. The organizational field literature depicts adaptation as difficult to achieve and rare. Hence, when it does occur, scholarly accounts are typically used to highlight how the under-lying social order within the field has been disturbed. An event like the UNCF's formation must shift the inequalities and power centers within the field in some meaningful manner. To the contrary, the chapters in this volume suggest that black colleges constantly shifted shape, char-acter, and form. Yet, the underlying inequality regimes within the field were hardly affected at all. Determining why organizational adaptation had such little impact on field-level inequality requires further analyses.

Some might speculate that as social actors black colleges lacked the requisite social skill to alter field-level dynamics. Social skill refers to whether an actor possesses "a highly developed cognitive capacity for reading people and environments, framing lines of action, and mo-bilizing people in the service of broader conceptions of the world and of themselves."[3] Building on this perspective, one could reason that the inequality regimes within the field remained stable because the black col-leges misread the crises precipitating each adaptive episode and therefore chose strategies and tactics ill suited to shift the field's systems of in-equality. However, we must account for the context in which black col-leges adapted if we are to understand the role of social skill or the lack thereof on reconfiguring inequality regimes.

Fields consist of incumbents and challengers. Incumbents "are those actors who wield a disproportionate influence within a field and whose interests and views tend to be heavily reflected in the dominant organi-zation" of the field.[4] Comparatively, challengers "occupy less privileged niches within the field and ordinarily wield little influence over its op-eration." While challengers typically go along with the dominant logic, as the term suggests, they also wait for "opportunities to challenge the structure and logic of the system." This imagery of a field and classifica-tion of the actors within it sheds light on why the types of adaptive ef-forts in which black colleges engaged, though capable of disrupting the inequality regime, ultimately failed to do so.

Within the black higher education field, students, sponsors, donors, the state, and the judiciary are best understood as the incumbents. Time and again, the rules of the black higher education field privileged these groups relative to black colleges. For instance, constitutional law privi-leges the rights of individuals, not organizations. As a result, even relative to black students, black colleges have less power within the field. Court rulings affirmed the right of black students to attend any school of their choosing. Meanwhile, the Southern states and the courts characterized black colleges as culprits that prevented black students from choosing

to attend traditionally white colleges and thus integrating higher education. Naturally, eliminating black colleges was a viable means to ensure
that black students made the "right" choice. That is, the choice to attend
better-resourced and more prestigious traditionally white colleges. The
states and courts had the power to interpret laws to the detriment of
black colleges. Notwithstanding their seemingly central role in this field,
black colleges occupied a challenger position.

The organizational field literature typically posits that adaptations
undertaken by challengers have the capacity to alter power dynamics
within fields. However, this is most likely to occur when the challengers
emanate from outside as opposed to within the field under observation.
Invasions from groups that had not been players in the field are effective
because such actors "are not bound by the conventions" of the field.[5] That
black colleges' efforts to adapt originated from within the field undoubtedly limited their ability to shift the prevailing inequities and power
dynamics. To illustrate, recent scholarship has explicated the ability of
collective action to destabilize fields. Though it is important to note that
in the cases used to develop this theoretical perspective collective action
happened to a field, it was not generated from within it. For instance,
corporations often find themselves subject to protests and boycotts emanating from external parties. These activists draw upon repertoires of
contention available from national-level social movements to launch a
fundamental critique of corporate practices perceived to have a deleterious effect on society. These efforts often result in corporations instituting
new, more socially conscious business practices.[6]

Alternatively, though collective, the UNCF was generated from
within the black higher education field and the organization's critique
of the status quo was limited and drew upon repertoires of conciliation,
not of contention. Similarly, black college advocate efforts to maintain
a position in the post-*Brown* landscape, concentrated on reemphasizing
legal precedents and theories present within the field prior to that ruling.
It was not a lack of social skill that hampered the black colleges' ability to
use organizational adaptation to shift the underlying inequality regimes
within the field. To the contrary, according to current theoretical understanding, the decision to build a political coalition among those willing
to financially support black colleges demonstrated keen social skill, as
did the decision to work toward reasserting institutional logics that supported students' choice to attend black colleges.

The real problem appears to have been that black colleges used
their social skill toward the wrong ends. The adaptations black colleges

undertook had little chance of unseating the incumbents within the black higher education field. None of the adaptations studied herein caused other field members to cede power to black colleges. Had an actor other than industrial philanthropists entered the field and proposed a new way to procure black college financial stability, then a new status system might have emerged and black colleges might have had room to critique racial inequality on a broader scale. Had advocates been able to engage an entity other than the Southern states in the aftermath of *Brown*, then black colleges' advocates might have stood a better chance of asserting an institutional logic that better supported the role of black colleges in a racially integrated system of higher education. Following the end of state-sanctioned racial segregation, it is not difficult to imagine a scenario in which a group of education leaders focused their attention on creating an organizational form not linked to the deleterious outcomes of the system; an alternative to the dichotomy of black or traditionally white colleges. However, this did not occur—traditionally white colleges remained the standard to which black colleges were compared. Groups historically committed to maintaining white racial dominance remained the primary interlocutor of black college advocates.

Ultimately, the structure of the field constrained organizational adaptation's potential to alter the inequality regimes at play. Essentially, black colleges were unable to mount a successful challenge. Still, this is not to suggest that black colleges failed completely. The contrast between success and failure does not capture the situation's full complexity. In each instance, it is possible to see how partial adaptation led to partial success, especially at the organizational level. At the same time, it is also possible to see that had the underlying inequality regime within the field shifted, success at the organizational level could have been greater and the inequality regime would have weakened.

The UNCF's formation enabled participating schools to increase financial control, and through its annual campaigns the UNCF created greater social acceptance for black colleges generally and above all for the idea that Americans had a moral responsibility to support black colleges. At the organizational level, this was a great success. Even so, at the level of the field, the status system remained intact. This meant that lower status schools were not able to better control their resource environment. Moreover, the UNCF did not use the campaigns to critique a racially motivated system responsible for this situation. America of the 1940s offered little space for that type of argument. Attacking the system potentially alienated white donors. Again, at the level of the field, the regime that made it difficult for black colleges to claim rewards relative to traditionally white ones by and large went unchecked.

Focusing on where the black colleges partially succeeded highlights the paradox inherent to adapting amidst inequality. Inequality regimes are not strong enough to prevent adaptation outright. Stranger still, the regimes themselves produce circumstances that all but require adaptation. Nevertheless, the inequality regimes are insulated enough so as not to be truly affected or challenged by such adaptation. For instance, within the black higher education field the inequality regime shifted from being guided by a theory of color-conscious to color-blind policy. This shift necessitated that black colleges change, but without producing a more favorable environment for black colleges. In some ways, black colleges were worse off than when the field was decidedly race-conscious. Black colleges had to adapt in ways that reduced racial distinctions between themselves and traditionally white colleges. This resulted in black colleges sacrificing things that once made them unique and special, further fueling speculation that black colleges were poor substitutes for traditionally white colleges. The inequality regime was stronger than ever, for it purported to be and was deemed race-neutral by the highest court in the land, yet still managed to cultivate an environment detrimental to black college progress.

Black college advocates wanted the courts to direct the states to abide by the "cumulative effect" logic of past discriminatory acts that would require states to rectify past funding disparities. In addition, black college advocates wanted the courts to focus on ensuring that colleges and universities removed racist policies and practices that barred black students from attending traditionally white colleges. Black college advocates did not want courts to focus on the racial identifiability of schools. The advocates' institutional work did not alter the inequality regime that pitted the black colleges against the Southern states and the judiciary. The judiciary responsible for ruling in these cases had come to favor a more conservative interpretation of civil rights law that supported the reconstituted white racial project of the post-*Brown* era. The Southern states' insistence that inequality was no longer a problem and that states could not be held accountable for past discrimination in the present day resonated with a judiciary already leaning toward color-blind public policy.

Black college efforts to adapt illustrate the organizational literature's inability to account for the experience of relatively powerless and highly stigmatized actors. Much of what we know about adaptation is based on the experience of powerful, nonstigmatized actors. As a result, the adaptive maneuvers undertaken by such actors allow them to lay claim to rewards and shift the field dynamics in their favor. For instance, organizational scholars Timothy Vogus and Gerald F. Davis chronicled the events leading to a wave of corporate anti-takeover legislation. Like black college advocates following *Brown*, business elites worked collectively to influence the institutional space. Business elites argued that hostile takeovers, that is, efforts to buy a company from its current shareholders without the approval of current managers, were bad for firms and destabilized the communities in which taken-over firms resided. Elites pushed for states to adopt legislation that made it difficult for hostile takeovers to take place. Business elites were successful in their effort to transform the institutional space—states adopted legislation that favored corporate rather than shareholder interests. Crucial to these elites' success was the field's structure—the interconnections among corporations and the existence of laws already privileging corporate interests facilitated the spread of anti-takeover legislation.

This finding is not anomalous. The literature on the proliferation of equal employment, maternity leave, domestic partner, and other rights-based practices within organizations attests to this. Corporations have been granted incredible leeway in developing policies to remedy discrimination on the basis of race, gender, and sexual orientation. In fact, field members in charge of regulating (e.g., the federal government, the judiciary) view the solutions enacted by corporations as evidence of fulfilling federal and state law. Effectively, corporations get to define the terms of compliance with the law. Comparatively, black colleges did not operate from a position that allowed them to define their compliance with color-blind legal policies in the last decades of the twentieth century, nor did black colleges have the ability to control the definitions of legitimacy that historically prevailed within the black higher education field. On the contrary, be it their decision to include both pre- and postsecondary courses within their curricula, their emphasis on teacher-training, or the decision to remain focused on the education of black students, the adaptations black colleges undertook were consistently perceived as illegitimate among the field of actors.

That what little we know about adaptation is based on the actions of powerful field members stifles the organization studies literature. Often depicting them as spaces of contestation,[7] scholars characterize fields as spaces that have winners and losers. Those for whom the field's structure works are the winners, and the rest losers. The foregoing chapters suggest that this imagery does not capture the fluidity of the situation.

Black colleges were both winners and losers simultaneously. At the organizational level, adapting did partially improve the black colleges' outlook. The UNCF brought in more donations, the advocacy work created a post-*Brown* narrative for the colleges, and updating their organizational capacity to facilitate student access to a wider range of degree offerings brought the colleges into the twentieth century. At the field level, because it did not drastically shift the patterns of domination among the actors, black college adaptation had less of an impact.

The potential of this duality can go unnoticed because most of the criteria used to judge an adaptation's success are based on organization-level outcomes. Resource dependence theorists would argue that an adaptation is successful to the extent that it affords an organization more control over its inputs and outputs. Institutional theorists would argue that an adaptation is successful if it helps an organization gain social acceptance. Little attention is given to the notion that success at the organizational level does not translate to that of the field. In reality, success is not equally available at both levels. Particularly in the case of stigmatized field members, adaptation can occur, but it does not necessarily alter the pattern of subordination that defines the field. The inequality regimes' persistence within the black higher education field offers proof of this. The colleges changed, but the structure of the field remained more or less the same.

What is a stigmatized field member to do, then? That is, how can a stigmatized field member use adaptation to challenge the inequality regimes reigning within the field? Exploring paths partially followed by black colleges provides insight to these questions. Stigmatized actors are best served by using their social and entrepreneurial skills to bring new populations into the field. For instance, by making appeals to the American public, the UNCF did this in part. Cultivating a relationship with a group that had yet to make its mark on the black higher education field had the potential to alter the systems of inequality. However, as detailed in chapters 2 and 3, the way the UNCF went about formulating the organization and appeals reified the inequality regimes operating within the field. Though it would have taken longer to get the UNCF up and running, circumventing those field members who had shown antagonism toward black colleges altogether held greater promise with regard to shifting the pattern of subordination and domination within the field. Engaging groups less invested in the white racial project was key.

There were philanthropies that supported a more radical vision of black progress that black college leaders could have tried to cultivate.

The Garland Fund, for example, supported the NAACP.[8] However, the Garland Fund was not a traditional member of the black higher education field, thus black colleges would have had to spend an enormous amount of time and energy to build a bridge to such an organization. Yet, differentiating between those whose cooperation is needed to better organizational outcomes and those whose cooperation is needed to alter the structure of a field is a key component of social skill.[9] Because they were vested in the status quo, philanthropists who traditionally supported black colleges had little reason to challenge the systems of inequality operating within the field. New visions for the field are likely to come from actors not yet committed to or those that do not benefit from the existing order.[10] Furthermore, reconciling short- and long-term goals is also important. In the short run, turning to philanthropists already operating within the black higher education field to start the UNCF was a good idea. The endorsement of the Rockefeller family gave the UNCF credibility and stature typically reserved for more established entities; however, in the long run the presence of philanthropies made it difficult for the UNCF to speak out against racial inequality or to include member colleges that defied the status distinctions philanthropists preferred.

A modern-day example highlights the usefulness of circumventing field members that have proven themselves to be antagonistic toward black colleges. Though it started its ranking system more than a century after black colleges emerged, *U.S. News and World Report* refused to rank black colleges.[11] By using college presidents' subjective opinions of other colleges, *U.S. News and World Report* perpetuated the stereotypes about black colleges. Whether *U.S. News and World Report* intentionally did so, by refusing to rank black colleges the organization played into the white racial project that holds black colleges cannot be as good as traditionally white ones. Black colleges protested this ranking system and began supporting alternatives such as The Education Conservancy.[12] The Education Conservancy asked those responding to the *U.S. News and World Report* ranking survey to skip questions about subjective opinions of other colleges and to only provide data that had been collected in accordance with shared professional standards and reported to state or federal officials.[13] In 2011, *U.S. News and World Report* began to provide a separate listing of black colleges. This is not a perfect solution, but it is one that likely would not have come about without the agitation of an outside organization such as The Education Conservancy.

Developing links with social movement groups also represents a particularly promising means by which stigmatized actors within a field can challenge inequality. By cultivating such relationships, less powerful field members gain access to the social movement's mobilization experience. Social movements are "a set of opinions and beliefs in a population which represents preferences for changing some element of the structure and/or reward distribution of society."[14] For a social movement to meet with success, it must not only offer a compelling vision of the world, it must also recruit individuals and groups to engage in activities that will make the necessary changes come to fruition. Mobilizing individuals and groups to act or better yet agitate, then, accounts for much of what social movements do.

Scholars have long recognized the ability of social movements to transform organizations, and more recently scholars have extended this argument to entire fields.[15] Be they environmental groups rallying activists to protest corporate waste management practices or black power groups urging colleges and universities to develop black studies programs, social movements have the capacity to transform fields.[16] Despite the prevalent and well-documented involvement of many black college students and alumni with these movements,[17] black colleges as social actors unto themselves had complicated relationships with civil rights and black power movement organizations. As discussed in chapters 3 and 4, the NAACP, the largest civil rights group at the time,[18] advocated against single-race institutions. High-level NAACP executives, many of whom had received their education at black colleges, even went as far as to say that black colleges should be closed following the *Brown* decision. Black power activists critiqued black colleges as insular spaces encouraging apathy and an abandonment of black identity in favor of integration.[19] Known for their conservatism,[20] black college leaders often rebuffed student activism, especially the more militant strain taken by those affiliated with the black power movement.[21]

Just as black college advocates used institutional work to engage the Southern states in *Brown*'s aftermath, the advocates could have also used institutional work to engage corners of the civil rights and black power movements. Neither movement stood out as a natural ally to black colleges, yet this this does not mean that movements are not penetrable. The constant influx of new recruits and ideas to their causes all but guarantees that movement groups adopt new platforms, alter goals, and shift tactics midstream. In the case of the black colleges, cultivating stronger connections to the civil rights or black power movements would have been beneficial because both movements launched a greater critique of racism and inequality. Altering the pattern of domination and subordination within the black higher education field required the kind of sustained assault that black movement groups had used to upend racially discriminatory practices writ large. As the chapters of the book have shown, no amount of adapting by the black colleges produced fundamental change within the field. Bringing social movements to bear on the problem of the inequalities particular to the black higher education field could have led to a more favorable distribution of rewards for black colleges.

Black Colleges: One of Many Stigmatized Organizational Actors

Thus far, the discussion has been confined to the case at hand; however, it is important to understand whether and how this empirical investigation generalizes beyond the experience of black colleges. Black colleges are not the only stigmatized organizational actor. Higher education offers two cases that serve as useful comparisons to think through the boundary conditions of partial adaptation—women's and tribal colleges. Women's and tribal colleges exist within inequality regimes and as a result suffer from stigma, though the basis of this stigma is different from that which confronts black colleges.

Women's colleges highlight that race is not the only characteristic that provides the basis for an inequality regime. Whereas black colleges affronted the white racial project, women's colleges never sought to challenge America's racial order. To the contrary, women's college supporters and alumnae were quite happy to think of the best women's colleges as an extension of the Ivy League when there "was no such thing as coeducation."[22] Much like traditionally white colleges of the South, women's colleges did not purposefully recruit nonwhite students until the 1960s.[23] Therefore, we can think of women's colleges as natural affronts to the patriarchy project. These schools did not critique the racial project that relegated racial minority group members to the status of second-class citizens, but women's colleges did stand in opposition to the patriarchal inequality regime that made it difficult for white women to claim rewards relative to white men.

Tribal colleges are perhaps more similar to black colleges with regard to the racial project that both confront. Though even here things diverge. Tribal colleges are sovereign entities chartered by their affiliated nations, which too are sovereign from the larger socio-legal structure of the United States.[24] Thus, we can think of these schools as not just opposing the white racial project, but as also opposing an American project that makes it difficult if not impossible for indigenous people to lay claim to rewards without assimilating into American society. This is a key factor differentiating black and tribal colleges from one another. Black colleges have never aspired to offer their students an alternative to assimilating into American society after graduation. In fact, advocates at times argue that the value of black colleges is that they better facilitate black students' transition into American society than traditionally white colleges. Tribal colleges, on the other hand, seek to "turn the tables on . . . assimilation . . . by establishing [schools] charged with preserving traditional languages and cultures, promoting local economic development, and fostering political autonomy."[25] Black, women's, and tribal colleges all stand in opposition to particular inequality regimes. However, each engages a connected, yet slightly different regime.[26]

Critical organizational differences further distinguish these schools from one another. While the first women's and black colleges appeared in the pre–Civil war period, tribal colleges did not enter the educational scene until the second half of the twentieth century. As already mentioned, tribal colleges are sovereign and thus not subject to Supreme Court rulings that dictate schools lose their racial identity. Similarly, state-controlled women's colleges were few in number. In 1930, of the more than two hundred women's colleges in existence, only ten women's liberal arts colleges were publicly controlled.[27] By the late 1950s, only six of the ten remained.[28] Of the 9.6 percent of students attending women's colleges in the 1956–57 academic year, only 1.1 percent enrolled at public four-year schools.[29] Thus, we can think of women's colleges as relatively sovereign from state dictates. The vast majority of these colleges operate as privately controlled entities outside the purview of the state.

Black, women's, and tribal colleges faced different pressures to integrate their campuses. Tribal colleges are largely absent from conversations about racial integration within higher education. Their sovereign status protects them from the fate that has befallen black colleges. Tribal colleges are not characterized as obstacles to integrating traditionally white colleges. While women's colleges have faced difficulties racially integrating their campuses,[30] most conversations about these schools revolve around sex integration or the decision to become coeducational. Though even here, sexually integrating women's college campuses appears to have been less fraught than anything that occurred within the black higher education field. Scholar and longtime Vassar faculty member Mabel Newcomber argues that three trends facilitated the transition to coeducation among women's colleges.[31] First, women's colleges suffered declining enrollment. Admitting male students was a way to overcome this. Second, students increasingly wanted to attend college close to their homes. Local residents pressured nearby sex-segregated schools to open their doors to both men and women. Third, students themselves, especially women, wanted coeducational spaces. As a result, seventy-three of the 158 women's colleges in existence as of 1968 were coeducational by 1985.[32] The preference among men and women to attend the same schools or among local residents to have their white sons and daughters attend schools together did not translate when the situation involved black and white students. Instead, there was a clear desire to maintain separate spaces well beyond the *Brown* ruling.

The differences between the inequality regimes confronting each type of school as well as the organizational and historical particulars means that partial adaptation, especially toward the norm of the traditionally white model, may not be as necessary, constraining, or severe among women's and tribal colleges. Within the context of American education, the stigmatizing force of race has operated differently than that of either sex or nativity. For example, tribal colleges integrate more ethnocentric courses into their curriculum than black colleges.[33] In his analysis of ethnocentric content, sociologist Wade Cole found that between 1977 and 2002, an average of almost 20 percent of the courses at tribal colleges included ethnocentric content compared to less than 3 percent for black colleges.[34] Private black colleges had more ethnocentric content than public black colleges and traditionally white colleges. However, private black colleges had far less ethnocentric content than tribally controlled ones. Private black colleges have more freedom than public black colleges, yet constraint still exists. Scholars of black colleges often argue that if government funding is the measure by which we judge a college as public then it is difficult to classify private black colleges as truly private. This helps explain why, though they tend to be slightly less homogenous to traditionally white colleges than public black colleges (see chapter 4), private black colleges still exhibit the same patterns as public black colleges.

Whereas tribal colleges get to have organizational outcomes that clearly distinguish them from other minority-serving institutions and traditionally white colleges, the institutional environment surrounding black colleges requires them to become homogenous to traditionally white colleges. Their sovereignty moderates the need for tribal colleges to adapt toward the curricular models espoused by traditionally white colleges. Tribal colleges can and do build a distinct identity around preserving tribal culture. The field of actors precludes public and private black colleges from doing the same around black culture.

Black and women's colleges were challenged by racial and sex integration respectively. Chapter 4 of this book highlighted the difficulties black colleges faced as they adapted in an environment that privileged non–racially identifiable schools. Black colleges could only ever partially adapt within this framework for they did not desire to give up their focus on the education of black students. Moreover, desegregation rulings required public black colleges to integrate their campuses. Some rulings even stipulated that certain monies be withheld until white enrollment reached a court-mandated threshold.

Alternatively, the sex integration of higher education played out quite differently. Even when coeducation was uncommon, many men's schools had coordinating relationships with women's colleges, such as Harvard and Radcliffe. Some public universities, such as the University of Michigan, cordoned off sections of the campus for women students.[35] By 1870, eight state universities within the Midwest and West were open to women.[36] In important ways, the worlds of white male and female higher education were less discrete than black and white higher education. During times of war, especially World War II, surging female enrollment enabled many colleges to remain open. Though college and university administrators typically viewed women as substitutes for men and fully expected women to cede their spots to returning veterans,[37] these administrators did gain experience operating sexually integrated college campuses.

Just as the civil rights movement caused some to question the relevance of single-race educational settings, the feminist movement of the 1960s and 1970s prompted many women's college administrators, faculty, students, and alumnae to question the need for and relevance of single-sex educational spaces.[38] Publicly supported women's colleges faced lawsuits that required the admission of men.[39] However, unlike the black higher education field in which public colleges represented half the schools and educated the majority of students attending black colleges, the field of women's colleges was for all intents and purposes privately controlled. Not only did this mean that as a field of actors, women's colleges were relatively free to choose how to respond to the sex integration of higher education, it also meant that there was no actor equivalent to the Southern states within the black higher education field doing all that it could to prevent women's colleges from integrating their campuses.

The actions of the Southern states post-*Brown* made it incredibly difficult for black colleges, whether public or private, to recruit white students. Again, as chapter 4 documented, preventing the Southern states from doing this is what initially drove black college advocates to the courts and what led the U.S. Department of Health, Education, and Welfare to argue that a dual system of higher education persisted well into the 1960s. On the one hand, the institutional environment demanded that black colleges adapt toward the norms of racially integrated education. On the other hand, the Southern states made this task near-impossible to achieve. This dynamic was absent for women's colleges. Recruiting men or merging with men's college represented strategies that women's colleges could utilize if they desired to go coeducational. Comparatively, merger was at times forced upon black colleges as a means of enabling a neighboring traditionally white college to racially integrate.

The relative freedom that women's colleges had in deciding to adapt toward the coeducational norm sweeping higher education provided women's colleges with the opportunity to learn from one another. For instance, Smith College learned a great deal from Vassar's efforts to become coeducational. Vassar officials at first looked to form a coordinate relationship with Yale University that would have required Vassar to relocate from Poughkeepsie, New York, to New Haven, Connecticut.[40] This deal fell through in 1967. Vassar then decided to admit men, yet the college had trouble attracting qualified male applicants.[41] Reflecting on this period, Smith president Mary Dunn recalled that "[t]he early years of Vassar were very tough, which illustrated for people the difficulty of trying to go coed."[42] In the end, Smith remained a women's college.

Learning of this type was not possible within the black higher education field. The number and dominance of public colleges within the field resulted in increased scrutiny and pressure once higher education desegregation was cast as a systemic issue that could not be achieved by protecting an individual's choice to attend any school of their choosing. Officials in charge of black public colleges could not take a "wait and see" approach. Those leading black public colleges could not look at a failed merger between a public black and traditionally white college in one state and halt efforts in another. Unlike women's colleges, a nontrivial number of black colleges are connected to the state and, therefore, are not in control of merging or closing their schools. Even after courts stipulated that integrating higher education should not place a greater burden on black colleges than it did on traditionally white ones, black colleges continued to operate under the threat of merger and closure. Furthermore, those leading black colleges could not take failed attempts to recruit white students as evidence that it was best for black colleges to stay single-race. Again, the public colleges' connection to public authorities and the reliance of private colleges on government funding made this an implausible response to environmental trends. Women's colleges' capacity to choose their own fate in the wake of sex integration was greater than black colleges trying to adapt in the wake of racial integration.

Reflecting on the financial state of black and women's colleges offers another opportunity to contemplate whether the stigmatizing forces of race and gender have operated differently within higher education. In tracing how partial adaptation arises, this book has given particular attention to the notion that inequality regimes force black colleges into nonoptimal adaptation strategies. Of particular concern has been how inequality regimes hamper the organizing process, or black colleges' ability to claim rewards relative to their competitors. Students attending black colleges exist within an inequality regime in which blacks earn less than whites.[43] Consequently, blacks attending college cannot afford to pay as much as whites. This reality has resulted in tuition and fees charged by black colleges lagging behind inflationary trends.[44] That is, student fees at black colleges have not kept pace with the cost of operating these schools. This is particularly troublesome for private black colleges, as these schools derive much less revenue from student fees than do other private colleges.[45] On the whole, black colleges partially adapted to inflationary trends within higher education. Tuition and fees have increased but not at levels that will support black college revenue needs. This results in black colleges, public and private, relying much more on government aid as a revenue stream than do traditionally white colleges.

How much black colleges can charge students offers insight into whether these schools can reap financial rewards comparable to their competitors. In 2013–14, Smith, a women's college, charged $43,114 in tuition and fees compared to $24,634 and $17,130 respectively for Spelman and Bennett, both private black women's colleges. By contrast, Smith charged $1,000 more for tuition than Harvard University. Smith is able to construct claims about the educational work that it does that enables it to charge roughly what Harvard University charges its students to attend. Still predominantly white, women's colleges draw from within communities that are empowered to make claims for better jobs, wages, and promotions that enable their children to attend schools that charge significantly more than black colleges. Relative to other stigmatized organizational actors, because women's colleges are by and large products of the white racial project, be it an all-female version, they are more able to claim financial rewards than those schools that stand in opposition of white racial projects. Though stigmatized in their own right, tribal and women's colleges have had a greater capacity to choose more optimal, and therefore less partial adaptation strategies than black colleges.

The black college experience is unique because although they account for a small proportion of higher education organizations, the schools have found themselves at the center of debates within American higher education, legislation, and jurisprudence more than other stigmatized actors such as women's or tribal colleges. Perhaps because they aspired to do something as militant as educate the formerly enslaved and their descendants, some with public monies no less, black colleges have faced stiff opposition whenever they have attempted to expand their resources and capabilities or express their rights in ways not deemed appropriate by powerful field members.

Only with this in mind is it possible to understand why black colleges took the shape and form that they did. Hence, it is not enough to advise black colleges and their advocates about how the schools should change or to criticize the schools for a perceived lack of development. Anyone looking to improve black colleges must account for the field of actors' ability to make partial adaptive responses more likely than others. For instance, after chronicling the problems confronting black colleges in the twenty-first century (e.g., accreditation lapses, revenue shortfalls, layoffs, etc.) Brooks and Starks recommended among other things that black colleges institute more transparent governance procedures, diversify their student populations, and develop diverse revenue streams. At no point did the authors discuss whether the field of actors creates a context in which any of these outcomes are possible or sustainable.

In theory, it is a good idea for black colleges to have open and flexible administrative procedures and to publicize decisions of interest to core constituencies. In practice, historically the field of actors has made open governance less possible. Only in secret were black college officials able to maintain liberal arts courses within their curriculums while simultaneously accepting from philanthropists funds conditioned upon the removal of them.[46] Understanding why secrecy was a necessity then leads to determining if the field of actors has shifted such that transparency is now more feasible. Like open governance, diversifying the student populations is a good idea. However, the proliferation of publicly controlled affiliate campuses of traditionally white flagship universities across the South continues to make diverse recruitment a difficult strategy for black colleges to pursue. Until the Southern state changes its behaviors, black colleges will continue to face obstacles to recruiting nonblack students. Black colleges have worked to diversify their revenue streams since their beginnings. The UNCF was just one of many attempts to garner more resources. However, be it the judiciary ruling that states do not need to remunerate funding discrepancies or federal programs that routinely fund black colleges at lower levels than traditionally white ones,[47] the field of actors has consistently rebuffed black colleges' efforts to lay claim to financial rewards. When the field of actors divests from a racial project that intentionally stunts the growth of organizations dedicated to the progress of black Americans, black colleges will no longer have to choose between the lesser of nonoptimal adaptation strategies. Once the field of actors changes its stance toward black colleges, these schools will grow and develop to the fullest potential imaginable. Questions regarding the necessity for black colleges will be a thing of the past.

Appendix 1

Population of Black Colleges and Universities[1]

School Name	State	Founded
Lincoln University	Pennsylvania	1854
Wilberforce University	Ohio	1856
Atlanta University	Georgia	1860
Atlanta School of Social Work	Georgia	1865
Shaw University	North Carolina	1865
Walden College	Tennessee	1865
Fisk University	Tennessee	1865
Virginia Union University	Virginia	1865
Lincoln University	Missouri	1866
Talladega College	Alabama	1867
Howard University	Washington, D.C.	1867
Morehouse College	Georgia	1867
Johnson C Smith University	North Carolina	1867
St. Augustine's College	North Carolina	1867
Roger Williams	Tennessee	1867
Storer College	West Virginia	1867
Straight College	Louisiana	1868
Hampton Normal & Agricultural Institute (Hampton University)	Virginia	1868
New Orleans University	Louisiana	1869
Tougaloo College	Mississippi	1869
Claflin University	South Carolina	1869
Clark University	Georgia	1870
Leland University	Louisiana	1870
Barber-Scotia College	North Carolina	1870
Allen University	South Carolina	1870

School Name	State	Founded
Benedict College	South Carolina	1870
LeMoyne College	Tennessee	1870
Alcorn Agricultural & Mechanical College (Alcorn A&M University)	Mississippi	1871
Brewer Junior College	South Carolina	1872
Knoxville College	Tennessee	1872
Wiley College	Texas	1873
State Teachers College (Alabama State University)	Alabama	1874
State Agricultural & Mechanical Institute (Alabama A&M University)	Alabama	1875
Arkansas State College (University of Arkansas, Pine Bluff)	Arkansas	1875
Stillman College	Alabama	1876
Morgan College (Morgan State University)	Maryland	1876
Meharry Medical College	Tennessee	1876
Philander Smith College	Arkansas	1877
Western University	Kansas	1877
Jackson College (Jackson State University)	Mississippi	1877
State Normal School (Fayetteville State University)	North Carolina	1877
Tillotson College	Texas	1877
Selma University	Alabama	1878
Lane College	Tennessee	1878
Simmons Bible College	Kentucky	1879
Voorhees Normal & Industrial Institute (Voorhees College)	South Carolina	1879
Tuskegee Normal & Industrial Institute (Tuskegee University)	Alabama	1881
Spelman College	Georgia	1881
Southern Christian Institute	Mississippi	1881
Bettis College	South Carolina	1881
Morristown Normal and Industrial College (Knoxville College – Morristown)	Tennessee	1881
Bishop College	Texas	1881
Paul Quinn College	Texas	1881
Gammon Theological Seminary	Georgia	1882
Paine College	Georgia	1882
Livingstone College	North Carolina	1882
Edward Waters College	Florida	1883
Swift Memorial College	Tennessee	1883
Virginia State College (Virginia State University)	Virginia	1883
Arkansas Baptist College	Arkansas	1885

School Name	State	Founded
Morris Brown College	Georgia	1885
Natchez College	Mississippi	1885
Kittrell College	North Carolina	1885
Shorter College	Arkansas	1886
Princess Anne Academy (University of Maryland— Eastern Shore)	Maryland	1886
Rust College	Mississippi	1886
Mary Allen Seminary	Texas	1886
Prairie View State College (Prairie View Agricultural & Mechanical University)	Texas	1886
Florida Agricultural & Mechanical College (Florida A&M University)	Florida	1887
Central State University	Ohio	1887
Guadalupe College	Texas	1887
St. Paul's Normal & Industrial School (St. Paul's College)	Virginia	1888
Virginia College & Seminary (Virginia University of Lynchburg)	Virginia	1888
Daniel Payne College	Alabama	1889
State Normal School (Elizabeth City State University)	North Carolina	1889
Georgia State Industrial College (Savannah State University)	Georgia	1890
Coleman College	Louisiana	1890
Western College	Missouri	1890
Stowe Teachers College (Harris-Stowe State University)	Missouri	1890
Campbell College	Mississippi	1890
State College for Colored Youth (Delaware State University)	Delaware	1891
Agricultural & Technical College (North Carolina A&T State University)	North Carolina	1891
West Virginia State College (West Virginia State University)	West Virginia	1891
Florida Normal & Industrial College (Florida Memorial University)	Florida	1892
Mary Holmes College	Mississippi	1892
Lomax-Hannon Junior College	Alabama	1893
Fort Valley Normal & Industrial Institute (Fort Valley State University)	Georgia	1893
Clinton Junior College	South Carolina	1894
Texas College	Texas	1894
Joseph K. Brick Junior College	North Carolina	1895
State Agricultural & Mechanical College (South Carolina State University)	South Carolina	1895

School Name	State	Founded
Barber College	Alabama	1896
Oakwood College	Alabama	1896
Kentucky State Industrial College (Kentucky State University)	Kentucky	1896
Colored Agricultural & Normal University (Langston University)	Oklahoma	1897
Seneca Junior College	South Carolina	1898
St. Philip's Junior College (St. Philip's College)	Texas	1898
Central City College	Georgia	1899
Samuel Huston College	Texas	1900
Miles Memorial College	Alabama	1902
Coppin Normal School (Coppin State University)	Maryland	1902
Okolona Industrial School	Mississippi	1902
Palmer Memorial Institute	North Carolina	1902
Utica Junior College	Mississippi	1903
Immanuel Lutheran College	North Carolina	1903
Conroe Normal & Industrial Institute	Texas	1903
Bethune-Cookman College (Bethune-Cookman University)	Florida	1904
Georgia Normal & Agricultural College (Albany State University)	Georgia	1905
Louisiana Normal & Industrial College (Grambling State University)	Louisiana	1905
Morris College	South Carolina	1905
Butler College	Texas	1905
Mississippi Industrial College	Mississippi	1906
Prentiss-Normal and Industrial Institute	Mississippi	1907
Piney Woods School	Mississippi	1909
Jarvis Christian College	Texas	1909
West Kentucky Industrial College	Kentucky	1910
Maryland Normal School (Bowie State University)	Maryland	1911
Lincoln Institute of Kentucky	Kentucky	1912
Agricultural & Industrial State College (Tennessee State University)	Tennessee	1912
Cheyney Training School (Cheyney State University of Pennsylvania)	Pennsylvania	1913
Southern University and Agricultural & Mechanical College	Louisiana	1914
Xavier University	Louisiana	1915
Beda Eta Academy	Georgia	1921
Bluefield State Teachers College (Bluefield State College)	West Virginia	1921
Concordia College	Alabama	1922

School Name	State	Founded
North Carolina College for Negroes (North Carolina Central University)	North Carolina	1925
Winston-Salem State Teachers College (Winston-Salem State University)	North Carolina	1925
Bennett College for Women	North Carolina	1926
Houston Colored Junior College	Texas	1927
Dunbar Junior College	Arkansas	1929
Miner Teachers College (University of District of Columbia)	Washington D.C.	1929
Louisville Municipal College	Kentucky	1931
Coulter Junior College	South Carolina	1931
Friendship College	South Carolina	1935
Norfolk State University	Virginia	1942
Mississippi Valley State University	Mississippi	1946
Texas Southern University	Texas	1947
Southwestern Christian College	Texas	1948
Coahoma Junior College	Mississippi	1949
Southern University at New Orleans	Louisiana	1956
Interdenominational Theological Center	Georgia	1958
Southern University at Shreveport	Louisiana	1964
SD Bishop State Junior College	Alabama	1965
Lawson State Community College	Alabama	1965
Morehouse School of Medicine	Georgia	1981
Morris Booker College	Arkansas	?
Washington Junior College	Florida	?
State Technical & Agricultural College	Georgia	?
Kansas City Junior College, Sumner Branch	Kansas	?
Carver Junior College	Maryland	?
Lincoln Junior College	Missouri	?
Mississippi Negro Training School	Mississippi	?
Central Mississippi College	Mississippi	?
Harbison Junior College	South Carolina	?

Appendix 2

UNCF Membership and Organizational Meetings

I obtained the list of colleges that participated in the UNCF and the date that participation began from the United Negro College Fund Archives located in the Robert Woodruff Library of the Atlanta University Center. I constructed the list of private schools that did not participate in the UNCF from the *Journal of Negro Education, The Evolution of the Negro College*, and government-sponsored surveys of black colleges. For those schools that did not participate in the UNCF, I determined their eligibility to do so from reports in the *Journal of Negro Education* during the years 1939–1943. These reports confirmed each school's accreditation status and that the thirty-six schools offered membership were the only ones eligible to participate during the time period under investigation.

The UNCF held its first organizational meeting in April 1943. At this meeting, fifteen college representatives worked out the details regarding the aforementioned membership criteria. Fourteen of these schools became UNCF members. Another organizational meeting took place in November 1943. Meeting attendees solidified the distribution scheme for funds raised and returned to the issue of membership. Those present decided eligible schools currently not participating could join the coalition at a later date and developed a membership path for schools deemed ineligible at this point. This ensured all private black colleges that became accredited would have the opportunity to join the coalition. After this meeting, all colleges had to confirm their commitment to the UNCF. All twenty-five colleges present at this meeting participated in the first campaign.

Organizational Data

I gathered data on enrollment from the 1943 *Journal of Negro Education* annual report "Enrollment in Institutions of Higher Education of Negroes." I obtained information on the total number of college-level students in attendance from the 1939 *College Blue Book* section entitled "Colleges Especially for Negro Youth" and used this information to calculate the percentage of a school's enrollment accounted for by college-level students. I gathered data on school income from the 1939 *College Blue Book* section entitled "Colleges Especially for Negro Youth." To calculate the percentage of black trustees, I obtained information on the total number of trustees and the number of black trustees at the colleges from the 1929 *Survey of Negro Colleges and Universities*.

Finding organizational data for black private colleges in this time period proved difficult. For example, a 1939 *College Blue Book* report included information on school income; however, the report did not include income data for ten schools within this population. I did not obtain information on the percentage of black trustees for three schools and information on enrollment for four schools.[1] I utilized single variable imputation techniques to fill in these missing values. The missing values of each variable were imputed using a set of predictor variables for which data were complete, such as college enrollment. In addition to these data, I included information on school age in 1944, GEB affiliation, 1958 enrollment, and 1958 endowment in the regression equation to obtain point estimates for the missing values. I performed additional analyses in which the minimum value of a particular variable was substituted and analyses that utilized complete cases only. I chose minimum substitution as opposed to mean substitution on the theory that schools missed by government surveyors and other groups were smaller than the average school within the population. The pattern of results from the three analyses indicated that school income, the percentage of black trustees, and total enrollment differentiated participants from nonparticipants.

Several of the variables came from data sources compiled much earlier than the year preceding the UNCF's formation. Data concerning the percentage of black trustees were obtained from a government report issued in 1929, and data concerning the proportion of college students were obtained from a 1939 report. Within the organizational literature, much attention is devoted to the concept of inertia.[2] From this perspective, organizational characteristics are not likely to experience rapid change. Therefore, even if collected between four and fourteen years earlier, the organizational characteristics under investigation are not likely to have changed much. For instance, among private black colleges the overall percentage of black trustees did not change much between the 1920s and the 1960s. Samuel M. Nabrit and Julius S. Scott Jr.'s 1967–68 study of private black college trustees found that of the 1,255 trustees 730, or 58 percent, were black.[3] Data from the 1929 survey of black colleges used for my analyses indicate that 57 percent of the trustees were black; if focus remains on those data that were not missing a similar percentage (61 percent) emerges.

Analyses

I used the Wilcoxin-Mann-Whitney (Wilcoxin) test as an analytic technique. The normality assumption underlying parametric models proved difficult to uphold with these data. With large samples, researchers can assume that the variable under consideration is normally distributed, yet the limited number of cases made it difficult to assume this and the normal probability plots confirmed this suspicion. Because it does not assume the variables are drawn from a normally distributed population and it is better suited for small sample sizes, the Wilcoxin test offered the best alternative to parametric ones. Strictly speaking, Wilcoxin models do not test for the equality of means but instead test for whether two samples have the same distribution. The data from samples n_1 and n_2, are ranked from 1 to n_1+n_2. The mean of these ranks is then computed for each sample. If the mean rank from one sample is significantly larger than the other, this is taken as evidence that the two samples have a different distribution, or, in parametric terms, that the means are not equal to one another. For ease of understanding the mean, proportion, or the percentage for each variable, not the mean of the ranks from the Wilcoxin test, is reported in Table 2.1.

Appendix 3

Frame Analyses

I utilized the work of various scholars who focused on frame identification in their work as a model for conducting the analysis. In an analysis of white separatist rhetoric, Mitch Berbrier documented three specific frames used by separatist groups to build ethnic affinity among whites. In another work, David Pellow utilized interview data to document the two frames environmental activists employed to assign blame for their problems. Finally, Joseph Gerteis documented three frames utilized by the Knights of Labor to organize workers across racial and class lines. Using these works as a reference, I sought to identify and enumerate the dominant frames within the UNCF campaign documents.

I read all of the UNCF campaign documents between 1944 and 1954 to develop the framing categories. In *Content Analysis* Klaus Krippendorf recommends working with units of text smaller than the sampling unit itself. Thus, if entire pages are sampled, as was the case here, researchers should consider analyzing the words, sentences, or paragraphs within the page to detect the frame categories. When determining the unit of analysis, Krippendorf suggests researchers rely upon syntactical distinctions that reflect the structure of the text. In particular, the paragraph provides necessary context for understanding the meanings attached to words or sentences and also represents a syntactically defined unit within text.

Each page of the UNCF brochures contained multiple paragraphs that were clearly delineated by spacing breaks and/or paragraph indentation. Following Krippendorf's recommendation, I utilized these paragraphs as the context units to identify frames. I created frame categories and added categories until I reached saturation that according to Matthew Miles and Michael Huberman is the point at which I could go through the paragraphs in the brochures without adding a new category.

After reading each paragraph, I determined which frames occurred within it and assigned it to the appropriate frame category. Three possibilities existed. First, a paragraph could contain no frames. Second, a paragraph could contain only one frame. Third, a paragraph could contain multiple frames. After I completed the analysis, I used the data to focus on identifying the "internal logic of the narrative"[1] in light of the prevailing structures of opportunity.

Appendix 4

Earned Degree Data

The sample for chapter 5 includes colleges from four distinct groups—black public and black private colleges, traditionally white public colleges of the South, and Northeastern private colleges. A common method to determine the boundaries of the population of black colleges is to include those colleges that began with the primary mission of providing blacks with a postsecondary education prior to 1964 within the limits. To determine the listing of black four-year colleges that were still in existence during the first year of data collection for this study, I consulted *The Evolution of the Negro College* and *America's Black and Tribal Colleges*.[1] This generated a list of ninety black colleges (39 public and 51 private). Because of missing data and school closures, the number of schools included in the analyses ranged between thirty-eight and thirty-nine for the black public colleges and between forty-seven and fifty-one for the black private colleges.

I used the Higher Education General Information Survey to determine the listing of private Northeastern and public Southern schools. This survey contains regional categorizations for U.S. colleges and universities. I began with all private four-year institutions in New England. The New England region represents those schools located in Connecticut, Maine, Massachusetts, New Hampshire, Rhode Island, and Vermont. I removed from the list those schools that began operating after 1964. I used this year as my cutoff point because the main argument laid out in chapter 5 draws on the historical connection between the black private colleges and their Northeastern liberal arts counterparts. If the black colleges emulated the behavior of these schools, it seems fair to assume that the black colleges looked to those Northeastern schools that had existed for at least as long as they had and not those Northeastern schools that had a more recent history than the black colleges themselves.

I removed the Ivy League schools from the sample because prior organizational research by Matthew Kraatz and Edward Zajac indicates that Ivy League schools exhibit a different pattern of isomorphism than the average private liberal arts colleges and the private black colleges.[2] This study calls for a comparison of students attending schools situated within similar institutional contexts, so as to understand isomorphic patterns. Thus, removing the Ivy League schools allows for a comparison of the behavior exhibited by students and organizations that faced similar institutional and opportunities and constraints. This generated an initial list of seventy-two Northeastern private liberal arts colleges. Because of missing data and school closures, the number of schools included in the analyses ranged between fifty-nine and sixty-five.

To construct the listing of traditionally white public schools to use as comparisons for the black public colleges, I started with the list of all publicly controlled universities located in the states that maintained racially segregated systems of education and began operating before 1964: Alabama, Arkansas, Delaware, Florida, Georgia, Kentucky, Louisiana, Maryland, Missouri, Mississippi, North Carolina, Oklahoma, South Carolina, Tennessee, Texas, Virginia, and West Virginia. As part of the sample, I included the most prestigious or "flagship" university from each state (e.g., University of Georgia, University of Alabama, and the University of Mississippi) and when possible one other publicly controlled college from the state. This generated a list of twenty-eight publicly controlled traditionally white universities.

I gathered the data for this study using the Higher Education General Information Survey (1968, 1973, 1978, and 1983) and the Integrated Postsecondary Education Data System Survey (1988). I used the Earned Degree Survey from both series to determine the number of degrees granted in each educational program offering at the bachelor level by each college and university under investigation. The list of educational programs includes the following: agriculture, architecture, biological sciences, business administration, computer science, education, English literature, engineering, fine art, foreign languages, health sciences, home economics, law, library sciences, mathematics, military sciences, physical sciences, psychology, theology, social sciences, and general studies. I combined several educational programs to create twenty uniform categories across the different time periods. For instance, the 1968 survey included separate program listings for forestry, geography, philosophy, records management, and trades. In subsequent surveys, other educational offerings such as social science and business administration subsumed these categories from the 1968 survey. With this in mind, I combined 1968 degree data with the educational programs that these degrees were categorized under in future surveys. These combinations resulted in the following educational program classifications: agriculture, biology, business, computer science, education, engineering, English literature, fine art, foreign language, health science, home economics, law, library science, mathematics, military science, physical science, psychology, theology, social science, and general studies.

Statistical Technique

To determine the level of degree diversity for each population, I used a measure of qualitative variation that would allow me to ascertain how widely dispersed the degrees were across the educational programs available in a given year. I selected the index of diversity as specified by Agresti and Agresti in their 1978 article "Statistical Analysis of Qualitative Variation."[3] This index allowed me to determine how widely dispersed the degrees are within one group (e.g., how widely the degrees are dispersed at the black public colleges) or between two groups (e.g., how widely the degrees are dispersed at the black public and private colleges).

The calculation of both the within and between group levels of diversity requires the same data. Using the data contained in the Earned Degree Surveys I calculated (1) the number of degrees a college awarded in each educational program offering and (2) the total number of degrees awarded by the same college. I then used these figures to create an aggregate measure for each of the four types of colleges under investigation. For example, I created one measure that represented the number of students that obtained bachelor's degrees in engineering from the public black colleges and another measure that represented the number of students that obtained degrees in biological sciences from the black public colleges, and so on, until I had covered all the educational programs, k, available in the academic year. Then for each of the program offerings, i, I determined the proportion, p, of students that graduated with degrees in i. I used this information to compute the index of diversity within one group as follows:

$$D = 1 - \Sigma\, p_i^2 \quad _{where\ i\ =\ 1\ ...\ k;} \quad (1)$$

and the index of diversity between two groups as follows:

$$D = 1 - \Sigma\, (p_i{\cdot}q_i) \quad _{where\ i\ =\ 1\ ...\ k;} \quad (2)$$

The index of diversity indicates the probability that two students will graduate with degrees from distinct educational programs.

To determine how the degree diversity of one population compared to another, I used the inference techniques specified by Agresti and Agresti as well. The inference procedures can determine the equality of the diversity indices for two groups. These inference procedures are similar to equality of means tests in which two or more sample means are compared to one another to determine if they significantly differ. The hypothesis for these inference tests centers on testing the proposition that the level of diversity between two groups differs. Therefore, the variance and standard deviation of the distributions are calculated and used to obtain a z-statistic that determines if the null hypothesis that the diversity levels are equal to one another should be rejected.

The first inference method compares the within group diversity levels of two independent groups. This allowed me to determine if the degree diversity of one type of college (e.g., black public colleges) significantly differed from the degree diversity of another type of college (e.g., black private colleges).

The procedure involves two steps, calculating the variance and calculating a z-statistic. The variance is calculated as follows:

$$\sigma^2 = 4[\Sigma p_i^3 - (\Sigma p_i^2)^2], \text{ where } i = 1 \dots k; \quad (1)$$

To determine if $D_1 = D_0$, the z-statistic is calculated as follows:

$$Z = \sqrt{n_1} * (D_1 - D_0)/\sigma_1, \quad (2)$$

In this scenario, D_0 would represent one of the other diversity indices obtained in the same time period.

The second method compares the level of diversity between two groups to the level of diversity between two other groups. This method allowed me to determine if the between group degree diversity of two types of colleges taken as one group (e.g., black public and private colleges) significantly differed from the between group degree diversity of two other types of colleges taken as one group (e.g., traditionally white public and private colleges).

The procedure involves two steps, calculating the variance and calculating a z-statistic. The variance is calculated as follows:

$$\sigma^2 = ((n_1+n_2)/n_1) * \Sigma p_i \cdot q_i^2 + ((n_1 + n_2)/n_2)$$
$$* \Sigma q_i \cdot p_i^2 - ((n_1 + n_2)^2 /n_1 , n_2)$$
$$* (\Sigma p_i \cdot q_i)^2, \text{ where } i = 1 \dots k \quad (4)$$

To determine the equality of two between group diversity indices (i.e., $D_b = D_0$), the z-statistic is calculated as follows:

$$Z = \sqrt{(n_{1+} n_2)} * (D_b - D_0)/ \sigma_b, \quad (5)$$

To understand the level of homogeneity between the degree distributions for two school populations, I calculated a measure that captured the amount of deviation between the proportions of degrees earned per educational program for the two populations. This measure was calculated as follows:

$$\sigma = \sqrt{(\Sigma\ (p_i - q_i)^2/ k)}, _{where\ i = 1 \dots k} \quad (3)$$

To determine if the level of homogeneity changed significantly over time, I used the deviation measures to compare the degree distributions in the 1968–69 academic year to the distributions obtained in the 1988–89 academic year. I used the deviation measures to calculate an F-statistic to test the hypothesis that the deviation among the 1968–69 distributions was greater than the deviation among the 1988–89 distributions.

Table A4.1 Complete Degree Distributions, 1968–1969

Program Name	White Public Colleges	Black Public Colleges	Black Private Colleges	White Private Colleges
Agriculture	4%	1%	1%	0%
Biology	5%	5%	8%	5%
Business	16%	9%	9%	16%
Computer Science	0%	0%	0%	0%
Education	17%	45%	28%	9%
Engineering	11%	2%	2%	9%
English Literature	9%	5%	7%	12%
Fine Art	3%	1%	2%	4%
Foreign Language	2%	2%	2%	4%
Health Science	4%	1%	2%	2%
Home Economics	2%	2%	2%	0%
Law	0%	0%	0%	0%
Library Science	0%	0%	0%	0%
Mathematics	4%	5%	5%	3%
Military Science	0%	0%	0%	0%
Physical Science	3%	1%	3%	3%
Psychology	3%	2%	3%	5%
Theology	0%	0%	1%	1%
Social Science	16%	18%	26%	27%
General Studies	2%	0%	1%	1%

Table A4.2 Complete Degree Distributions, 1988–1989

Program Name	White Public Colleges	Black Public Colleges	Black Private Colleges	White Private Colleges
Agriculture	5%	2%	1%	0%
Biology	3%	3%	6%	4%
Business	24%	27%	29%	26%
Computer Science	2%	7%	5%	2%
Education	9%	13%	7%	3%
Engineering	12%	8%	3%	7%
English Literature	12%	5%	10%	11%
Fine Art	3%	1%	2%	4%
Foreign Language	1%	0%	0%	2%
Health Science	4%	4%	7%	6%
Home Economics	2%	2%	1%	1%
Law	0%	3%	0%	0%
Library Science	0%	0%	0%	0%
Mathematics	1%	2%	3%	1%
Military Science	0%	0%	0%	0%
Physical Science	2%	2%	3%	2%
Psychology	4%	3%	4%	5%
Theology	0%	0%	1%	0%
Social Science	13%	15%	15%	23%
General Studies	3%	2%	5%	3%

Notes

Introduction

1. For an explanation of the sociohistorical processes leading to the stigmatization of black and urban spaces see Massey, Doug and Nancy Denton. 1993. *American Apartheid: Segregation and the Making of the Underclass.* Cambridge: Harvard University Press. For an explanation of the psychological processes leading people to associate blackness with crime and poverty see Sampson, Robert J. and Stephen W. Raudenbush. 2004. "Seeing Disorder: Neighborhood Stigma and the Social Construction of 'Broken Windows.'" *Social Psychological Quarterly* 67:319–342. For an explanation of the processes that lead white felons to have better job opportunities than blacks without a criminal history see Pager, Devah. 2003. "The Mark of a Criminal Record." *American Journal of Sociology* 108:937–975.

2. National Association for Equal Opportunity in Higher Education Web site. http://www.nafeo.org/community/web2010/news_vedder.html. HBCU Leaders Respond! Accessed on May 2, 2013.

3. Minor, James T. 2008. *Contemporary HBCUs: Considering Institutional Capacity and State Priorities. A Research Report.* Michigan State University, College of Education, Department of Educational Administration. East Lansing, MI.

4. I borrow the terminology from Scott, Richard W., Martin Ruef, Peter J. Mendel, and Carol A. Caronna. 2000. *Institutional Change and Healthcare Organizations: From Professional Dominance to Managed Care.* Chicago: University of Chicago Press. P. 2. The authors describe organizations as collective actors in possession of resources, rights, and distinctive capabilities and limitations. This is a useful way to think about organizational adaptation. When organizations adapt they are attempting to grow and change their ability to access resources, express rights, and develop distinctive capabilities.

5. Omi, Michael and Howard Winant. 1994. *Racial Formation in the United States: From the 1960s to the 1990s.* New York: Routledge. Omi and Winant developed the concept of "racial project" as a means of understanding "the

sociohistorical process by which racial categories are created, inhabited, transformed and destroyed." Racial projects do the ideological work of making links between structure and representation. "A racial project is simultaneously an interpretation, representation, or explanation of racial dynamics, and an effort to reorganize and redistribute resources along particular racial lines." Pp. 56–57.

6. Wooten, Melissa E. 2006. "Race and Strategic Organization." *Strategic Organization* 4: 191–199.

7. Acker, Joan. 2006. "Inequality Regimes: Gender, Class, and Race in Organizations." *Gender and Society* 20:441–464. P. 443.

8. Branch, Enobong H. 2011. *Opportunity Denied: Limiting Black Women to Devalued Work.* New Brunswick, NJ: Rutgers University Press.

9. Avent-Holt, Dustin and Donald Tomaskovic-Devey. 2010. "The Relational Basis of Inequality: Generic and Contingent Wage Distribution Processes." *Work and Occupations* 37:162–193.

10. Scott, W. Richard. 1995. *Institutions and Organizations.* Thousand Oaks, CA: Sage.

11. Ibid.

12. Hannan, Michael T. and John Freeman. 1977. "The Population Ecology of Organizations." *American Journal of Sociology* 82:929–964. Hannan and Freeman borrowed the biological metaphor "population" to "refer to aggregates of organizations" that are "alike in some respect." They directed researchers to concentrate on those organizations that share a common fate with respect to environmental variation. The black higher education field consists of multiple populations. For instance, philanthropists represent one population and the colleges another.

13. Meyer, John and Brian Rowan. 1977. "Institutionalized Organizations: Formal Structure as Myth and Ceremony." *American Journal of Sociology* 83:41–62.

14. Ibid.

15. See Anderson, James D. 1988. *The Education of Blacks in the South, 1860–1935.* Chapel Hill, NC: University of North Carolina Press, for a full history of the relationship between factions within the South and its implications for black primary, secondary, and postsecondary education.

16. See Anderson, James D. 1997. "Philanthropy, the State and the Development of Historically Black Public Colleges: The Case of Mississippi." *Minerva* 35295–309, for an example of how this affected black colleges in Mississippi especially.

17. Anderson, James D. 1988.

18. Brooks, F. Erik and Glenn L. Starks. 2011. *Historically Black Colleges and Universities: An Encyclopedia.* Oxford: Greenwood.

19. Anderson, Eric and Alfred A. Moss Jr. 1999. *Dangerous Donations: Northern Philanthropy and Southern Black Education, 1902–1930.* Columbia, MO: University of Missouri Press.

20. President Maxson Bishop College Vision Statement, July 7, 1919, folder 1523, box 163, series 1, General Education Board Archives, RAC.

21. Irons, Jenny. 2010. *Reconstituting Whiteness.* Nashville: Vanderbilt University Press. Irons uses the case of Mississippi to illustrate how Southern whites created goals for what would be considered acceptable forms of racism and white supremacy in the wake of desegregation. Thus, the white racial project was not done away with, but rather reconstituted or reinvented in segregation's aftermath.

22. From Scott's 1995 book, institutions consist of three pillars or three elements that make up and support them. The regulative pillar highlights the ways in which rules and laws constrain behavior. The normative pillar highlights the ability of ideals that specify how things should be done to constrain behavior. The cultural-cognitive pillar highlights the taken-for-granted nature of routines and how this constrains behavior.

23. Jones, Thomas Jesse. 1929. *Negro Education: A Study of the Private and Higher Schools for Colored People in the United States.* Washington, DC: U.S. Department of the Interior.

24. Though on first glance it seems as though whites would not have been willing to attend black colleges, the data following desegregation suggest otherwise, particularly in border states such as West Virginia. The drastic increase of white enrollment in West Virginia's black colleges following the *Brown* ruling suggests that some whites in other states would have enrolled in black colleges if given the opportunity. Current white enrollment in Bluefield State College of West Virginia and West Virginia State University exceeds 80 percent; from Gasman, Marybeth, Benjamin Baez, Noah D. Drezner, Katherine V. Sedgwick, Christopher Tudico, and Julie M. Schmid. 2007. "Historically Black Colleges and Universities: Recent Trends". A Report of the American Association of University Professors.

25. Anderson, James D. 1988.

26. Statistics from Minor, James T. 2008.

27. Allen, Walter R. 1992. "The Color of Success: African-American College Student Outcomes at Predominantly White and Historically Black Public Colleges and Universities." *Harvard Educational Review* 62:26–44; Fries-Britt, Sharon and Bridget Turner. 2002. "Uneven Stories: Successful Black Collegians at a Black and a White Campus." *The Review of Higher Education* 25:315–330; Kim, Mikyong Minsun. 2002. "Historically Black vs. White Institutions: Academic Development among Black Students." *The Review of Higher Education* 25:385–407; Outcalt, Charles L. and Thomas E. Skewes-Cox. 2002. "Involvement, Interaction, and Satisfaction: The Human Environment at HBCUs." *The Review of Higher Education* 25:331–347.

28. Humphreys, Jeffrey and Roslyn Korb. 2006. *Economic Impact of the Nation's Historically Black Colleges and Universities.* Washington, DC: U.S. Department of Education, National Center for Education Statistics.

29. Tushnet, Mark V. 1987. *The NAACP's Legal Strategy against Segregated Education, 1925–1950.* Chapel Hill, NC: University of North Carolina Press.

30. Psychologists, sociologist, and higher education researchers have added to historical works by focusing more on the internal dynamics of black colleges opting to investigate issues related to student and faculty development, curriculum, and campus leadership.

31. Holmes, Dwight O. W. 1934. *The Evolution of the Negro College.* New York: Columbia University Press.

32. Samuels, Albert. 2004. *Is Separate Unequal? Black Colleges and the Challenge to Desegregation.* Lawrence, KS: University Press of Kansas; From Tushnet, Mark V. 1997. Only one student attended the Oklahoma law school for blacks during the eighteen months in which it remained open. P. 123. In Texas, the space for the black law school could accommodate no more than ten students. P. 126.

33. Gasman, Marybeth. 2007. *Envisioning Black Colleges: A History of the United Negro College Fund.* Baltimore, MD: Johns Hopkins University Press.

Chapter 1. The Black Higher Education Field

1. http://www.lincoln.edu/about.html; Though Cheyney University of Pennsylvania claims itself as the oldest historically black college, the institution did not begin with the intent to offer postsecondary education to black Americans when it opened in 1837. Not until 1913 did Cheyney brand itself as a college.

2. See Appendix 1 for a listing of the schools.

3. Figure 1.1 represents a histogram of founding dates for the 145 schools for which founding dates were identified.

4. Anderson, James. 1988.

5. Tarrow, Sidney. 1998. *Power in Movement: Social Movements and Contentious Politics.* Cambridge: Cambridge University Press; Rao, Hayagreeva, Calvin Morrill, and Mayer N. Zald. 2000. "Power Plays: How Social Movements and Collective Action Create New Organizational Forms." *Research in Organizational Behaviour* 22:239–282.

6. Wacquant, Loïc. 2002. "From Slavery to Mass Incarceration: Rethinking the 'Race Question' in the US." *New Left Review* 13:41–59. P. 46.

7. Meyer, John and Brian Rowan. 1977.

8. Anderson, James D. 1988; Anderson, Eric, and Alfred A. Moss Jr. 1999.

9. According to the population ecology perspective espoused by Michael Hannan and John Freeman, the carrying capacity of any population is fixed, that is, the environment can only sustain a certain number and type of organizations. This appears to have been true for the black colleges. Though 154 schools were identified, it appears as though no more than 120 of these schools existed at any one moment. Most lists of black colleges in the current day include 105–116 schools.

10. Anderson, James D. 1988.

11. Ibid.

12. The religious societies included the Colored Methodist Episcopal, American Missionary Association, Black Baptist, Methodist Episcopal Church, African Methodist Episcopal, American Baptist Home Missionary Society, Catholic, Disciples of Christ, Presbyterian, and Episcopal.

13. Holmes, Dwight O. W. 1934.

14. Du Bois, W. E. B. 1903. *Souls of Black Folk*. New York: Bantam Books; Anderson, James D. 1988.

15. Holmes, Dwight O. W. 1934; Anderson, James D. 1988.

16. Sixteen schools would go on to obtain the land grant designation.

17. Anderson, James D. 1997.

18. Stinchcombe, Arthur. 1965. "Social Structure and Organizations." Pp. 142–193 in *Handbook of Organizations*, edited by J. March. Chicago: Rand McNally. P. 172.

19. Holmes, Dwight O. W. 1935, p. 85.

20. Ibid., p. 87.

21. U.S. Department of the Interior. 1929; Anderson, James D. 1988.

22. McPherson, James M. 1992. *Abraham Lincoln and the Second American Revolution*. Oxford: Oxford University Press. P. 19.

23. Holmes, Dwight O. W. 1934; U.S. Department of Education. 1982. "The Traditionally Black Institutions of Higher Education." Washington DC: National Center for Education Statistics.

24. Anderson, James D. 1988, p. 73.

25. Ibid., p. 77.

26. Ibid., p. 33.

27. Ibid., p. 80.

28. Ibid., p. 33.

29. DiMaggio, Paul and Walter Powell. 1983. "The Iron Cage Revisited: Institutional Isomorphism and Collective Rationality in Organizational Fields." *American Sociological Review* 48:147–160.

30. Rockefeller Archive Center, GEB archives.

31. Johnson, Donald. 2000. "W. E. B. Du Bois, Thomas Jesse Jones, and the Struggle for Social Education, 1900–1930." *Journal of Negro History* 85:71–95.

32. Woodson, Carter G. 1950. "Thomas Jesse Jones." *Journal of Negro History* 35: 107–109.

33. Ibid.

34. U.S. Department of the Interior, Bureau of Education. 1916. "Negro Education: A Study of the Private and Higher Schools for Colored People in the United States." Washington, DC: U.S. Government Printing Office.

35. Du Bois, W. E. B. 1900. *The College Bred Negro*. Atlanta, GA: Atlanta University Press. P. 3.

36. *Journal of Negro Education* Web site. http://www.journalnegroed.org /generalinfo.html.

37. Anderson, Eric and Alfred A. Moss Jr. 1999.

38. The black colleges had such meager endowments that in his 1922 book *College and University Finance*, General Education Board officer Trevor Arnett did not even request information from the black colleges. Arnett argued that the book intended to speak to the challenges of endowed schools and the black colleges did not fit this criterion. GEB, Series 1, Subseries 2, Box 271, Folder 2801, RAC.

39. Figures from Holmes, Dwight O. W. 1934, p. 185.

40. U.S. Department of Interior, 1916 report, I, p. 55.

41. Holmes, Dwight O. W. 1934, p. 161.

42. Anderson, James D. 1988, p. 197.

43. Ibid., p. 202.

44. Ibid., p. 236–237. Figures from Tables 6.5 and 6.6.

45. Jenkins, Martin D. 1943. "Enrollment in Institutions of Higher Education for Negroes, 1942–43." *The Journal of Negro Education* 12:687–693.

46. Anderson, James D. 1988.

47. Not all schools provided detailed information on the area in which a degree was awarded. Among those that provided this information, education accounted for 256, agriculture 84, home economics 62, and theology 53 of the bachelor degrees awarded between 1922 and 1927.

48. Anderson, James D. 1988; Gaines, Kevin G. 1996. *Uplifting the Race: Black Leadership, Politics, and Culture in the Twentieth Century.* Chapel Hill, NC: University of North Carolina Press.

49. The Supreme Court cited the changes in the role of the state as a major provider of education for the nation as a whole and blacks in particular as a factor that contributed to its ruling in favor of plaintiffs in *Brown.*

50. Tushnet, Mark V. 1987.

51. Ibid., p. 122.

52. U.S. Department of Education. 1982.

53. Anderson, James D. 1997.

54. Ibid; Samuels, Albert. 2004.

55. Anderson, James D. 1997, p. 302.

56. Ibid., p. 305.

57. Ibid., p. 307.

58. Ibid., p. 308.

59. U. S. Department of Education. 1982.

60. Gasman, Marybeth. 2007.

61. Samuels, Albert. 2004.

62. Roebuck, Julian B. and Komanduri S. Murty. 1993. *Historically Black Colleges and Universities: Their Place in American Higher Education.* Westport, CT: Praeger; Brooks, F. Erik and Glenn L. Starks. 2011.

63. Roebuck, Julian and Komanduri Murty. 1993; Brooks, F. Erik and Glenn Starks. 2011.

64. U.S. Department of Education. 1982.

65. Figures come from U.S. Department of Education. 1996 report, Table 45 contains data related to private colleges. P. 74.

66. Brooks, F. Erik and Glenn Starks. 2011.

67. Ibid.

68. Ibid; U.S. Department of Education. 1982.

69. To comply with Title VI of the 1964 Civil Rights Act, colleges began to provide enrollment data by race to the U.S. Department of Education. Beginning in 1976, the Higher Education General Information Survey later named the Integrated Postsecondary Education Data Survey collected this data from colleges on an annual basis.

70. Brooks, F. Erik and Glenn Starks. 2011.

Chapter 2. Collective Action and Status Inequality

1. 1944 Financial Report for Benedict College, Columbia South Carolina To the Board of Education of the Northern Baptist Convention, folder 4170, box 317, series 1, General Education Board Archives, RAC.

2. C. E. Lucas to Edward Sage, May 12, 1923, folder 304, box 33, series 1, General Education Board Archives, RAC.

3. W. S. Scarborough to Edward Sage, September 29, 1911, folder 6340, box 597, series 1, General Education Board Archives, RAC.

4. Jackson Davis to David D. Jones, November 2, 1945, folder 1059, box 117, series 1, General Education Board Archives, RAC.

5. Folder 1059, box 117, series 1, General Education Board Archives, RAC.

6. Gasman, Marybeth. 2007.

7. Ibid.

8. UNCF Certificate of Incorporation, folder 5238, box 491, series 1, General Education Board Archives, RAC.

9. Gasman, Marybeth. 2007; General Education Board Archives, RAC.

10. Gasman, Marybeth. 2007.

11. Pfeffer, Jeffrey and Gerald Salancik. 1978. *The External Control of Organizations: A Resource Dependence Perspective.* New York: Harper and Row.

12. Ninety-four percent of the black colleges had a relationship with the GEB.

13. Stinchcombe, Arthur. 1965. P. 172. In this essay, Stinchcombe called for a theory of status specific to organizations.

14. Roth, Guenther and Claus Wittich, eds. 1978. *Economy and Society: An Outline of Interpretive Sociology.* Berkeley, CA: University of California Press. P. 305.

15. The summary that follows is taken from Sauder, Michael. 2006. "Third Parties and Status Position: How the Characteristics of Status Systems Matter." *Theory and Society* 35:299–321.

16. Washington, Marvin and Edward Zajac. 2006. "Status Evolution and Competition: Theory and Evidence." *Academy of Management Journal* 48:282–296.

17. Meyer, John, David Tyack, Joane Nagel, and Audri Gordon. 1979. "Public Education as Nation-Building in America." *American Journal of Sociology* 85:591–613.

18. Ibid.

19. Notice of GEB Beginning, folder 163, box 17, Educational interest series, RG 2 OMR, Rockefeller Family Archives, RAC.

20. Anderson, James D. 1988.

21. Ibid.

22. Ibid., p. 86.

23. Gates, Frederick. T. 1977. *Chapters in My Life: Frederick Taylor Gates.* New York: The Free Press.

24. The UNCF developed a membership path for those schools deemed ineligible at this point, ensuring that all private black colleges that became accredited would have the opportunity to affiliate with the UNCF.

25. Proceedings from the Association of Colleges and Secondary Schools for Negroes, folder 4017, box 391, series 1, General Education Board Archives, RAC.

26. By using reports issued by the *Journal of Negro Education,* the Association of College and Secondary Schools for Negroes, and the College Blue Book, I identified fifty private black colleges that existed at the time of the UNCF's formation. Of these fifty, fourteen schools did not meet the UNCF's rating requirement.

27. Holmes, Dwight. O. W. 1934; Anderson, James D. 1988.

28. An account of the General Education Board activities from 1902 thru June 30, 1914, folder 3, box 1, series 918, General Education Board Archives, RAC.

29. Ibid.

30. Ibid.

31. Jenkins, Martin D. 1943.

32. Gilmartin, Kevin. J. 1981. *Development of Indicators of the Viability of Higher Education Institutions.* Palo Alto, CA: Statistical Analysis Group in Education.

33. Baum, Joel. A. C. 1996. "Organizational Ecology." Pp. 77–114 in *Handbook of Organizational Studies,* edited by S. R. Clegg, C. Hardy, and W. R. Nord. Thousand Oaks, CA: Sage Press. P. 79.

34. Ibid; Stinchcombe, Albert. 1965.

35. Meeting minutes from United Negro College Fund Exploratory Committee, April 19, 1943, folder 655, box 94, Educational Interests series, RG 2 OMR, Rockefeller Family Archives, RAC.

36. A. R. Mann to Jackson Davis, September 12, 1941, folder 457, box 51, series 1, General Education Board Archives, RAC.

37. Gilmartin, Kevin. 1981.

38. Southern Association of Colleges and Secondary Schools Brochure, folder 4993, box 468, series 1, General Education Board Archives, RAC.

39. Arnett, Trevor. 1922. *College and University Finance*, p. 14; Report of Florida Black College Ratings by Southern Association of Colleges and Secondary Schools from D. E. Williams to J. Henry Highsmith, November 25, 1947, folder 4992, box 467, series 1, General Education Board Archives, RAC.

40. Holmes, Dwight O. W. 1934, p. 189.

41. Abraham Flexner to William Graves, March 19, 1917, folder 1227, box 133, series, 1, General Education Board Archives, RAC.

42. Abraham Flexner to Henry Pritchett, April 22, 1921, folder 1229, box 133, series, 1, General Education Board Archives, RAC.

43. Conference regarding support for Meharry Medical College between Albert Mann, Robert Lambert, and Jackson Davis, February 14, 1944, folder 1245, box 135, series 1, General Education Board Archives, RAC.

44. Raymond Fosdick to Winthrop Aldrich Rockefeller, February 15, 1944, folder 1245, box 135, series 1, General Education Board Archives, RAC.

45. Report on the Investment Committee of Meharry Medical College between Albert Mann and Chancellor O. C. Carmichael, March 14, 1944, folder 1245, box 135, series 1, General Education Board Archives, RAC.

46. Anderson, James. 1988; Anderson, Eric and Alfred Moss Jr. 1999.

47. J. F. Lane to Leo Favrot, May 19, 1937, folder 1430, box 154, series 1, General Education Board Archives, RAC.

48. Leo Favrot to J. F. Lane, May 25, 1937, folder 1430, box 154, series 1, General Education Board Archives, RAC.

49. Personal Correspondence between General Education Board officers, 1937, folder 457, box 50, series 1, General Education Board Archives, RAC.

50. Meeting minutes from United Negro College Fund Exploratory Committee, April 19, 1943, folder 655, box 94, Educational Interests series, RG 2 OMR, Rockefeller Family Archives, RAC.

51. Gasman, Marybeth. 2007.

52. Stuart, Toby, Ha Hoang, and Ralph Hybels. 1999. "Interorganizational Endorsements and the Performance of Entrepreneurial Ventures." *Administrative Science Quarterly* 44:315–349.

53. Ibid.

54. Report on the activities at Talladega College, Jackson Davis visit, December 1926, folder 86, box 11, series 1, General Education Board Archives, RAC.

55. William Brierly to Fred Brownlee, January 19, 1932, folder 88, box 11, series 1, General Education Board Archives, RAC.

56. William Brierly to Buel G. Gallagher, April 1, 1936, folder 89, box 12, series 1, General Education Board Archives, RAC.

57. October 1939, folder 5123, box 481, series 1, General Education Board Archives, RAC.

58. Leo Favrot to George A. Works, October 6, 1938, folder 5125, box 481, series 1, General Education Board Archives, RAC.

59. Report on the activities at Talladega College, Jackson Davis visit, December 1927, Folder 86, Box 11, series 1, General Education Board Archives, RAC.

60. Report on the activities at Wilberforce University, Trevor Arnett visit, April 1922, folder 6341, box 597, series 1, General Education Board Archives, RAC.

61. Leo Favrot to Gilber H. Jones, March 2, 1929, folder 6342, box 597, series 1, General Education Board Archives, RAC.

62. Correspondence 1932, box 11, folder 88, series 1, General Education Board Archives, RAC.

63. Leo Favrot to D. Ormonde Walker, January 15, 1938, folder 6342, box 597, series 1, General Education Board Archives, RAC.

64. Abraham Flexner to William Graves, March 19, 1917, folder 1227, box 133, series, 1, General Education Board Archives, RAC.

65. Edward Sage to George W. Hubbard, December 10, 1917, folder 1228, box 133, series 1, General Education Board Archives, RAC. Wallace Buttrick to Thomas Nichols, March 3, 1919, folder 1228, box 133, series 1, General Education Board Archives, RAC.

66. Conference regarding support for Meharry Medical College between Albert Mann, Robert Lambert, and Jackson Davis, February 14, 1944, folder 1245, box 135, series 1, General Education Board Archives, RAC.

67. Officer diary entry, Robert A. Lambert, November 23, 1943, folder 1244, box 135, series 1, General Education Board Archives, RAC.

Chapter 3. Advocacy and Racial Inequality

An earlier version of this chapter, "Mobilizing Elites: The Framing Activities of the United Negro College Fund" appeared in the September 2010 issue of *Mobilization.*

1. Nationally, the UNCF's leadership consisted of a chairman, vice-chairman, the Chairman's Advisory Committee, a national treasurer, the Campaign Executive Committee, and the Committee of College Presidents. A mix of blacks and whites served throughout the organization, though during the first ten years, when present, black leaders were mainly found on the Committee of College Presidents.

2. Rockefeller Archive Center. 1952. General Education Board Archives, Series 1.3, Box 492, Folder 5241. Sleepy Hollow, NY. United Negro College Fund Publicity Guide.

3. Rockefeller Archive Center. 1952. General Education Board Archives, Series 1.3, Box 492, Folder 5241. Sleepy Hollow, NY. United Negro College Fund Chairman's Desk Book.

4. Rockefeller Archive Center. 1947. Office of the Messers Rockefeller, Educational Interests, Record Group III2G, Box 94, Folder 655C. Sleepy Hollow, NY. Correspondence of Laurance S. Rockefeller.

5. Rockefeller Archive Center. 1951. General Education Board Archives, Series 1.3, Box 490, Folder 5243. Sleepy Hollow, NY. Memo regarding New York Men's committee work, January.

6. Jenkins, Martin D. 1944. "Current Trends and Events of National Importance in Negro Education: Section A: Enrollment in Institutions of Higher Education for Negroes." *The Journal of Negro Education,* 13:227–233; United Negro College Fund. 1946. "A Memorandum Concerning the United Negro College Fund, Inc." In *United Negro College Fund Archives,* Robert W. Woodruff Library, Atlanta University Center, Atlanta, GA.

7. Goffman, Erving. 1974. *Frame Analysis: An Essay on the Organization of Experience.* New York: Harper and Row. Pp. 10–11.

8. Benford, Robert and David Snow. 2000. "Framing Processes and Social Movements: An Overview and Assessment." *Annual Review of Sociology* 26:611–639.

9. Goffman, Erving. 1974.

10. McAdam, Doug. 1982. *Political Process and the Development of Black Insurgency 1930–1970.* Chicago: University of Chicago Press; Tarrow, Sidney. 1998.

11. Ferree, Myra Marx. 2003. "Resonance and Radicalism: Feminist Framing in the Abortion Debates of the United States and Germany." *American Journal of Sociology* 109:304–334; Ferree, Myra M., William A. Gamson, Jurgen Gerhards, and Dieter Rucht. 2002. *Shaping Abortion Discourse: Democracy and the Public Sphere in Germany and the United States.* Cambridge: Cambridge University Press; Gerhards, Jurgen and Dieter Rucht. 1992. "Mesomobilization: Organizing and Framing in Two Protest Campaigns in West Germany." *American Journal of Sociology* 98:555–595.

12. Three questions served as a guide: How did the UNCF describe the social condition of black Americans? How did the UNCF describe the social condition of black Americans seeking a higher education? What role did the UNCF suggest black higher education has in mediating the social condition of black Americans? See Appendix 3 for further details.

13. Gaines, Kevin G. 1996.

14. Baker, Lee D. 1998. *From Savage to Negro: Anthropology and the Construction of Race, 1896–1954.* Berkeley: University of California Press.

15. Ibid., p. 31.

16. Ibid; Behrens, Angela, Christopher Uggen, and Jeff Manza. 2003. "Ballot Manipulation and the 'Menace of Negro Domination': Racial Threat and Felon Disenfranchisement in the United States, 1850–2002." *American Journal of Sociology* 109:559–605.

17. Baker, Lee. 1998, p. 36.

18. Gaines, Kevin. 1996.

19. United Negro College Fund. 1954. "If You Have Built Castles in the Air, Your Work Need Not Be Lost." *United Negro College Fund Archives*, Robert W. Woodruff Library, Atlanta University Center, Atlanta, GA.

20. United Negro College Fund. 1954. "A Statement of the Work of the United Negro College Fund and Its Member Colleges." *United Negro College Fund Archives*, Robert W. Woodruff Library, Atlanta University Center, Atlanta, GA.

21. United Negro College Fund. 1945. "Thirty-Two Steps Forward to a Better America." *United Negro College Fund Archives*, Robert W. Woodruff Library, Atlanta University Center, Atlanta, GA.

22. United Negro College Fund. 1954. "If You Have Built Castles in the Air, Your Work Need Not Be Lost."

23. United Negro College Fund, 1948. "Much with Little." *United Negro College Fund Archives*, Robert W. Woodruff Library, Atlanta University Center, Atlanta, GA.

24. United Negro College Fund. 1946. "Tomorrow's Generation." *United Negro College Fund Archives*, Robert W. Woodruff Library, Atlanta University Center, Atlanta, GA.

25. United Negro College Fund. 1945. "Thirty-Two Steps Forward to a Better America."

26. Ibid.

27. United Negro College Fund. 1946. "Tomorrow's Generation."

28. United Negro College Fund. 1951. "Abroad in the Land." *United Negro College Fund Archives*, Robert W. Woodruff Library, Atlanta University Center, Atlanta, GA.

29. United Negro College Fund. 1953. "A Statement of the Work of the United Negro College Fund and Its Member Colleges." *United Negro College Fund Archives*, Robert W. Woodruff Library, Atlanta University Center, Atlanta, GA.

30. United Negro College Fund. 1954. "If You Have Built Castles in the Air, Your Work Need Not Be Lost."

31. United Negro College Fund. 1945. "Thirty-Two Steps Forward to a Better America."

32. United Negro College Fund. 1947. "A Memorandum Concerning the United Negro College Fund, Inc." *United Negro College Fund Archives*, Robert W. Woodruff Library, Atlanta University Center, Atlanta, GA.

33. United Negro College Fund. 1954. "If You Have Built Castles in the Air, Your Work Need Not Be Lost."

34. United Negro College Fund. 1947. "A Memorandum Concerning the United Negro College Fund, Inc."

35. United Negro College Fund. 1954. "If You Have Built Castles in the Air, Your Work Need Not Be Lost."

36. United Negro College Fund. 1947. "Teach Hope to All." *United Negro College Fund Archives*, Robert W. Woodruff Library, Atlanta University Center, Atlanta, GA.

37. Du Bois, W. E. B. 1903; Anderson, James. 1988.

38. Sociologist Mario Diani posits that particular framing strategies have a higher likelihood of success dependent upon the divisions and opportunities for action within the political environment. Diani, Mario. 1996. "Linking Mobilization Frames and Political Opportunities: Insights from Regional Populism in Italy." *American Sociological Review* 61:1053–1069.

39. United Negro College Fund. 1949. "A Statement of the Work of the United Negro College Fund and Its Member Colleges." *United Negro College Fund Archives*, Robert W. Woodruff Library, Atlanta University Center, Atlanta, GA.

40. United Negro College Fund. 1953. "A Statement of the Work of the United Negro College Fund and Its Member Colleges." *United Negro College Fund Archives*, Robert W. Woodruff Library, Atlanta University Center, Atlanta, GA.

41. United Negro College Fund. 1950. "A Part of the American Harvest." *United Negro College Fund Archives*, Robert W. Woodruff Library, Atlanta University Center, Atlanta, GA.

42. United Negro College Fund. 1952. "A Statement of the Work of the United Negro College Fund and Its Member Colleges." *United Negro College Fund Archives*, Robert W. Woodruff Library, Atlanta University Center, Atlanta, GA.

43. Ibid.

44. United Negro College Fund. 1949. "A Statement of the Work of the United Negro College Fund and Its Member Colleges."

45. Gaines, Kevin. 1996.

46. United Negro College Fund. 1953. "Ten Best Years." *United Negro College Fund Archives*, Robert W. Woodruff Library, Atlanta University Center, Atlanta, GA.

47. Valocchi, Steve. 1996. "The Emergence of the Integrationist Ideology in the Civil Rights Movement." *Social Problems* 43:116–130.

48. Tushnet, Mark. 1987, p. 34.

49. Ibid.

50. Ibid.

51. Ibid.

52. Rockefeller Archive Center. 1951. General Education Board Archives, Series 1.3, Box 491, Folder 5239. Sleepy Hollow, NY. Speech by Charles Dollard at the United Negro College Fund Convocation, October 8.

53. United Negro College Fund. 1954. "A Statement of the Work of the United Negro College Fund and Its Member Colleges."

54. Anderson, Eric and Alfred Moss Jr. 1999, p. 28.

55. United Negro College Fund. 1946. "Evaluation of the 1946 Case." *United Negro College Fund Archives*, Robert W. Woodruff Library, Atlanta University Center, Atlanta, GA.

56. Ibid.

57. Meier, August, and Elliott Rudwick. 1976. "Attorneys Black and White: A Case Study of Race Relations within the NAACP." *The Journal of American History* 62:913–946.

58. Rockefeller Archive Center. 1947. Office of the Messers Rockefeller, Educational Interests, Record Group III2G, Box 94, Folder 655C. Sleepy Hollow, NY. Correspondence between Lindsey F. Kimball and Arthur W. Packard, June 23.

59. United Negro College Fund. 1946. "Tomorrow's Generation."

60. Data on donations came from UNCF brochures and reports. Individual donation totals for 1944, 1946, 1947, 1950, 1951, and 1952.

Chapter 4. Adapting to a World without State-Sanctioned Racial Inequality

1. Lynne Zucker's 1977 experimental study, "The Role of Institutionalization in Cultural Persistence." *American Sociological Review* 42:726–743, documented the process of cultural transmission between individuals. The more official a practice appeared, the easier it was to transmit from one set of participants to the next. Moreover, it was harder to deviate from such practices over time as well. The state's endorsement of racial inequality and the practices associated with it aided the transmission of these practices from generation to generation.

2. Thomas Lawrence and Roy Suddaby define institutional work as the creative and knowledgeable work of actors that may or may not achieve its desired ends and which interacts with existing social and technological structures in unintended and unexpected ways. 2006. "Institutions and Institutional Work." Pp. 215–254 in In *Handbook of Organization Studies*, edited by S. Clegg, C. Hardy, T. Lawrence, and W. R. Nord, 2nd ed. Thousand Oaks, CA: Sage.

3. Text of ruling cited from 1954 NAACP Annual Report: *The Year of the Great Decision*, pp. 81–85.

4. Samuels, Albert L. 2004, p. 62.

5. Jenkins, Martin D. 1958. "The Future of the Desegregated Negro College: A Critical Summary." *Journal of Negro Education* 27:419–429. P. 419.

6. Ibid., p. 419; emphasis in the original.

7. Johnson, Guy B. 1958. "Desegregation and the Future of the Negro College: A Critical Summary." *Journal of Negro Education* 27:430–435. P. 434.

8. Samuels, Albert L. 2004, p. 66.

9. Ibid.

10. Taylor, Edward and Steven Olswang. 1999. "Peril or Promise: The Effect of Desegregation Litigation on Historically Black Colleges." *The Western Journal of Black Studies* 23:73–82.

11. Samuels, Albert L. 2004, p. 79.

12. Ibid.

13. Ibid.

14. Ibid., p. 81.

15. Ibid.

16. Ibid., p. 83.

17. Schneiberg, Marc. 2007. "What's on the Path? Path Dependence, Organizational Diversity and the Problem of Institutional Change in the US Economy, 1900–1950." *Socio-Economic Review* 5:47–80. P. 52.

18. Samuels, Albert L. 2004, p. 80.

19. Friedland, Roger and Robert R. Alford. 1991. "Bringing Society Back In: Symbols, Practices, and Institutional Contradictions." Pp. 232–263 in *The New Institutionalism in Organizational Analysis*, edited by W. W. Powell and P. J. DiMaggio. Chicago: University of Chicago Press. P. 248.

20. Ibid.

21. Samuels, Albert L. 2004, p. 81.

22. Ibid., p. 84; emphasis in the original.

23. Taylor, Edward and Steven Olswang. 1999, p. 75.

24. Moreover, according to legal scholar Anthony Ngula Luti, "because of the extent to which the contemporary HBCU is publicly funded, there is no tangible difference between it and a public institution of higher education. As a result, there is a need to demonstrate why . . . 'private' HBCUs are constitutionally sound." P. 471. Luti, Anthony N. 1999. "When a Door Closes, a Window Opens: Do Today's Private Historically Black Colleges and Universities Run Afoul of Conventional Equal Protection Analysis?" *Howard Law Journal* 42:469–504.

25. Ware, Leland. 1994. "The Most Visible Vestige: Black Colleges after Fordice." *Boston College Law Review* 35:633–680. P. 648.

26. Samuels, Albert L. 2004., p. 85.

27. Ibid.

28. Ware, Leland. 1994, p. 651.

29. Ibid.

30. Samuels, Albert L. 2004, p. 86.

31. Ware, Leland. 1994.

32. Ibid., p. 654.

33. Samuels, Albert L. 2004, p. 104, Table 4.

34. Ibid., pp. 104–105.

35. Ibid., p. 110.

36. Ibid., p. 112.

37. Ibid., p. 124.

38. The *Ayers* case was initiated in 1975. The parties attempted to negotiate an agreement for many years. After these negotiations failed, the case came to trial in 1987. See Samuels, Albert L. 2004. p. 125.

39. Ibid.

40. Smith, Tarvald A. 1993. "*United States v. Fordice*: The Interpretation of Desegregation in Higher Education and the Struggle for the Survival of the Historically Black College in America." *Southern University Law Review* 20:407–439.

41. Ibid.: 413.

42. Ibid.

43. Samuels, Albert L. 2004, p. 127.

44. Ibid.

45. Ibid., p. 128.

46. Ibid., p. 129.

47. Ibid., p. 130.

48. Ibid., p. 131.

49. Ibid., p. 136.

50. Ware, Leland. 2004.

51. Samuels, Albert L. 2004, p. 137.

52. Zietsma, Charlene and Brent McKnight. 2009. "Building the Iron Cage: Institutional Creation Work in the Context of Competing Proto-Institutions." Pp. 143–177 in *Institutional Work: Actors and Agency in Institutional Studies of Organization*, edited by T. B. Lawrence, R. Suddaby, and B. Leca. Cambridge: Cambridge University Press. P. 144.

53. Lawrence, Thomas B., Roy Suddaby, and Bernard Leca. 2009. "Introduction: Theorizing and Studying Institutional Work." Pp. 1–28 in *Institutional Work: Actors and Agency in Institutional Studies of Organizations*, edited by T. B. Lawrence, R. Suddaby, and B. Leca. Cambridge: Cambridge University Press. P. 20.

54. Smith, Tarvald A. 1993, p. 412.

55. Brown-Scott, Wendy. 1994. "Race Consciousness in Higher Education: Does "Sound Educational Policy" Support the Continued Existence of Historically Black Colleges?" *Emory Law Journal* 43:1–81. P. 54.

56. Adams, Frank, Jr. 1996. "Why Brown v. Board of Education and Affirmative Action can Save Historically Black Colleges." *Alabama Law Review* 47:481–511. P. 488.

57. Smith, Tarvald A. 1993, p. 408.

58. McKenzie, Thomas L. 1993. "United States v Fordice: Does the End of 'Separate and Unequal' also Spell the End of Historically Black Colleges." *Western State University Law Review* 20:735–747. P. 746.

59. Smith, Tarvald A. 1993, p. 420.

60. Ibid., p. 421.

61. McKenzie, Thomas L. 1993, p. 746.

62. Ibid.

63. Brown-Scott, Wendy. 1994, p. 8.

64. Smith, Tarvald A. 1993, p. 434.

65. Brown-Scott, Wendy. 1994, p. 35.

66. Ibid.

67. Adams, Frank, Jr. 1996, p. 495. Even Albert Samuels argued that litigators in the *Sweatt* and *McLaurin* cases underestimated the amount of progress that the "hastily created" black graduate and professional schools had made since their opening. Critics failed to recognize that once created, organizations take on a life of their own and the people employed by them tend to pursue the goal to which they have been assigned.

68. Samuels, Albert L. 2004, p. 56.

69. Adams, Frank, Jr. 1996, p. 497.

70. Schneiberg, Marc. 2007, p. 66.

71. Ibid.: 64.

72. Brown-Scott, Wendy. 1994, p. 25.

73. Ibid.

74. Smith, Tarvald A. 1993, p. 435.

75. Brown-Scott, Wendy. 1994.

76. Ibid.

77. Samuels, Albert L. 2004, p. 118.

78. Ibid.

79. Ibid.

80. Ibid.

81. Ibid.

82. Ibid., p. 119.

83. Ibid.

84. Brown-Scott, Wendy. 1994, p. 18.

85. Samuels, Albert L. 2004, p. 120.

86. Ibid.

87. Ibid, p. 117.

88. Ibid.

89. Anderson, James D. 1988.

90. Minor, James T. 2008. "A Contemporary Perspective on the Role of Public HBCUs: Perspicacity from Mississippi." *Journal of Negro Education* 77:323–335. P. 330.

91. Brown II, M. Christopher. 2001. "Collegiate Desegregation and the Public Black College: A New Policy Mandate." *Journal of Higher Education* 72:42–62. P. 52.

92. Ibid.

93. Ibid.

94. Gasman. 2007, p. 70.

95. Brown II, M. Christopher. 2001.

96. Hebel, Sara. 2004. "Supreme Court Clears Way for Settlement of College-Desegregation Case." *The Chronicle of Higher Education,* Oct. 29, 2004.

97. Ibid.

98. Gasman et al. 2007, p. 70.

99. Hebel, Sara. 2004.

100. Gasman et al. 2007, p. 70.

101. Minor, James T. 2008, p. 330.

102. Ibid.

103. Hebel, Sara. 2004.

104. Iaschik, Scott. 2009. "Threat to Black Colleges." *Inside Higher Ed.,* Nov. 17, 2009.

105. Palmer, Robert T., Ryan J. Davis, and Marybeth Gasman. 2011. "A Matter of Diversity, Equity, and Necessity: The Tension between Maryland's Higher Education System and its Historically Black Colleges and Universities over the

Office of Civil Rights Agreement." *Journal of Negro Education* 80:121–133. P. 125.

106. Ibid.

107. Ibid.: 126.

108. Ibid.: 127.

109. Ibid.: 128.

110. Ibid.

111. Brown-Scott, Wendy. 1994, p. 20.

112. Ibid.

113. Ibid., p. 42.

114. Minor, James T. 2008.

115. Ibid.: 331.

116. Perna, Laura W., Jeffrey Milem, Danette Gerald, Evan Baum, Heather Rowan, and Neal Hutchens. 2006. "The Status of Equity for Black Undergraduates in Public Higher Education in the South: Still Separate and Unequal." *Research in Higher Education* 47:197–228.

117. Perna and colleagues measured using the Academic Equity Index. The index represents a particular racial/ethnic group among all those with a particular outcome (e.g., blacks enrolled in college) relative to the representation of that group among the reference group (e.g., black high school graduates). Perna and colleagues focused on three categories of civil rights oversight: states monitored by the Office of Civil Rights (OCR), states ruled in compliance by OCR, and states under court order. No category of oversight improved black equity outcomes.

118. Minor, James T. 2008, p. 327.

119. Palmer et al., 2011.

120. Minor, James T. 2008, p. 331.

121. Ibid.

Chapter 5. Building Legitimacy amid Inequality

1. I am not endorsing the perspective that the policies associated with this time period were in actuality racially neutral. As discussed in chapter 4, the policies disadvantaged black colleges relative to traditionally white ones. However, these policies did require colleges to have racially neutral outcomes. Colleges were not supposed to be racially identified by their outcomes.

2. Meyer, John W. and Brian Rowan. 1977.

3. Suchman, Mark. 1995. "Managing Legitimacy: Strategic and Institutional Approaches." *Academy of Management Review* 20:571–610. P .574.

4. Hannan and Freeman. 1977.

5. DiMaggio, Paul and Walter Powell. 1983.

6. For an alternative perspective on the causes of isomorphism stemming from competitive influences, refer to the population ecology approach as espoused by Hannan and Freeman 1977.

7. Meyer and Rowan. 1977.

8. As discussed in chapter 4, the institutional environment refers to the regulatory, normative, and cultural-cognitive scripts that guide everyday action.

9. Data come from Ruggles, Steven, Matthew Sobek, Trent Alexander, Catherine A. Fitch, Ronald Goeken, Patricia Kelly Hall, Miriam King, and Chad Ronnander. 2009. Integrated Public Use Microdata Series: Version 4.0 (machine-readable database). Minneapolis: Minnesota Population Center. Teaching-related occupations included all occupations listed as art teachers, college presidents and deans, professors and instructors, dance teachers, music teachers, and the general category of teachers.

10. See Appendix 4 for methodological details.

11. When evaluated against their northeastern counterparts, private black colleges tended to offer their students more equivalent opportunities, yet differences still existed. Take Fisk University and Amherst College—both private institutions with approximately 1,200 students enrolled in the 1968–69 academic year. Students at the black college, Fisk, had access to twenty-two bachelor degree programs whereas those at Amherst, the traditionally white college, had access to thirty-two programs.

12. Barman, Emily and Heather MacIndoe. 2012. "Institutional Pressures and Organizational Capacity: The Case of Outcome Measurement." *Sociological Forum* 72:70–90. P. 72.

13. Tillman, Linda C. 2004. "(Un)Intended Consequences?: The Impact of the Brown v. Board of Education Decision on the Employment Status of Black Educators." *Education and Urban Society* 36:280–303. P. 281.

14. Ibid.

15. Freeman, Richard B. 1976. *Black Elite: The New Market for Highly Educated Black Americans.* New York: McGraw-Hill.

16. Anderson, James D. 1988.

17. Ethridge, Samuel. 1979. "Impact of the 1954 *Brown v. Topeka Board of Education* Decision on Black Educators." *Negro Educational Review* 30:217–32. P. 220.

18. Smith, G. 1987. "The Effects of Competency Testing on the Supply of Minority Teachers." Washington, DC: National Education Association and the Council of Chief State School Officers.

19. Freeman, Richard B. 1976.

20. Webster, David S., Russell L. Stockard, and James W. Henson. 1981. "Black Student Elite: Enrollment Shifts of High-Achieving, High Socioeconomic Status Black Students from Black to White Colleges During the 1970s." *College and University: Journal of the American Association of Collegiate Registrars* 56:283–291. P. 286.

21. Stevens, Mitchell, Elizabeth Armstrong, and Richard Arum. 2008. "Sieve, Incubator, Temple, Hub: Empirical and Theoretical Advances in the Sociology of Higher Education." *Annual Review of Sociology* 43:127–151.

22. Edelman, Lauren. 1992. "Legal Ambiguity and Symbolic Structures: Organizational Mediation of Civil Rights Law." *American Journal of Sociology* 97: 1531–1576; Kelly, Erin and Frank Dobbin. 1998. "How Affirmative Action Became Diversity Management: Employer Response to Antidiscrimination Law, 1961–1996." *American Behavioral Scientist* 41: 960–984; Stainback, Kevin and Donald Tomaskovic-Devey. 2012. *Documenting Desegregation: Racial and Gender Segregation in Private-Sector Employment Since the Civil Rights Act.* New York: Russell Sage Foundation.

23. Data from Stainback, Kevin and Donald Tomaskovic-Devey. 2012. Figure 3.3, P. 95.

24. According to Stainback and Tomaskovic-Devey's analysis, while black men and women continued to face barriers obtaining managerial jobs, professional occupations—those requiring specific educational credentials—offered more promising opportunities for college-educated blacks (p. 135). Between 1973 and 1980, black men and women's representation in professional occupations increased by 6 and 9 percent respectively (p. 136). The numbers may seem small, but given their virtual exclusion from such positions the gains were large. Between 1966 and 2005, the authors found that black men and women increased their presence in industries where credentials became a more prominent selection mechanism (pp. 238–240).

25. Brown-Scott, Wendy. 1994, p. 25.

26. Ibid.

27. Perna et al., p. 198.

28. Ibid., p. 207.

29. The correlation between occupational data from the 1970, 1980, and 1990 census and the percentage of earned degrees in business and education for the academic year prior to the census (1968–69, 1978–79, and 1988–89) was confirmed using a Spearman analysis. The spearman analysis tests for the null hypothesis that two variables are not correlated with one another. The results suggested a strong positive relationship between the percentage of college-educated blacks working as teachers and the percentage of earned degrees in education at black colleges. The results also suggested a strong positive relationship between the percentage of college-educated blacks working as managers and professionals and the percentage of earned degrees in business at black colleges.

30. http://rockarch.org/collections/rockorgs/geb.php.

31. GEB had planned to spend down its funds and dissolve itself.

32. Drewry, Henry N. and Humphrey Doermann. 2001. *Stand and Prosper: Private Black Colleges and Their Students.* Princeton, NJ: Princeton University Press. P. 108.

33. http://rockarch.org/collections/ford/.

34. Drewry, Henry N. and Humphrey Doermann. 2001.

35. Ibid., p. 263.

36. Albert E. Manley to James Armsey. Report concerning the Fine Arts as they relate to Negroes generally in the United States and to the predominantly

Negro colleges. Part I, Survey of the Problems. October 5, 1966. L67-458. Ford Foundation Archives. Rockefeller Archive Center. P. 8.

37. Ibid., p. 4.

38. Ibid.

39. Ibid., pp. 6–7.

40. Benjamin E. Mays to Robert Weaver. A Proposed Program of Training and Research in Public and International Affairs. March 23, 1960. L60-1142. Ford Foundation Archives. Rockefeller Archive Center. P. 6.

41. Ivy F. Steber to Benjamin F. Payton. Close-Out Memo. May 4, 1979. Ford Foundation Archive. Rockefeller Archive Center.

42. Joseph N. Gayles to Marilyn Coolen. Final Report on the Ford Foundation Grant Number 700-0502 in support of Strengthening the Social Sciences at Talladega College Talladega, Alabama. November 7, 1977. Evaluation pp. 3–4. Ford Foundation Archive. Rockefeller Archive Center.

43. Samuels, Albert. 2004, p. 35.

44. Ibid., pp. 53–54.

45. Ibid., pp. 84–86.

46. Jackson, Jerlando F. L., Michael T. Snowden, and Suzanne E. Eckes. 2002. "Fordice as a Window of Opportunity: The Case for Maintaining Historically Black Colleges and Universities (HBCUS) as Predominantly Black Institutions." West's Education Law Reporter 1:1–19.

47. Cass, James and Max Birnbaum. 1965. Comparative Guide to American Colleges: For Students, Parents, and Counselors. New York: Harper and Row.

48. Using procedures specified by Agresti and Agresti, 1978, the index of diversity was calculated by determining the proportion, p, of students that graduated with degrees in i, for all programs, k and then subtracting this sum from 1.

49. The variance and standard deviation of the earned degree distributions are calculated and used to obtain a z-statistic, which determines if the null hypothesis that the variation levels are equal to one another should be rejected.

50. $z = 2.78$, one-tailed, $\alpha = 0.05$.

51. The comparisons of the diversity indices no longer yield significantly different results ($z = 0.27$).

52. Meyer, John W., and Brian Rowan. 1977.

53. Philips, Damon J. and Ezra W. Zuckerman. 2001. "Middle-Status Conformity: Theoretical Restatement and Empirical Demonstrations in Two Markets." American Journal of Sociology 107:379–429.

54. Ibid., p. 382.

55. Gurin, Patricia. 1966. "Social Class Constraints on the Occupational Aspirations of Students Attending Some Predominantly Negro Colleges." Journal of Negro Education 35:336–350. Gurin argued that instead of facilitating student access to majors linked to new career opportunities, black colleges could continue to focus on developing the next generation of black social and political leadership by further emphasizing traditional majors such as education.

56. Albert, Stuart and David A. Whetten. 1985. "Organizational Identity." Pp. 263–295 in *Research in Organizational Behavior*, edited by R. Sutton and B. Staw. Greenwich, CT: JAI Press. P. 265.

Chapter 6. The Story of Organizational Adaptation

1. Donation figures obtained from UNCF brochures and correspondence records. These documents did not always separate out the total amounts raised from particular groups and therefore the figures for the percentage of philanthropic giving were calculated using data from the following years 1944, 1946, 1947, 1950, 1951, and 1952.

2. Meyer, Allen D. 1982. "Adapting to Environmental Jolts." *Administrative Science Quarterly* 27:515–537.

3. Fligstein, Neil and Doug McAdam. 2012. *A Theory of Fields*. Oxford: Oxford University Press. P. 17.

4. Ibid., p. 13.

5. Ibid., p. 99.

6. King, Brayden. 2011. "The Tactical Disruptiveness of Social Movements: Sources of Market and Mediated Disruption in Corporate Boycotts." *Social Problems* 58:491–517. King, Brayden. 2008. "A Political Mediation Model of Corporate Response to Social Movement Activism." *Administrative Science Quarterly* 50:395–421.

7. Bourdieu, Pierre and Loïc J. D. Wacquant. 1992. *An Invitation to Reflexive Sociology*. Chicago: University of Chicago Press.

8. Meier, August and John H. Bracey Jr. 1993. "The NAACP as a Reform Movement, 1909–65: 'To Reach the Conscience of America.'" *Journal of Southern History* 59:3–30. The Garland Fund supported the NAACP's legal strategy aimed at securing black access to graduate and professional programs in the South and the NAACP's equalization strategy. According to the NAACP's 25th Annual Report for 1934, the money was to be "used exclusively for a campaign of legal action and public education against unequal apportionment of public funds for education and discrimination in public transportation." P. 22.

9. In *Theory of Fields*, Fligstein and McAdam argue that having the social skill to induce cooperation and appeal to others is key to both creating and sustaining fields. P. 46.

10. According to Fligstein and McAdam, opportunities for transformation exist when dominant field members have trouble reproducing their privilege. Dominant field members are likely to cling to the status quo and manipulate "the same symbols, identities, and tactics that have always proved successful in the past." P. 112.

11. Brooks, F. E. and Glenn L. Starks. 2011.

12. Ibid.

13. Ibid.

14. McCarthy, John D. and Mayer Zald. 1977. "Resource Mobilization and Social Movements: A Partial Theory." *American Journal of Sociology* 82:1212–1241. P. 1217.

15. As early as 1978, Mayer N. Zald and Michael A. Berger, in "Social Movements in Organizations: Coup d'Etat, Insurgency, and Mass Movements," *American Journal of Sociology* 83:823–861, argued that much of what accounted for organizational change could be attributed to movement-like forces emanating from both within and outside of organizations. The 2005 volume *Social Movements and Organization Theory*, edited by Gerald F. Davis, Doug McAdam, W. Richard Scott, and Mayer N. Zald (New York: Cambridge University Press) documented the processes by which social movements infiltrate and ultimately transform field-level behavior and outcomes.

16. See Hoffman, Andrew J. 1997. *From Heresy to Dogma: An Institutional History of Corporate Environmentalism.* San Francisco: The New Lexington Press for a study of the relationship between the environmental movement and corporate practices. See Rojas, Fabio. 2007. *From Black Power to Black Studies: How a Radical Social Movement Became an Academic Discipline.* Baltimore, MD: Johns Hopkins University Press for an investigation of the relationship between the Black Power movement and the rise of black studies.

17. In his book *From Black Power to Black Studies: How a Radical Social Movement Became an Academic Discipline*, Fabio Rojas chronicles Stokely Carmichael's time at Howard University, the four students from North Carolina A&T who led the 1960 Greensboro lunch counter sit-in, and H. Rap Brown's time at Southern University. Doug McAdam also cited the black colleges as organizational bases of strength for the civil rights movement in his book *Political Processes and the Development of Black Insurgency, 1930–1970.*

18. Based on data from Doug McAdam's *Political Processes and the Development of Black Insurgency, 1930–1970,* the NAACP and the NAACP Legal Defense Fund had significantly larger income than groups such as the Student Non-Violent Coordinating Committee, the Congress On Racial Equality, and the Southern Christian Leadership Committee.

19. Rojas, Fabio. 2007, p. 32.

20. See Wolters, Raymond. 1975. *The New Negro on Campus.* Princeton, NJ: Princeton University Press for a historical perspective on the conservative reaction of black college officials to student unrest.

21. Rojas, Fabio. 2007, p. 27.

22. Greene, David A. 2004. *The Women's Movement and the Politics of Change at a Women's College: Jill Ker Conway at Smith, 1975–1985.* New York: Routledge Falmer. P. 23.

23. Kendall, Elaine. 1976. *"Peculiar Institutions": An Informal History of the Seven Sister Colleges.* New York: G. P. Putnam's Sons.

24. Cole, Wade M. 2011. *Uncommon Schools: The Global Rise of Postsecondary Institutions for Indigenous Peoples.* Stanford, CA: Stanford University Press.

25. Ibid., p. 2.

26. For a theoretical perspective on the way in which inequality regimes intersect see Patricia Hill Collins. 2005. *Black Sexual Politics: African Americans, Gender, and the New Racism.* New York: Routledge.

27. Newcomber, Mabel. 1959. *A Century of Higher Education for American Women.* New York: Harper and Brothers. Statistics from p. 37, Table 1, and p. 39.

28. Ibid., p. 39.

29. Ibid., p. 49, Table 3.

30. Kendall. Elaine. 1976.

31. Newcomber, Mabel. 1959, pp. 38–40.

32. Heaphy, Emily D. 2003. "Repertoires of Organizational Identity: Women's Colleges and Decisions Regarding Coeducation and Closure, 1968–1985." Unpublished manuscript. University of Michigan.

33. Cole, Wade M. 2011.

34. Ibid., p. 189.

35. Newcomer, Mabel. 1959.

36. Ibid.

37. Eisenmann, Linda. 2006. *Higher Education for Women in Postwar America, 1945–1965.* Baltimore, MD: Johns Hopkins University Press.

38. Newcomer, Mabel. 1959; Kendall, Elaine. 1976.

39. Harwarth, Irene, Mindi Maline, and Elizabeth DeBra. 1997. "Women's Colleges in the United States: History, Issues, and Challenges." Washington, D.C: National Institute of Postsecondary Education.

40. Greene, David A. 2004.

41. Ibid.

42. Ibid, p. 24.

43. Avent-Holt, Dustin and Donald Tomaskovic-Devey. 2010.

44. Brooks, F. Erik and Glenn L. Stark. 2011.

45. National Center for Education Statistics. 1996. *Historically Black Colleges and Universities: 1976 to 1994.* Washington, DC: U.S. Department of Education.

46. Anderson, Eric and Alfred Moss Jr. 1999.

47. Brooks, F. E. and Glenn L. Starks. 2011.

Appendix 1

1. For some of the schools I found nothing more than a name, perhaps a founding date, during archival research, but I was unable to identify any related statistical information; conflicting founding dates existed for many schools. In most cases, the conflicting dates were a few years apart, likely reflecting the difference between the first attempts to organize a school and the official chartering. Holmes reported Morris College of South Carolina's founding date as 1905 whereas Brooks and Starks reported the school's founding date as 1908. In other

instances, conflicting dates resulted from rechartering. Originally opened as a private college in 1909, North Carolina College for Negroes was later chartered as a public school by the state in 1925. Disagreements exist regarding how to designate the list of black colleges. The 1982 report issued by the U.S. Department of Education designated 105 schools founded prior to 1954 for the purpose of educating blacks as black colleges while recognizing the presence of other more and less inclusive listings. If the date of 1964 is chosen, a more expansive listing of black colleges results, as in Roebuck and Murty's 1993 study of 109 black colleges. Still other lists put the number beyond 110, opting to include those schools founded after 1964 for the purpose of educating black students and schools whose student bodies are majority black regardless of this intention. When HEGIS and or IPEDS data were used, in this study, I focused those colleges founded prior to 1964 and located within the continental United States.

Appendix 2

1. I was able to obtain enrollment information for two schools from correspondence files of the General Education Board; thus, the imputations were performed for two schools.

2. Baum. 1996; Hannan and Freeman. 1984; Stinchcombe. 1965.

3. Figures reported in Drewry and Doermann. 2001. P. 269.

Appendix 3

1. Gerteis, Joseph. 2002. "The Possession of Civic Virtue: Movement Narratives of Race and Class in the Knights of Labor." *American Journal of Sociology* 108: 580–615.

Appendix 4

1. Holmes, Dwight O. W. 1934; Bowman, J. Wilson. 1999. *America's Black and Tribal Colleges*. Quality Books.

2. Kraatz, Matthew S. and Edward J. Zajac. 1996. "Exploring the Limits of the New Institutionalism: The Causes and Consequences of Illegitimate Organizational Change." *American Sociological Review*, 61(5):812–836.

3. Agresti, Alan and Barbara F. Agresti. 1978. "Statistical Analysis of Qualitative Variation." *Sociological Methodology* 9:204–237.

References

Acker, Joan. 2006. "Inequality Regimes: Gender, Class, and Race in Organizations." *Gender and Society* 20(2):441–464. P. 443.

Adams, Frank Jr. 1996. "Why *Brown v. Board of Education* and Affirmative Action Can Save Historically Black Colleges." *Alabama Law Review* 47(2):481–511.

Agresti, Alan and Barbara F. Agresti. 1978. "Statistical Analysis of Qualitative Variation." *Sociological Methodology* 9:204–237.

Albert, Stuart and David A. Whetten. 1985. "Organizational Identity." Pp. 263–95 in *Research in Organizational Behavior*, edited by R. Sutton and B. Staw. Greenwich, CT: JAI Press.

Allen, Walter R. 1992. "The Color of Success: African-American College Student Outcomes at Predominantly White and Historically Black Public Colleges and Universities." *Harvard Educational Review* 62 (1):26–44.

Anderson, Eric and Alfred A. Moss. 1999. *Dangerous Donations: Northern Philanthropy and Southern Black Education, 1902–1930.* Columbia, MO: University of Missouri Press.

Anderson, James D. 1988. *The Education of Blacks in the South, 1860–1935.* Chapel Hill, NC: University of North Carolina Press.

———. 1997. "Philanthropy, the State, and the Development of Historically Black Public Colleges: The Case of Mississippi." *Minerva* 35(3):295–309.

Arnett, Trevor. 1922. *College and University Finance.* New York: General Education Board.

Avent-Holt, Dustin and Donald Tomaskovic-Devey. 2010. "The Relational Basis of Inequality: Generic and Contingent Wage Distribution Processes." *Work and Occupations* 37(2):162–193.

Baker, Lee D. 1998. *From Savage to Negro: Anthropology and the Construction of Race, 1896–1954.* Berkeley, CA: University of California Press.

Barman, Emily and Heather MacIndoe. 2012. "Institutional Pressures and Organizational Capacity: The Case of Outcome Measurement." *Sociological Forum* 72(1):70–90.

Baum, Joel A. C. 1996. "Organizational Ecology." Pp. 77–114 in *Handbook of Organizational Studies*, edited by S. R. Clegg and W. R. Nord. Thousand Oaks, CA: Sage.

Behrens, Angela, Christopher Uggen, and Jeff Manza. 2003. "Ballot Manipulation and the 'Menace of Negro Domination': Racial Threat and Felon Disenfranchisement in the United States, 1850–2002." *American Journal of Sociology* 109(3):559–605.

Benford, Robert D. and David A. Snow. 2000. "Framing Processes and Social Movements: An Overview and Assessment." *Annual Review of Sociology* 26:611–639.

Berbrier, Mitch. 1998. "'Half the Battle': Cultural Resonance, Framing Processes, and Ethnic Affectations in Contemporary White Separatist Rhetoric." *Social Problems* 45(4):431–450.

Bourdieu, Pierre and Loïc J. D. Wacquant. 1992. *An Invitation to Reflexive Sociology*. Chicago: University of Chicago Press.

Bowman, J. Wilson. 1999. America's Black and Tribal Colleges. Quality Books.

Branch, Enobong H. 2011. *Opportunity Denied: Limiting Black Women to Devalued Work*. New Brunswick, NJ: Rutgers University Press.

Brooks, F. E. and Glenn L. Starks. 2011. *Historically Black Colleges and Universities: An Encyclopedia*. Santa Barbara, CA: Greenwood.

Brown II, M. Christopher. 2001. "Collegiate Desegregation and the Public Black College: A New Policy Mandate." *Journal of Higher Education* 72(1):42–62.

Brown-Scott, Wendy. 1994. "Race Consciousness in Higher Education: Does "Sound Educational Policy" Support the Continued Existence of Historically Black Colleges?" *Emory Law Journal* 43(1):1–81.

Cass, James and Max Birnbaum. 1965. *Comparative Guide to American Colleges: For Students, Parents, and Counselors*. New York: Harper and Row.

Cole, Wade M. 2011. *Uncommon Schools: The Global Rise of Postsecondary Institutions for Indigenous Peoples*. Stanford, CA: Stanford University Press.

Davis, Gerald F. Doug McAdam, W. Richard Scott, and Mayer N. Zald, editors. 2005. *Social Movements and Organization Theory*. New York: Cambridge University Press.

Diani, Mario. 1996. "Linking Mobilization Frames and Political Opportunities: Insights from Regional Populism in Italy." *American Sociological Review* 61(6):1053–1069.

DiMaggio, Paul J. and Walter W. Powell. 1983. "The Iron Cage Revisited: Institutional Isomorphism and Collective Rationality in Organizational Fields." *American Sociological Review* 48(2):147–160.

Drewry, Henry N. and Humphrey Doermann. 2001. *Stand and Prosper: Private Black Colleges and Their Students*. Princeton, NJ: Princeton University Press.

Du Bois, W. E. B. Atlanta University and Schomburg Collection of Negro Literature and History. 1900. *The College-Bred Negro Report of a Social Study*

Made under the Direction of Atlanta University Together with the Proceedings of the Fifth Conference for Study of the Negro Problems Held at Atlanta University, May 29–30, 1900. Atlanta: Atlanta University Press.

———. 1903. *The Souls of Black Folk.* New York: Bantam Books.

Edelman, Lauren B. 1992. "Legal Ambiguity and Symbolic Structures: Organizational Mediation of Civil Rights Law." *American Journal of Sociology* 97(6):1531–1576.

Eisenmann, Linda. 2006. *Higher Education for Women in Postwar America, 1945–1965.* Baltimore, MD: Johns Hopkins University Press.

Ethridge, Samuel. 1979. "Impact of the 1954 *Brown v. Topeka Board of Education* Decision on Black Educators." *Negro Educational Review* 30(4):217–232.

Ferree, Myra M. 2002. *Shaping Abortion Discourse: Democracy and the Public Sphere in Germany and the United States.* New York: Cambridge University Press.

———. 2003. "Resonance and Radicalism: Feminist Framing in the Abortion Debates of the United States and Germany." *American Journal of Sociology* 109(2):304–344.

Fligstein, Neil and Doug McAdam. 2012. *A Theory of Fields.* Oxford: Oxford University Press.

Freeman, Richard B. 1976. *Black Elite: The New Market for Highly Educated Black Americans.* New York: McGraw-Hill.

Friedland, Roger and Robert R. Alford. 1991. "Bringing Society Back In: Symbols, Practices, and Institutional Contradictions." Pp. 232–263 in *The New Institutionalism in Organizational Analysis*, edited by W. W. Powell, and P. J. DiMaggio. Chicago: University of Chicago Press.

Fries-Britt, Sharon and Bridget Turner. 2002. "Uneven Stories: Successful Black Collegians at a Black and a White Campus." *The Review of Higher Education* 25(3):315–330.

Gaines, Kevin G. 1996. *Uplifting the Race: Black Leadership, Politics, and Culture in the Twentieth Century.* Chapel Hill, NC: University of North Carolina Press.

Gasman, Marybeth. 2007. *Envisioning Black Colleges: A History of the United Negro College Fund.* Baltimore, MD: Johns Hopkins University Press.

Gasman, Marybeth, Benjamin Baez, Noah D. Drezner, Katherine V. Sedgwick, Christopher Tudico, and Julie M. Schmid. 2007. "Historically Black Colleges and Universities: Recent Trends." A Report of the American Association of University Professors.

Gates, Frederick T. 1977. *Chapters in My Life.* New York: Free Press.

Gerhards, Jurgen and Dieter Rucht. 1992. "Mesomobilization: Organizing and Framing in Two Protest Campaigns in West Germany." *American Journal of Sociology* 98(3):555–595.

Gerteis, Joseph. 2002. "The Possession of Civic Virtue: Movement Narratives of Race and Class in the Knights of Labor." *American Journal of Sociology* 108(3):580–615.

Gilmartin, Kevin J., American Institutes for Research and National Center for Education Statistics. 1981. *Development of Indicators of the Viability of Higher Education Institutions.* Palo Alto, CA: American Institutes for Research.

Goffman, Erving. 1974. *Frame Analysis: An Essay on the Organization of Experience.* New York: Harper and Row.

Greene, David A. 2004. *The Women's Movement and the Politics of Change at a Women's College: Jill Ker Conway at Smith, 1975–1985.* New York: Routledge Falmer.

Gurin, Patricia. 1966. "Social Class Constraints on the Occupational Aspirations of Students Attending Some Predominantly Negro Colleges." *Journal of Negro Education* 35(4):336–350.

Hannan, Michael T. and John Freeman. 1977. "The Population Ecology of Organizations." *American Journal of Sociology* 82(5):929–964.

Hannan, Michael T. and John Freeman. 1984. "Structural Inertia and Organizational Change." *American Sociological Review* 49(2):149–164.

Harwarth, Irene, Mindi Maline, and Elizabeth DeBra. 1997. *Women's Colleges in the United States: History, Issues, and Challenges.* Washington, D.C: National Institute of Postsecondary Education.

Haydu, Jeffrey. 1998. "Making use of the Past: Time Periods as Cases to Compare and as Sequences of Problem Solving." *American Journal of Sociology* 104(2): 339–371.

Heaphy, Emily D. 2003. "Repertoires of Organizational Identity: Women's Colleges and Decisions Regarding Coeducation and Closure, 1968–1985." Unpublished manuscript. University of Michigan.

Hebel, Sara. 2004. "Supreme Court Clears Way for Settlement of College-Desegregation Case." *The Chronicle of Higher Education* Oct. 29, 2004.

Hill Collins, Patricia. 2005. *Black Sexual Politics: African Americans, Gender, and the New Racism.* New York: Routledge.

Hirsch, Paul M. and Y. Sekou Bermiss. 2009. "Institutional "Dirty" Work: Preserving Institutions Through Strategic Decoupling." Pp. 262–283 in *Institutional Work: Actors and Agency in Institutional Studies of Organizations,* edited by T. B. Lawrence, R. Suddaby, and B. Leca.

Holmes, Dwight O. W. 1934. *The Evolution of the Negro College.* New York: Teachers College, Columbia University.

Hoffman, Andrew J. 1997. *From Heresy to Dogma: An Institutional History of Corporate Environmentalism.* San Francisco: The New Lexington Press.

Humphreys, Jeffrey and Roslyn Korb. 2006. *Economic Impact of the Nation's Historically Black Colleges and Universities.* Washington, DC: U.S. Department of Education, National Center for Education Statistics.

Hurt, Huber W. 1939. *The College Blue Book.* De Land: The College Blue Book.

Iaschik, Scott. 2009. "Threat to Black Colleges." *Inside Higher Ed.* Nov. 17, 2009.

Irons, Jenny. 2010. *Reconstituting Whiteness.* Nashville, TN: Vanderbilt University Press.

Jackson, Jerlando F. L., Michael T. Snowden, and Suzanne E. Eckes. 2002. "Ford-ice as a Window of Opportunity: The Case for Maintaining Historically Black Colleges and Universities (HBCUS) as Predominantly Black Institutions." *West's Education Law Reporter* 1:1–19.

Jenkins, Martin D. 1938. "Enrollment in Negro Colleges and Universities, 1937–38." *The Journal of Negro Education* 7(2):118–123.

———. 1939. "Higher Education: Enrollment in Negro Colleges and Universities, 1938–39." *The Journal of Negro Education* 8(3):247–253.

———. 1942. "Enrollment in Institutions of Higher Education of Negroes 1941–42." *The Journal of Negro Education* 11(2):217–223.

———. 1943. "Enrollment in Institutions of Higher Education for Negroes, 1942–43." *The Journal of Negro Education* 12(4):687–693.

———. 1944. "Current Trends and Events of National Importance in Negro Education: Section A: Enrollment in Institutions of Higher Education for Negroes, 1943–44." *The Journal of Negro Education* 13(2):227–233.

———. 1945. "Enrollment in Institutions of Higher Education for Negros, 1944–45." *The Journal of Negro Education* 14(2):238–244.

———. 1946. "Enrollment in Institutions of Higher Education for Negroes, 1945–46." *The Journal of Negro Education* 15(2):231–239.

———. 1947. "Enrollment in Institutions of Higher Education for Negroes, 1946–47." *The Journal of Negro Education* 16(2):224–232.

———. 1948. "Enrollment in Institutions of Higher Education for Negroes, 1948." *The Journal of Negro Education* 17(2):206–215.

———. 1949. "Enrollment in Institutions of Higher Education for Negroes, 1948–49." *The Journal of Negro Education* 18(4):568–575.

———. 1950. "Enrollment in Institutions of Higher Education for Negroes, 1949–50." *The Journal of Negro Education* 19(2):197–208.

———. 1951. "Enrollment in Institutions of Higher Education for Negroes, 1950–51." *The Journal of Negro Education* 20(2):207–222.

———. 1952. "Enrollment in Institutions of Higher Education for Negroes, 1951–52." *The Journal of Negro Education* 21(2):205–219.

———. 1953. "Enrollment in Institutions of Higher Education for Negroes, 1952–53." *The Journal of Negro Education* 22(2):188–200.

———. 1954. "Enrollment in Institutions of Higher Education for Negroes, 1953–54." *The Journal of Negro Education* 23(2):139–151.

———. 1958. "The Future of the Desegregated Negro College: A Critical Summary." *Journal of Negro Education* 27(3):419–429.

Johnson, Donald. 2000. "W. E. B. DuBois, Thomas Jesse Jones and the Struggle for Social Education, 1900–1930." *The Journal of Negro History* 85(3):71–95.

Johnson, Guy B. 1958. "Desegregation and the Future of the Negro College: A Critical Summary." *Journal of Negro Education* 27(3):430–435.

The Journal of Negro Education. 2013. "A Howard University Quarterly Review of Issues Incident to the Education of Black People." Retrieved April 20, 2013. http://www.journalnegroed.org/generalinfo.html.

Kelly, Erin and Frank Dobbin. 1998. "How Affirmative Action Became Diversity Management: Employer Response to Antidiscrimination Law, 1961–1996." *American Behavioral Scientist* 41(7): 960–984.

Kendall, Elaine. 1976. *"Peculiar Institutions": An Informal History of the Seven Sister Colleges.* New York: G. P. Putnam's Sons.

Kim, Mikyong Minsun. 2002. "Historically Black vs. White Institutions: Academic Development among Black Students." *The Review of Higher Education* 25(4):385–407.

King, Brayden. 2008. "A Political Mediation Model of Corporate Response to Social Movement Activism." *Administrative Science Quarterly* 50(3):395–421.

———. 2011. "The Tactical Disruptiveness of Social Movements: Sources of Market and Mediated Disruption in Corporate Boycotts." *Social Problems* 58(4):491–517.

Krippendorf, Klaus. 2004. *Content Analysis: An Introduction to its Methodology.* Thousand Oaks, CA: Sage.

Lawrence, Thomas and Roy Suddaby. 2006. "Institutions and Institutional Work." Pp. 215–254 in *Handbook of Organization Studies*, edited by S. Clegg, C. Hardy, T. Lawrence, and W. R. Nord., 2nd ed. Thousand Oaks, CA: Sage.

Lawrence, Thomas B., Roy Suddaby, and Bernard Leca. 2009. "Introduction: Theorizing and Studying Institutional Work." Pp. 1–28 in in *Institutional Work: Actors and Agency in Institutional Studies of Organizations*, edited by T. B. Lawrence, R. Suddaby, and B. Leca. Cambridge: Cambridge University Press.

Lincoln University of the Commonwealth of Pennsylvania. 2013. "About Lincoln: A Legacy of Producing Leaders." Retrieved April 20, 2013. http://www.lincoln.edu/about.html.

Luti, Anthony N. 1999. "When a Door Closes, a Window Opens: Do Today's Private Historically Black Colleges and Universities Run Afoul of Conventional Equal Protection Analysis?" *Howard Law Journal* 42(Spring):469–504.

Massey, Douglas S. and Nancy A. Denton. 1993. *American Apartheid: Segregation and the Making of the Underclass.* Cambridge, MA: Harvard University Press.

McAdam, Doug. 1982. *Political Process and the Development of Black Insurgency, 1930–1970.* Chicago: University of Chicago Press.

McCarthy, John D. and Mayer N. Zald. 1977. "Resource Mobilization and Social Movements: A Partial Theory." *American Journal of Sociology* 82(6):1212–1241.

McKenzie, Thomas L. 1993. *"United States v Fordice*: Does the End of 'Separate and Unequal' also Spell the End of Historically Black Colleges?" *Western State University Law Review* 20:735–747.

McPherson, James M. 1992. *Abraham Lincoln and the Second American Revolution.* New York: Oxford University Press.

Meier, August and John H. Bracey Jr. 1993. "The NAACP as a Reform Movement, 1909–65: "To Reach the Conscience of America." *Journal of Southern History* 59(1):3–30.

Meier, August and Elliott Rudwick. 1976. "Attorneys Black and White: A Case Study of Race Relations Within." *The Journal of American History,* 62(4):913–946.

Meyer, Allen D. 1982. "Adapting to Environmental Jolts." *Administrative Science Quarterly* 27(4):515–537.

Meyer, John W. and Brian Rowan. 1977. "Institutionalized Organizations: Formal Structure as Myth and Ceremony." *American Journal of Sociology* 83(2):340–363.

Meyer, John W., David Tyack, Joane Nagel, and Audri Gordon. 1979. "Public Education as Nation-Building in America: Enrollments and Bureaucratization in the American States, 1870–1930." *American Journal of Sociology* 85(3):591–613.

Miles, Matthew B. and A. M. Huberman. 1994. *Qualitative Data Analysis: An Expanded Sourcebook.* Thousand Oaks, CA: Sage.

Minor, James T. 2008. "A Contemporary Perspective on the Role of Public HBCUs: Perspicacity from Mississippi." *Journal of Negro Education* 77(4):323–335.

———. 2008. *Contemporary HBCUs: Considering Institutional Capacity and State Priorities. A Research Report.* Michigan State University, College of Education, Department of Educational Administration. East Lansing, MI.

National Association for the Advancement of Colored People. 1954. Annual Report: *The Year of the Great Decision.* New York.

Newcomber, Mabel. 1959. *A Century of Higher Education for American Women.* New York: Harper and Brothers.

Omi, Michael and Howard Winant. 1994. *Racial Formation in the United State: From the 1960s to the 1990s.* New York: Routledge.

Orfield, Gary. 1969. *The Reconstruction of Southern Education: The Schools and the 1964 Civil Rights Act.* New York: John Wiley and Sons.

Outcalt, Charles L. and Thomas E. Skewes-Cox. 2002. "Involvement, Interaction, and Satisfaction: The Human Environment at HBCUs." *The Review of Higher Education* 25(3):331–347.

Palmer, Robert T., Ryan J. Davis, and Marybeth Gasman. 2011. "A Matter of Diversity, Equity, and Necessity: The Tension between Maryland's Higher Education System and its Historically Black Colleges and Universities over the Office of Civil Rights Agreement." *Journal of Negro Education* 80(2):121–133.

Pager, Devah. 2003. "The Mark of a Criminal Record." *American Journal of Sociology* 108(5):937–975.

Pellow, David N. 1999. "Framing Emerging Environmental Movement Tactics: Mobilizing Consensus, Demobilizing Conflict." *Sociological Forum* 14(4):659–683.

Perna, Laura W., Jeffrey Milem, Danette Gerald, Evan Baum, Heather Rowan, and Neal Hutchens. 2006. "The Status of Equity for Black Undergraduates in Public Higher Education in the South: Still Separate and Unequal." *Research in Higher Education* 47(2):197–228.

Pfeffer, Jeffrey and Gerald R. Salancik. 1978. *The External Control of Organizations: A Resource Dependence Perspective.* New York: Harper and Row.

Philips, Damon J. and Ezra W. Zuckerman. 2001. "Middle-Status Conformity: Theoretical Restatement and Empirical Demonstrations in Two Markets." *American Journal of Sociology* 107(2):379–429.

Rao, Hayagreeva, Calvin Morrill, and Mayer N. Zald. 2000. "Power Plays: How Social Movements and Collective Action Create New Organizational Forms." *Research in Organizational Behaviour* 22:239–282.

Roebuck, Julian B. and Komanduri S. Murty. 1993. *Historically Black Colleges and Universities: Their Place in American Higher Education.* Westport, CT: Praeger.

Rojas, Fabio. 2007. *From Black Power to Black Studies: How a Radical Social Movement Became an Academic Discipline.* Baltimore, MD: Johns Hopkins University Press.

Roth, Guenther and Claus Wittich, eds. 1978. *Economy and Society: An Outline of Interpretive Sociology.* Berkeley, CA: University of California Press.

Sampson, Robert J. and Stephen W. Raudenbush. 2004. "Seeing Disorder: Neighborhood Stigma and the Social Construction of 'Broken Windows.'" *Social Psychological Quarterly* 67(4):319–342.

Samuels, Albert L. 2004. *Is Separate Unequal? Black Colleges and the Challenge to Desegregation.* Lawrence, KS: University Press of Kansas.

Sauder, Michael. 2006. "Third Parties and Status Position: How the Characteristics of Status Systems Matter." *Theory and Society* 35(3):299–321.

Scott, W. R. 1995. *Institutions and Organizations.* Thousand Oaks, CA: Sage.

———. 2000. *Institutional Change and Healthcare Organizations: From Professional Dominance to Managed Care.* Chicago; London: The University of Chicago Press.

Scott, Richard W., Martin Ruef, Peter J. Mendel, and Carol A. Caronna. 2000. *Institutional Change and Healthcare Organizations: From Professional Dominance to Managed Care.* Chicago: University of Chicago Press.

Sealander, Judith. 1997. *Private Wealth & Public Life: Foundation Philanthropy and the Reshaping of American Social Policy from the Progressive Era to the New Deal.* Baltimore, MD: Johns Hopkins University Press.

Schneiberg, Marc. 2007. "What's on the Path? Path Dependence, Organizational Diversity and the Problem of Institutional Change in the US Economy, 1900–1950." *Socio-Economic Review* 5(1):47–80.

Smith, G. 1987. "The Effects of Competency Testing on the Supply of Minority Teachers." Washington, DC: National Education Association and the Council of Chief State School Officers.

Smith, Tarvald A. 1993. "*United States v. Fordice*: The Interpretation of Desegregation in Higher Education and the Struggle for the Survival of the Historically Black College in America." *Southern University Law Review* 20(2):407–439.

Stainback, Kevin and Donald Tomaskovic-Devey. 2012. *Documenting Desegregation: Racial and Gender Segregation in Private-Sector Employment Since the Civil Rights Act.* New York: Russell Sage Foundation.

Stevens, Mitchell, Elizabeth Armstrong, and Richard Arum. 2008. "Sieve, Incubator, Temple, Hub: Empirical and Theoretical Advances in the Sociology of Higher Education." *Annual Review of Sociology* 43:127–151.

Stinchcombe, Arthur. 1965. "Social Structure and Organization." Pp. 142–193 in *Handbook of Organizations*, edited by J. March. Chicago: Rand McNally.

Stuart, Toby E., Ha Hoang, and Ralph C. Hybels. 1999. "Interorganizational Endorsements and the Performance of Entrepreneurial Ventures." *Administrative Science Quarterly* 44(2):315–349.

Suchman, Mark. 1995. "Managing Legitimacy: Strategic and Institutional Approaches." *Academy of Management Review* 20(2):571–610.

Tarrow, Sidney G. 1998. *Power in Movement: Social Movements and Contentious Politics.* New York: Cambridge University Press.

Taylor, Edward and Steven Olswang. 1999. "Peril or Promise: The Effect of Desegregation Litigation on Historically Black Colleges." *The Western Journal of Black Studies,* 23(2):73–82.

Tillman, Linda C. 2004. "(Un)Intended Consequences?: The Impact of the *Brown v. Board of Education* Decision on the Employment Status of Black Educators." *Education and Urban Society* 36(3):280–303.

Tushnet, Mark V. 1987. *The NAACP's Legal Strategy against Segregated Education, 1925–1950.* Chapel Hill, NC: University of North Carolina Press.

Valocchi, Steve. 1996. "The Emergence of the Integrationist Ideology in the Civil Rights Movement." *Social Problems* 43(1):116–130.

Veblen, Thorstein. 1994 [1899]. *The Theory of the Leisure Class.* New York: Dover.

Vogus, Timothy J. and Gerald F. Davis. 2005. "Elite Mobilizatios for Antitakeover Legislation, 1982–1990." Pp. 96–121 in *Social Movements and Organization Theory*, edited by G. F. Davis, D. McAdam, W. R. Scott, and M. Zald.

Wacquant, Loïc. 2002. "From Slavery to Mass Incarceration." *New Left Review* (13):41–60.

Ware, Leland. 1994. "The Most Visible Vestige: Black Colleges after *Fordice.*" *Boston College Law Review* 35(3):633–680.

Washington, Marvin and Edward J. Zajac. 2005. "Status Evolution and Competition: Theory and Evidence." *The Academy of Management Journal* 48(2):282–296.

Webster, David S., Russell L. Stockard, and James W. Henson. 1981. "Black Student Elite: Enrollment Shifts of High-Achieving, High Socioeconomic Status Black Students from Black to White Colleges During the 1970s." *College and University: Journal of the American Association of Collegiate Registrars* 56(3):283–291.

Wolters, Raymond. 1975. *The New Negro on Campus: Black College Rebellions of the 1920s.* Princeton, NJ: Princeton University Press.

Woodson, Carter G. 1950. "Thomas Jesse Jones." *Journal of Negro History* 35(1):107–109.

Wooten, Melissa. 2006. "Race and Strategic Organization." *Strategic Organization* 4(2):191–199.

Zald, Mayer N. and Michael A. Berger. 1978. "Social Movements in Organizations: Coup d'Etat, Insurgency, and Mass Movements." *American Journal of Sociology* 83(4):823–861.

Zietsma, Charlene and Brent McKnight. 2009. "Building the Iron Cage: Institutional Creation Work in the Context of Competing Proto-Institutions." Pp. 143–177 in *Institutional Work: Actors and Agency in Institutional Studies of Organization*, edited by T. B. Lawrence, R. Suddaby, and B. Leca. Cambridge: Cambridge University Press.

Zucker, Lynne G. 1977. "The Role of Institutionalization in Cultural Persistence." *American Sociological Review* 42(5):726–743.

Archival Sources

Rockefeller Archive Center. 1902–1953. General Education Board Archives, Series 1.1, Boxes 49–50. Correspondence between Atlanta University and General Education Board Officials.

———. 1911. General Education Board Archives, Series 1.1, Box 597, Folder 6340. W. S. Scarborough to Edward Sage dated September 29, 1911.

———. 1914. General Education Board Archives, Administration, Program and Policy, Series 918, Box 1, Folder 3. An Account of the General Education Board Activities dated 1902–June 30, 1914.

———. 1917a. General Education Board Archives, Series 1.1, Box 133, Folder 1227. Abraham Flexner to William Graves, dated March 19.

———. 1917b. General Education Board Archives, Series 1.1, Box 133, Folder 1228. Edward Sage to George W. Hubbard, dated December 10.

———. 1919a. General Education Board Archives, Series 1.1, Box 133, Folder 1228. Wallace Buttrick to Thomas Nichols, dated March 3.

———. 1919b. General Education Board Archives, Series 1.1, Box 163, Folder 1523. President Maxsom Bishop College Vision Statement dated July 7.

———. 1921. General Education Board Archives, Series 1.1, Box 133, Folder 1229. Abraham Flexner to Henry Pritchett, dated April 22.

———. 1922a. General Education Board Archives, Series 1.1, Box 497, Folder 6341. Report on the Activities at Wilberforce University, Trevor Arnett visit, dated April 1922.

———. 1922b. General Education Board Archives, Series 1.1, Subseries 2, Box 271, Folder 2801. College and University Finance, Trevor Arnett, dated 1922.

———. 1923. General Education Board Archives, Series 1.1, Box 33, Folder 304. C. E. Lucas to Edward Sage dated May 12.

———. 1926. General Education Board Archives, Series 1.1, Box 11, Folder 86. Report on the Activities at Talladega College, Jackson Davis visit, dated December 1926.

———. 1927. General Education Board Archives, Series 1.1, Box 11, Folder 86. Report of the Activities at Talladega College by Jackson Davis, dated December 1927.

———. 1929. General Education Board Archives, Series 1.1, Box 597, Folder 6342. Leo Favrot to Gilber H. Jones, dated March 2.

———. 1932. General Education Board Archives, Series 1.1, Box 11, Folder 88. William Brierly to Fred Brownlee, dated January 19.

———. 1936. General Education Board Archives, Series 1.1, Box 12, Folder 89. William Brierly to Buel G. Gallagher, dated April 1.

———. 1937a. General Education Board Archives, Series 1.1, Box 154, Folder 1430. Personal Correspondence between Leo Favrot and Lane College President J. F. Lane, dated May 19.

———. 1937b. General Education Board Archives, Series 1.1, Box 154, Folder 1430. Personal Correspondence between Leo Favrot and J. F. Lane, dated May 25.

———. 1937c. General Education Board Archives, Series 1.1, Box 50, Folder 457. Personal Correspondence between General Education Board Officers, dated 1937.

———. 1938a. General Education Board Archives, Series 1.1, Box 597, Folder 6342. Leo Favrot to D. Ormonde Walker, dated January 15.

———. 1938b. General Education Board Archives, Series 1.1, Box 481, Folder 5125. Leo Favrot to George A. Works, dated October 6.

———. 1939. General Education Board Archives, Series 1.1, Box 481, Folder 1523. Dated October 1939.

———. 1941a. General Education Board Archives, Series 1.1, Box 51, Folder 457. Personal Correspondence between A. R. Mann and Jackson Davis.

———. 1941b. General Education Board Archives, Series 1.1, Box 50, Folder 457. Personal Correspondence between General Education Board Officers.

———. 1943a. Office of the Messers Rockefeller, Educational Interests, Record Group III2G, Box 94, Folder 655. Meeting Minutes from United Negro College Fund Exploratory Committee, dated April 19.

———. 1943b. General Education Board Archives, Series 1.3, Box 492, Folder 5321. Sleepy Hollow, NY. Correspondence between Frederick Patterson and Jackson Davis, dated May 28.

———. 1943c. General Education Board Archives, Series 1.1, Box 135, Folder 1244. Officer Diary Entry, Robert A. Lambert, dated November 23.

———. 1943d. General Education Board Archives, Series 1.1, Box 491, Folder 5238. UNCF Certificate of Incorporation, dated 1943.

———. 1944a. General Education Board Archives, Series 1.1, Box 135, Folder 1245. Conference Regarding Support for the Meharry Medical College between Albert Mann, Robert Lambert, and Jackson Davis, dated February 14.

———. 1944b. General Education Board Archives, Series 1.1, Box 135, Folder 1245. Raymond Fosdick to Winthrop Aldrich Rockefeller, dated February 15.

———. 1944c. General Education Board Archives, Series 1.1, Box 135, Folder 1245. Report on the Investment Committee of Meharry Medical College between Albert Mann and Chancellor O. C. Carmichael, dated March 14.

———. 1944d. General Education Board Archives, Series 1.1, Box 317, Folder 4170. Financial Report for Benedict College, Columbia, South Carolina, To the Board of Education of the Northern Baptist Convention.

———. 1944e. Office of the Messrs Rockefeller, Educational Interests, Record Group III2G, Box 94, Folder 655. Sleepy Hollow, NY. Correspondence between John D. Rockefeller Jr. and Tougaloo College President Judson L. Cross.

———. 1945. General Education Board Archives, Series 1.1, Box 117, Folder 1059. Jackson Davis to David D. Jones, dated November 2.

———. 1946. General Education Board Archives, Series 1.3, Box 490, Folder 5232. Sleepy Hollow, NY. Correspondence between Frank M. Totton and W. E. Mitchell, dated March 18, April 23, and May 7.

———. 1947a. Office of the Messers Rockefeller, Educational Interests, Record Group III2G, Box 94, Folder 655C. Sleepy Hollow, NY. Letter to John D. Rockefeller, Jr., dated April 18.

———. 1947b. Office of the Messrs Rockefeller, Educational Interests, Record Group III2G, Box 94, Folder 655C. Sleepy Hollow, NY. Correspondence between Lindsey F. Kimball and Arthur W. Packard, dated June 23.

———. 1947c. General Education Board Archives, Series 1.1, Box 467, Folder 4992. Florida Black College Ratings by Southern Association of Colleges and Secondary Schools from D. E. Williams to Henry Highsmith, dated November 25.

———. 1947d. Office of the Messrs Rockefeller, Educational Interests, Record Group III2G, Box 94, Folder 655C. Sleepy Hollow, NY. Correspondence of Laurance S. Rockefeller.

———. 1948. General Education Board Archives, Series 1.3, Box 492, Folder 5241. Sleepy Hollow, NY. Speech by John D. Rockefeller Jr.

————. 1950a. General Education Board Archives, Series 1.3, Box 490, Folder 5234. Sleepy Hollow, NY. Correspondence between William J. Trent and Fred McCuistion, dated February 10.

————. 1950b. General Education Board Archives, Series 1.3, Box 492, Folder 5242. Sleepy Hollow, NY. Memorandum on Some Problems Concerning the Private Negro College, dated October 16.

————. 1951a. General Education Board Archives, Series 1.3, Box 491, Folder 5243. Sleepy Hollow, NY. Memo regarding New York Men's Committee Work, dated January.

————. 1951b. General Education Board Archives, Series 1.3, Box 491, Folder 5239. Sleepy Hollow, NY. Speech by Charles Dollard at the United Negro College Fund Convocation, dated October 8.

————. 1952a. General Education Board Archives, Series 1.3, Box 492, Folder 5241. Sleepy Hollow, NY. United Negro College Fund Publicity Guide.

————. 1952b. General Education Board Archives, Series 1.3, Box 492, Folder 5241. Sleepy Hollow, NY. United Negro College Fund Chairman's Desk Book.

————. 1952c. General Education Board Archives, Series 1.3, Box 492, Folder 5241. Sleepy Hollow, NY. United Negro College Fund Campaign Pledge Sheet.

Rockefeller Archive Center. 1960. Ford Foundation Archives, Benjamin E. Mays to Robert Weaver. A Proposed Program of Training and Research in Public and International Affairs. March 23, 1960. L60-1142.

————. Albert E. Manley to James Armsey. Report Concerning the Fine Arts as They Relate to Negroes Generally in the United States and to the Predominantly Negro Colleges. Part I, Survey of the Problems. October 5, 1966. L67-458.

————. Joseph N. Gayles to Marilyn Coolen. Final Report on the Ford Foundation Grant Number 700-0502 in Support of Strengthening the Social Sciences at Talladega College Talladega, Alabama. November 7, 1977.

————. Ivy F. Steber to Benjamin F. Payton. Close-Out Memo. May 4, 1979.

United Negro College Fund. 1945. United Negro College Fund Archives, Robert W. Woodruff Library, Atlanta University Center, Atlanta Ga. *Thirty-Two Steps Forward to a Better America.*

————. 1946a. United Negro College Fund Archives, Robert W. Woodruff Library, Atlanta University Center, Atlanta, GA. *A Memorandum Concerning the United Negro College Fund, Inc.*

————. 1946b. United Negro College Fund Archives, Robert W. Woodruff Library, Atlanta University Center, Atlanta, GA. *Tomorrow's Generation.*

————. 1946c. United Negro College Fund Archives, Robert W. Woodruff Library, Atlanta University Center, Atlanta GA. *The College Serves the Community.*

———. 1946d. United Negro College Fund Archives, Robert W. Woodruff Library, Atlanta University Center, Atlanta GA. *Evaluation of the 1946 Case.*

———. 1947a. United Negro College Fund Archives, Robert W. Woodruff Library, Atlanta University Center, Atlanta GA. *A Memorandum Concerning the United Negro College Fund, Inc.*

———. 1947b. United Negro College Fund Archives, Robert W. Woodruff Library, Atlanta University Center, Atlanta GA. *Teach Hope to All.*

———. 1948. United Negro College Fund Archives, Robert W. Woodruff Library, Atlanta University Center, Atlanta GA. *Much with Little.*

———. 1949a. United Negro College Fund Archives, Robert W. Woodruff Library, Atlanta University Center, Atlanta GA. *Only a Hope . . . A Hundred Years Ago.*

———. 1949b. United Negro College Fund Archives, Robert W. Woodruff Library, Atlanta University Center, Atlanta GA. *A Statement of the Work of the United Negro College Fund and its Member Colleges.*

———. 1950. United Negro College Fund Archives, Robert W. Woodruff Library, Atlanta University Center, Atlanta GA. *A Part of the American Harvest.*

———. 1951. United Negro College Fund Archives, Robert W. Woodruff Library, Atlanta University Center, Atlanta GA. *Abroad in the Land.*

———. 1952. United Negro College Fund Archives, Robert W. Woodruff Library, Atlanta University Center, Atlanta GA. *A Statement of the Work of the United Negro College Fund and its Member Colleges.*

———. 1953a. United Negro College Fund Archives, Robert W. Woodruff Library, Atlanta University Center, Atlanta GA. *Ten Best Years.*

———. 1953b. United Negro College Fund Archives, Robert W. Woodruff Library, Atlanta University Center, Atlanta GA. *A Statement of the Work of the United Negro College Fund and its Member Colleges.*

———. 1954a. United Negro College Fund Archives, Robert W. Woodruff Library, Atlanta University Center, Atlanta GA. *A Statement of the Work of the United Negro College Fund and its Member Colleges.*

———. 1954b. United Negro College Fund Archives, Robert W. Woodruff Library, Atlanta University Center, Atlanta GA. *If You Have Built Castles in the Air, Your Work Need Not Be Lost.*

———. 1971. United Negro College Fund Archives, Robert W. Woodruff Library, Atlanta University Center, Atlanta GA. American Philanthropy: *Weighted and Found Wanting.*

U.S. Department of Education, 1981. *Development of Indicators of the Viability of Higher Education Institutions.* Washington, DC: National Center for Education Statistics.

———. 1982. *The Traditionally Black Institutions of Higher Education.* Washington, DC: National Center for Education Statistics.

———. 1996. *Historically Black Colleges and Universities: 1976 to 1994.* Washington, DC: National Center for Education Statistics.

———. 2003. *A Study of Higher Education Instructional Expenditures: The Delaware Study of Instructional Costs and Productivity.* Washington, DC: National Center for Education Statistics.

U.S. Department of the Interior, Bureau of Education. 1916. *Negro Education: A Study of the Private and Higher Schools for Colored People in the United States.* Washington, DC: U.S. Government Printing Office.

———. 1929. *Survey of Negro Colleges and Universities.* Washington, DC: U.S. Government Printing Office.

U.S. Department of the Interior, Office of Education. 1942. "National Survey of the Higher Education of Negroes." Washington, DC: U.S. Government Printing Office.

Machine-Readable Files

Ruggles, Steven, Matthew Sobek, Trent Alexander, Catherine A. Fitch, Ronald Goeken, Patricia Kelly Hall, Miriam King, and Chad Ronnander. 2009. Integrated Public Use Microdata Series: Version 4.0 (machine-readable database). Minneapolis: Minnesota Population Center.

U.S. Department of Education, National Center for Education Statistics. 1973–1974. *Higher Education General Information Survey (HEGIS) IX: Degrees and Other Formal Awards Conferred Between July 1, 1973 and June 30, 1974* [Computer File]. ICPSR version. Washington, DC: U.S. Dept. of Education, National Center for Education Statistics [producer]. Ann Arbor, MI: Inter-university Consortium for Political and Social Research [distributor].

———. 1978–1979. *Higher Education General Information Survey (HEGIS) IX: Degrees and Other Formal Awards Conferred Between July 1, 1978 and June 30, 1979* [Computer File]. ICPSR version. Washington, DC: U.S. Dept. of Education, National Center for Education Statistics [producer]. Ann Arbor, MI: Inter-university Consortium for Political and Social Research [distributor].

———. 1988–1989. *Integrated Postsecondary Education Data System (IPEDS): Earned Degrees 1988–1989* [Computer File]. ICPSR version. Washington, DC: U.S. Dept. of Education, Office of Educational Research and Improvement [producer]. Ann Arbor, MI: Inter-university Consortium for Political and Social Research [distributor].

———. 1993–1994. *Integrated Postsecondary Education Data System (IPEDS): Earned Degrees 1993–1994* [Computer File]. ICPSR version. Washington, DC: U.S. Dept. of Education, National Center for Education Statistics [producer]. Ann Arbor, MI: Inter-university Consortium for Political and Social Research [distributor].

———. 1968. *Higher Education General Information Survey (HEGIS): Fall Enrollment 1968* [Computer File]. ICPSR version. Washington, DC: U.S. Dept. of Education, National Center for Education Statistics [producer].

Ann Arbor, MI: Inter-university Consortium for Political and Social Research [distributor].

———. 1968–1969. *Higher Education General Information Survey (HEGIS) IX: Degrees and Other Formal Awards Conferred Between July 1, 1968 and June 30, 1969* [Computer File]. ICPSR version. Washington, DC: U.S. Dept. of Education, National Center for Education Statistics [producer]. Ann Arbor, MI: Inter-university Consortium for Political and Social Research [distributor].

———. 1969. *Higher Education General Information Survey (HEGIS): Fall Enrollment 1969* [Computer File]. ICPSR version. Washington, DC: U.S. Dept. of Education, National Center for Education Statistics [producer]. Ann Arbor, MI: Inter-university Consortium for Political and Social Research [distributor].

———. 1970. *Higher Education General Information Survey (HEGIS): Fall Enrollment 1970* [Computer File]. ICPSR version. Washington, DC: U.S. Dept. of Education, National Center for Education Statistics [producer]. Ann Arbor, MI: Inter-university Consortium for Political and Social Research [distributor].

———. 1971. *Higher Education General Information Survey (HEGIS): Fall Enrollment 1971* [Computer File]. ICPSR version. Washington, DC: U.S. Dept. of Education, National Center for Education Statistics [producer]. Ann Arbor, MI: Inter-university Consortium for Political and Social Research [distributor].

———. 1972. *Higher Education General Information Survey (HEGIS): Fall Enrollment 1972* [Computer File]. ICPSR version. Washington, DC: U.S. Dept. of Education, National Center for Education Statistics [producer]. Ann Arbor, MI: Inter-university Consortium for Political and Social Research [distributor].

———. 1973. *Higher Education General Information Survey (HEGIS): Fall Enrollment 1973* [Computer File]. ICPSR version. Washington, DC: U.S. Dept. of Education, National Center for Education Statistics [producer]. Ann Arbor, MI: Inter-university Consortium for Political and Social Research [distributor].

———. 1974. *Higher Education General Information Survey (HEGIS): Fall Enrollment 1974* [Computer File]. ICPSR version. Washington, DC: U.S. Dept. of Education, National Center for Education Statistics [producer]. Ann Arbor, MI: Inter-university Consortium for Political and Social Research [distributor].

———. 1975. *Higher Education General Information Survey (HEGIS): Fall Enrollment 1975* [Computer File]. ICPSR version. Washington, DC: U.S. Dept. of Education, National Center for Education Statistics [producer]. Ann Arbor, MI: Inter-university Consortium for Political and Social Research [distributor].

———. 1976. *Higher Education General Information Survey (HEGIS): Fall Enrollment 1976* [Computer File]. ICPSR version. Washington, DC: U.S. Dept. of Education, National Center for Education Statistics [producer]. Ann Arbor, MI: Inter-university Consortium for Political and Social Research [distributor].

———. 1977. *Higher Education General Information Survey (HEGIS): Fall Enrollment 1977* [Computer File]. ICPSR version. Washington, DC: U.S. Dept. of Education, National Center for Education Statistics [producer]. Ann Arbor, MI: Inter-university Consortium for Political and Social Research [distributor].

———. 1978. *Higher Education General Information Survey (HEGIS): Fall Enrollment 1978* [Computer File]. ICPSR version. Washington, DC: U.S. Dept. of Education, National Center for Education Statistics [producer]. Ann Arbor, MI: Inter-university Consortium for Political and Social Research [distributor].

———. 1979. *Higher Education General Information Survey (HEGIS): Fall Enrollment 1979* [Computer File]. ICPSR version. Washington, DC: U.S. Dept. of Education, National Center for Education Statistics [producer]. Ann Arbor, MI: Inter-university Consortium for Political and Social Research [distributor].

———. 1980. *Higher Education General Information Survey (HEGIS): Fall Enrollment 1980* [Computer File]. ICPSR version. Washington, DC: U.S. Dept. of Education, National Center for Education Statistics [producer]. Ann Arbor, MI: Inter-university Consortium for Political and Social Research [distributor].

———. 1981. *Higher Education General Information Survey (HEGIS): Fall Enrollment 1981* [Computer File]. ICPSR version. Washington, DC: U.S. Dept. of Education, National Center for Education Statistics [producer]. Ann Arbor, MI: Inter-university Consortium for Political and Social Research [distributor].

———. 1982. *Higher Education General Information Survey (HEGIS): Fall Enrollment 1982* [Computer File]. ICPSR version. Washington, DC: U.S. Dept. of Education, National Center for Education Statistics [producer]. Ann Arbor, MI: Inter-university Consortium for Political and Social Research [distributor].

———. 1983. *Higher Education General Information Survey (HEGIS): Fall Enrollment 1983* [Computer File]. ICPSR version. Washington, DC: U.S. Dept. of Education, National Center for Education Statistics [producer]. Ann Arbor, MI: Inter-university Consortium for Political and Social Research [distributor].

———. 1983–1984. *Higher Education General Information Survey (HEGIS) IX: Degrees and Other Formal Awards Conferred Between July 1, 1983 and June 30, 1984* [Computer File]. ICPSR version. Washington, DC: U.S.

Dept. of Education, National Center for Education Statistics [producer]. Ann Arbor, MI: Inter-university Consortium for Political and Social Research [distributor].

———. 1984. *Higher Education General Information Survey (HEGIS): Fall Enrollment 1984* [Computer File]. ICPSR version. Washington, DC: U.S. Dept. of Education, National Center for Education Statistics [producer]. Ann Arbor, MI: Inter-university Consortium for Political and Social Research [distributor].

———. 1985. *Higher Education General Information Survey (HEGIS): Fall Enrollment 1985* [Computer File]. ICPSR version. Washington, DC: U.S. Dept. of Education, National Center for Education Statistics [producer]. Ann Arbor, MI: Inter-university Consortium for Political and Social Research [distributor].

———. 1986. *Integrated Postsecondary Education Data System (IPEDS): Fall Enrollment 1986* [Computer File]. ICPSR version. Washington, DC: U.S. Dept. of Education, National Center for Education Statistics [producer]. Ann Arbor, MI: Inter-university Consortium for Political and Social Research [distributor].

———. 1987. *Integrated Postsecondary Education Data System (IPEDS): Fall Enrollment 1987* [Computer File]. ICPSR version. Washington, DC: U.S. Dept. of Education, National Center for Education Statistics [producer]. Ann Arbor, MI: Inter-university Consortium for Political and Social Research [distributor].

———. 1988. *Integrated Postsecondary Education Data System (IPEDS): Fall Enrollment Analysis 1988* [Computer File]. ICPSR version. Washington, DC: U.S. Dept. of Education, National Center for Education Statistics [producer]. Ann Arbor, MI: Inter-university Consortium for Political and Social Research [distributor].

———. 1989. *Integrated Postsecondary Education Data System (IPEDS): Fall Enrollment Analysis 1989* [Computer File]. ICPSR version. Washington, DC: U.S. Dept. of Education, National Center for Education Statistics [producer]. Ann Arbor, MI: Inter-university Consortium for Political and Social Research [distributor].

———. 1990. *Integrated Postsecondary Education Data System (IPEDS): Fall Enrollment Analysis 1990* [Computer File]. ICPSR version. Washington, DC: U.S. Dept. of Education, National Center for Education Statistics [producer]. Ann Arbor, MI: Inter-university Consortium for Political and Social Research [distributor].

———. 1991–1992. *Integrated Postsecondary Education Data System (IPEDS): Fall Enrollment Analysis 1991–1992* [Computer File]. ICPSR version. Washington, DC: U.S. Dept. of Education, National Center for Education Statistics [producer]. Ann Arbor, MI: Inter-university Consortium for Political and Social Research [distributor].

———. 1992. *Integrated Postsecondary Education Data System (IPEDS): Fall Enrollment Analysis 1992* [Computer File]. ICPSR version. Washington, DC: U.S. Dept. of Education, National Center for Education Statistics [producer]. Ann Arbor, MI: Inter-university Consortium for Political and Social Research [distributor].

———. 1993. *Integrated Postsecondary Education Data System (IPEDS): Fall Enrollment Analysis 1993* [Computer File]. ICPSR version. Washington, DC: U.S. Dept. of Education, National Center for Education Statistics [producer]. Ann Arbor, MI: Inter-university Consortium for Political and Social Research [distributor].

———. 1994. *Integrated Postsecondary Education Data System (IPEDS): Fall Enrollment Analysis 1994* [Computer File]. ICPSR version. Washington, DC: U.S. Dept. of Education, National Center for Education Statistics [producer]. Ann Arbor, MI: Inter-university Consortium for Political and Social Research [distributor].

———. 1995. *Integrated Postsecondary Education Data System (IPEDS): Fall Enrollment Analysis 1995* [Computer File]. ICPSR version. Washington, DC: U.S. Dept. of Education, National Center for Education Statistics [producer]. Ann Arbor, MI: Inter-university Consortium for Political and Social Research [distributor].

Index

Page numbers in **bold** are tables.
Page numbers in *italics* are figures.

Made in the USA
Coppell, TX
09 February 2021

50015150R00133